D1520662

THE UNIVERSAL VAMPIRE

THE UNIVERSAL VAMPIRE
Origins and Evolution of a Legend

Barbara Brodman and James E. Doan

Fairleigh Dickinson University Press
Madison · Teaneck

Published by Fairleigh Dickinson University Press
Co-published with The Rowman & Littlefield Publishing Group, Inc.
4501 Forbes Boulevard, Suite 200, Lanham, Maryland 20706
www.rowman.com

10 Thornbury Road, Plymouth PL6 7PP, United Kingdom

British Library Cataloguing in Publication Information Available

Library of Congress Cataloging-in-Publication Data
The universal vampire : origins and evolution of a legend / edited by Barbara Brodman
and James E. Doan.
    pages cm
  Includes bibliographical references and index.
  ISBN 978-1-61147-580-7 (cloth : alk. paper) — ISBN 978-1-61147-581-4 (electronic) 1.
Vampires. I. Brodman, Barbara.
  GR830.V3U55 2013
  398.21—dc23   2013002327

Printed in the United States of America

Contents

Acknowledgments

THIS BOOK IS THE PRODUCT of a vampires-in-the-mist experience that began in July 2006, when we both presented papers at the Conference on Icons and Iconoclasts at the University of Aberdeen, Scotland. Neither paper we presented then—Brodman's on the evolution of the 17th-century Don Juan legend and Doan's on Shakespeare's use of history in his plays—dealt specifically with the vampire. Over a few pints of stout, we began discussing parallels between Don Juan and the Byronic vampire anti-hero, which led to a paper, "From the Sensual to the Damned: Legends of Don Juan and the Vampire," that we subsequently presented at the 2008 National Popular Culture & American Culture Associations Conference in San Francisco. The topic stuck and led us to develop a book project that would explore in detail the origins and evolution of the legend.

We took our proposal to the International Conference on Vampires: Myths of the Past and the Future at the University of London in November 2011, gave out calls for papers, and were overwhelmed by the quality and quantity of the essays we received. We circulated additional calls for papers with equally impressive results. And we've only just begun.

We would like to thank those friends and colleagues whose assistance made this book possible. Harry Keyishian, Director of Fairleigh Dickinson University Press, and Brooke Bascietto, Associate Editor for the Rowman & Littlefield Publishing Group, made the challenges of turning an idea into a book easy and enjoyable. Ruth Nemire set us on the right course. At Nova Southeastern University, Dean Don Rosenblum, and Director of Humanities,

Marlisa Santos, gave us institutional support without which completion of this project would have been impossible. And our dear friend and colleague, Suzanne Ferriss, helped us in more ways than we can express, sharing her vast publishing experience with us unreservedly.

Barbara Brodman
James E. Doan

Introduction

Barbara Brodman
James E. Doan

F OR ALMOST 200 YEARS, since the publication of John Polidori's *The Vampyre* (1819), the vampire has been a mainstay of Western culture, appearing consistently in literature, art, music (notably opera), film, television, graphic novels, and popular culture in general. Even before its entrance into the realm of arts and letters in the early 19th century, the vampire was a feared creature of Eastern European folklore and legend, rising from the grave at night to consume its living loved ones and neighbors, often converting them at the same time into fellow vampires. A major question exists within vampire scholarship: to what extent is this creature a product of European cultural forms or is the vampire indeed a universal, perhaps even archetypal, figure?

In *The Universal Vampire: Origins and Evolution of a Legend*, this question is discussed by tracing the development of the vampire in the West from the early Norse *draugr* figure to the medieval European revenant and ultimately to Dracula, who, of course, first appears as a vampire in Anglo-Irish Bram Stoker's novel, *Dracula*, published in 1897. The Romantic vampire first coalesced around the figure of Lord Byron and his associates in the early 1800s and from there morphed into the characteristic blood-sucking ghoul of penny dreadfuls, such as the one found in James Malcolm Rymer's *Varney the Vampyre*. What led to the continual transformations and retransformations of these figures? Did they constitute resistance to the dominant cultural norms of the time? Moreover, how did the accounts of exhumations, decapitations, and other mutilations of alleged vampires during the 18th century reflect the anxiety of Western European contact with Slavic, Turkish, and other non-Western societies? What can modern science tell about the causes of apparent vampirism as well as lycanthropy (werewolves)?

In addition to these investigations of the Western mythic, literary, and historic traditions, other essays in this volume will move outside Europe to explore vampire figures in Native American and Mesoamerican myth and ritual, as well as the existence of similar vampiric traditions in Japanese, Russian, and Latin American art, theatre, literature, film, and other cultural productions.

Part One contains four essays, which focus on the development of the Western literary tradition. In "Draugula": The *Draugr* in Old Norse-Icelandic Saga Literature and His Relationship to the Post-Medieval Vampire Myth," Matthias Teichert explores undead creatures called *draugar* (singular nominative *draugr*) who strongly resemble the "classical" vampires from later Eastern European lore. Using four Norse *draugr* narratives, he reconstructs the underlying myth, suggesting they formed a cohesive pattern in 13th- and 14th-century saga literature. He also speculates that there may be a distant connection between the *draugr* and the vampire depicted in Murnau's 1922 German Expressionist film, *Nosferatu*, linking both possibly to the outbreaks of plague epidemics.

Paul E. H. Davis's essay, "Dracula Anticipated: The 'Undead' in Anglo-Irish Literature," traces a different trajectory for the rise of the 19th-century literary vampire, namely the Anglo-Irish literary tradition, which includes such figures as Melmoth in *Melmoth the Wanderer* (1820), who sells his soul to the devil; Silas Ruthyn in *Uncle Silas* (1864); and Mircalla/Carmilla, the first lesbian vampire (in *Carmilla*, published in 1871). As Davis concludes, without these previous works *Dracula* would not exist in its current form.

Both Alexis Milmine's "Retracing the Shambling Steps of the Undead: The Blended Folklore Elements of Vampirism in Bram Stoker's *Dracula*" and Cristina Artenie's "Dracula's Kitchen: A Glossary of Transylvanian Cuisine, Language, and Ethnography" investigate the ways in which Stoker's vampire differs from the traditional Eastern European ones, which were presumably his models. For example, Milmine discusses the means used to dispatch Dracula in the novel. Whereas a stake is used to kill Lucy and release her soul, the same type of weapon is not used against Dracula. Both Jonathan Harker and Quincy Morris destroy an immobilized Dracula with great knives, after which the vampire's body crumbles into dust. Whereas in previous texts, such as in *Carmilla*, the vampire must be decapitated and then the body burned, in Stoker's work the knives used to dispatch Dracula may derive from their use in various folklore traditions as safeguards against the dead rising from their grave to haunt and kill the living. Artenie, on the other hand, looks at calendrical and culinary inconsistencies in Stoker's novel to suggest that he has deliberately misconstrued cultural elements to create an *Other*world, so that, since his time, Transylvania has been viewed as Europe's "heart of darkness," the land of the Undead.

In Part Two, the focus shifts toward medical explanations for the vampire and werewolves. In "Biomedical Origins of Vampirism," Edward O. Keith links the vampire to a universal fear of the unknown and a synthesis of attitudes toward the dualism of life and death. He proposes that vampire myths developed from a mounting fear of diseases communities encountered daily or from psychiatric illnesses that were rarely understood as such until the scientific era, when they became a focus of Jungian and Freudian theory and were linked scientifically to disorders of the brain. In "Evidence for the Undead: The Role of Medical Investigation in the 18th-Century Vampire Epidemic" and "Undead Feedback: Adaptations and Echoes of Johann Flückinger's Report, *Visum et Repertum* (1732), until the Millennium," Leo Ruickbie and Clemons Ruthner examine 18th-century efforts scientifically to record and "prove"—or disprove—the existence of vampirism. Both examine medical investigations into reports of vampirism in 18th-century Eastern Europe and the responses these reports elicited then and in modern times. The essays in this part of the collection are unique in that they reflect efforts to lend scientific credence to the vampire legend rather than to analyze manifestations of the legend in myth and the arts.

As opposed to the primarily male vampires so far explored, Part Three focuses on the female vampire, historically the most ancient and probably the most widespread geographically of vampires. Perhaps originating from the angst over the premature death of infants and the fear that the mother may somehow be responsible, as early as the 3rd millennium BCE, the Sumerian and Babylonian goddess Lilith makes her first appearance; in later Jewish Talmudic tradition she also drains men of their life force (i.e., semen), as discussed by Nancy Schumann in "Women with Bite: Tracing Vampire Women from Lilith to *Twilight*" and Angela Tumini in "*Vampiresse*: Embodiment of Sensuality and Erotic Horror in Carl Th. Dreyer's *Vampyr* and Mario Bava's *The Mask of Satan*." Both authors trace the development of the female vampire from her ancient Near-Eastern origins to 20th- and 21st-century film and television series, pointing out the impact feminism has had on the current perception of both female vampires and the women who consort with the male of the "species."

James E. Doan's "The Vampire in Native American and Mesoamerican Lore" deals primarily with the vampiric corn and other earth goddesses prevalent throughout North America. Perhaps deriving from an earlier mistress of the animals brought across Beringia by the Paleolithic peoples who settled the Americas, as early as 6,700 B.C.E. the corn goddess (with the cultivation of maize) begins to make her appearance. In Hopi myth and Skidi Pawnee ritual, manifestations of her are seen through victims drained of their blood to propitiate the goddess and ensure fertility. In Mesoamerican lore she also appears as Cihuacoatl ("Snake Woman") and is connected with childbirth. Spirits of women who died in childbirth were honored as warriors, known as Cihuatateo, who were thought to haunt crossroads at night to steal children and often resemble Cihaucoatl. They are probably a prototype for La Llorona ("The Weeping Woman") in modern Mexican folklore, sometimes viewed as a vampire herself. They also resemble quite closely the Malayan female vampires called *pontianak* or *langsuir*, ghosts of women who have died in childbirth.

Katherine Allocco's "Vampiric Viragoes: Villainizing and Sexualizing Arthurian Women in *Dracula vs. King Arthur* (2005)" examines early versions of the male monster–female victim in works such as Marie de France's *Bisclavret*, as well as the amenorrheic virago who obtains power through retaining her own blood. Alloco sees a short progression from these archetypal images in medieval literature to their manifestation as female vampires in the four-issue comic book series, *Dracula vs. King Arthur*. Both Guinevere and Morganna, as well as other female characters, are found, sexualized by their conversions and ultimately destroyed, which Allocco sees as a direct result of their attempts to usurp Arthur's power.

Jamieson Ridenhour, in "'If I Wasn't a Girl, Would You Like Me Anyway?' Le Fanu's *Carmilla* and Alfredson's *Let the Right One In*," investigates the close relationship between the central figures in Le Fanu's novella, Laura and Carmilla, and their counterparts (12-year-old Oskar and the young dark-haired girl, Eli, who moves in next door) in the celebrated Swedish film. Mediated through the image of the *femme fatale* (who underlies many of the modern depictions of the female vampire), both Carmilla and Eli are not what they initially seem. In fact, there are even further complications over gender, more explicit in the original novel on which the film is based, but at least suggested in the latter.

Further evidence of the universality of the vampire myth is incorporated into Part Four of this collection. Here the authors discuss manifestations of the vampire theme in the arts and cultures of Japan, Russia, and Mexico. In "A Cultural Dynasty of Beautiful Vampires: Japan's Acceptance, Modifications, and Adaptations of Vampires," Masaya Shimokusu discusses the introduction of the vampire theme into Japan in the early 20th century and its evolution from a purely Western construct to a "thing of beauty" with a decidedly Japanese stamp.

Tomas Jesús Garza, in "From Russia with Blood: Imagining the Vampire in Contemporary Russian Popular Culture," takes the reader to Russia and traces the evolution of the Slavic vampire legend from its origins to its trans-formations during the Soviet and Post-Soviet era. By placing his analysis within the context of Post-Soviet pop-gothic music and Russian-Ukrainian-Tatar author Sergei Lukyanenko's 21st-century *Night Watch* series of vampire films, he clearly establishes the role and uniquely regional quality of the New Russian vampire.

Turning again to the Mesoamerican vampire tradition, Adriana Gordillo and co-authors Raúl Rodríguez-Hernández and Claudia Schaefer examine the vampire theme in Mexican literature and film. In "Dracula Comes to Mexico: Carlos Fuentes's *Vlad*, Echoes of Origins, and the Return of Colonialism," Gordillo relates one of Carlos Fuentes's last works, the novella *Vlad*, to the universal themes of class, origins, and the quest for eternal life. In this version of the vampire legend, Gordillo states that Fuentes presents a glance at the past, present, and future through multiple and constantly reinvented ideas of origin, while challenging authoritarian beliefs that plead for a univocal and fixed idea of the world.

Using Freud's theories of the uncanny within aesthetics as a framework, Raúl Rodríguez-Hernández and Claudia Schaefer discuss the vampire theme in two seminal Mexican films, Fernando Méndez's *El Vampiro* (1957) and Guillermo del Toro's *La invención de Cronos* (1993). In these films, an imported technology, cinematography, and an imported legend, the vampire, unite to create a vision that is both universal and decidedly Mexican.

Though called by a variety of names and possessing different traits, the vampires described in the essays in this volume reflect age-old anxieties about death, the possibility of rebirth into a different existence, and the quest for immortality, though obtained at a tremendous cost. Each culture examined here, and the myths, arts, literature, films, and television series they have produced, explore these issues. The respective storytellers, authors, artists, and filmmakers have placed their individual stamps on the tradition so that, rather than seeing the vampire tradition as monolithic, which many assume when seeing their first *Dracula* film, readers of this volume will discover that there is no one being that may be categorically defined—or delimited—as a vampire. Though the vampire's thirst for blood remains a leitmotif through-out these narratives, often erotically charged and connected with other bodily substances such as semen, the vampire itself continues to morph into new forms as each age rediscovers it.

I

THE WESTERN VAMPIRE: FROM *DRAUGR* TO DRACULA

1

"Draugula": The *Draugr* in Old Norse-Icelandic Saga Literature and His Relationship to the Post-Medieval Vampire Myth

Matthias Teichert

EVEN THOUGH VAMPIRES ARE COMMONLY associated with early modern and modern Eastern Europe, particularly Transylvania, revenants and undead resembling the "classical" vampire are found in myths, folktales, and epic narrative of many cultures and regions from antiquity onward.[1] As far as Northern Europe is concerned, the prime evidence for the vampire's universal character is recorded in the saga literature of medieval Iceland, a corpus of prose narratives recorded from the late 12th to the 15th century. Saga literature is traditionally divided into several subgenres, including the prestigious sagas of the Icelanders (*Íslendingasögur*), the kings' sagas (*konungasögur*), the mythical-heroic sagas (*fornaldarsögur*, literally "sagas of the ancient times," with "ancient" referring to the time before the beginning of the settlement of Iceland [870 AD]), knights' sagas (*riddarasögur*, dealing with chivalric and Arthurian matters), and romances (*ævintýrasögur*, literally "adventure sagas," or *rómans*, purely fictitious bridal-quest stories involving a range of European and Oriental literary and fairy-tale motifs).

Generally speaking, the most elaborate and most instructive revenant episodes are to be found in the sagas of the Icelanders. This chapter will therefore concentrate on these texts, of which a total number of 36 are preserved. The plot of these narratives is based on events and persons from the early history of the Icelandic Free State (ca. 900–1050 AD). The main topics are conflicts among neighboring wealthy peasants, often resulting in feud, mutual killings, and other kinds of bloodshed; court scenes, primarily at the legendary Althing near present-day Reykjavík; and the fate of famous outlaws prosecuted and ultimately killed by their enemies. Despite their historical impact, the sagas of the Icelanders frequently refer to mysterious and supernatural phenomena, such as magical swords, prophetic dreams, berserkers, werewolves, and living dead. The latter can be divided into two major groups according to the names the saga narrators apply to describe them. There is, first, the so-called *haugbúi* (plural nominative form *haugbúar*), a compound formed of the two nouns *haugr* ("howe"; "burial site") and *búi* ("dweller"): the term *haugbúi* may thus be rendered as "howe-dweller." The *haugbúi* is an undead who "lives" his post-mortal existence in his howe, enjoying the conveniences his funerary goods offer him. The *haugbúi* does neither act aggressively or harmfully toward the living, nor does he affect living people and animals outside his howe; the *haugbúi* is a predominantly defensive creature. The only situation in which a *haugbúi* may become wrathful and exercise violence on others is when tomb raiders open the howe and try to steal the precious grave goods. Because the *haugbúar* are said to be in command of tremendous physical strength, overcoming a *haugbúi* and picking up some of his grave goods as a trophy sometimes occurs as an element of a hero's biography.

The second and potentially more dangerous type of living dead in the sagas is the *draugr* (plural nominative *draugar*), a designation sometimes used as an umbrella term for any undead but usually applied to walking undead who leave their grave and behave mischievously and physically or mentally threatening toward the living. This feature is mirrored in the word's etymology which may be traced back to an Indo-European root *dhreugh* "to harm; to damage."[2] Other Old Norse-Icelandic terms for undead are the rarely recorded compounds *aptrgangr* (corresponding exactly to English *revenant*, literally "after-goer") and *aptrgöngumaðr* (*maðr* "man"), the even more scarcely recorded *váfa* ("ghost"), and the *hapax legomenon*, *flyka* ("wraith," "phantom").

For decades saga research has emphasized the physical aspect of *draugar* depictions up to identifying the *draugr* with the concept of the living corpse.[3] However, a closer look at the sources reveals a cluster of "para-material" vampire-like characteristics of the *draugr* and the associated literary motifs on which the following synoptic view of a selection of major *draugar* episodes from saga fiction will primarily focus.

Laxdœla saga ("The Saga of the People of Laxárdalr"), composed around 1250 AD, tells of a peasant named Hrappr Sumarliðason, a rather grouchy and wicked person who is prone to violence, whence his cognomen Vígr-Hrappr ("Slaying-Hrappr") is derived. The reader is informed that Hrappr has immigrated to Iceland from the Hebrides—thus he is not an offspring of the old-established plutocracy of landowners but a newly arrived upstart from the fringe of the Viking Empire—who remains an outsider in the society he has entered. The narrator hereby delineates a typical background biography of future revenants including vampires: those who are bound to return un-dead after their decease were aggressive, anti-social, and egomaniacal persons while alive.

Hrappr threatens his neighbors immensely and becomes increasingly hostile toward his environment. Soon after his dying of old age, Hrappr begins to haunt the living in the district until his long-term rival Höskuldr exhumes Hrappr's corpse and reburies it in the wilderness area. Subsequently, Hrappr's blood-seeking escapades diminish. Nevertheless, the undead successfully attacks his son who now runs his father's former estate and drives him insane: *tók hann œrsl ok dó lítlu síðar* (ÍF 3: 40; "frenzy came upon him, and he died shortly afterwards").[4] Óláfr, the son of Höskuldr, moves to Hrappr's former place to establish his farmyard there. After a while, Óláfr has an encounter with the undead Hrappr during which the *draugr* breaks Óláfr's spear into pieces before vanishing mysteriously: *Hrappr fór þar niðr, sem hann var kominn* (ÍF 3: 69; "Hrapp sank into the earth where he stood"). The following morning Óláfr goes to see Hrappr's grave and opens it to find the corpse undecayed and next to it his own spearhead that Hrappr has chipped off. Óláfr now adopts drastic measures in order to finish Hrappr's haunting: *lætr hann gera bál; er Hrappr brenndr á báli, ok er aska hans flutt á sjá út* (ÍF 3: 69; "he had a bale made; Hrappr is burned on the bale, and his ashes are flung out to sea").

There are several notable features of the Norse *draugr* myth involved in the two-section story of Hrappr. The first is the aforementioned "socio-psychiatric" profile of the future *draugr*. The second is the *draugr*'s ability to recover physically from debilitation caused by a defective apotropaic. After his corpse has been banned from human habitation to the outpost, Hrappr temporarily decreases in strength. Note the narrator's careful wording: *eptir at nemask af heldr aptrgöngur Hrapps* ("After that the hauntings of Hrapp lessened somewhat"). As time passes, however, he regains his former powers and demonstrates them in the scene of his confrontation with Óláfr where he breaks his opponent's spear. Third, the *draugr*'s body is not subject to decomposition, hereby reacting against natural law. Fourth, the draugr is far from being merely a living corpse, judging from his capacity to sink into the solid ground similar to a hologram-like ghost able to walk through walls. Fifth and finally, *Laxdœla saga* provides in-depth information as for the apotropaics against the *draugr*. The principal strategy to pursue in order to exterminate the walking dead is to burn the body and to spread the ashes.

Eyrbyggja saga ("The Saga of the Inhabitants of Eyrr"), written around the same time as *Laxdœla saga* in the mid-13th century, is a particularly valuable source for Viking-age West Nordic lore, pagan beliefs, and medieval "Gothic fiction." As in *Laxdœla saga*, the future *draugr*, Þórólfr bægifótr (anglicized as Thorolf Clubfoot), appears as an unsociable, selfish farmer with a liability to crime and violence during his mortal existence. After Þórólfr's death, his son Arnkell, a far more balanced and positive character than Þórólfr himself, takes charge of his father's funeral. The first step is what the saga narrator calls *nábjargir* ("obsequies"; "corpse-help"): *tók Arnkell þá í herðar Þórólfi ok varð hann at kenna aflsmunar, áðr hann kœmi honum undir; síðan sveipaði hann klæðum at höfði Þórólfi ok bjó um hann eptir siðvenju. Eptir þat lét hann brjóta vegginn á bak honum ok draga hann þar út. Síðan váru yxn fyrir sleða beittir; var Þórólfr þar í lagiðir,* . . . (ÍF 4: 92; "Arnkell took Þórólfr by the shoulders, and he was forced to use all his strength before he was able to bring him under. Then he swept a cloth about Þórólfr's head, and then cared for him according to the old customs. Afterwards he let break down the wall behind him, and had him carried out thereby. Then there were oxen yoked to a sledge, and thereon Þórólfr was laid, . . .")

The cloaking of the head is to be regarded as an apotropaic against the evil eye.[5] Carrying out the dead body through a hole specially carved for this purpose (which was to be bricked up afterward) is probably based on a belief according to which the undead will not find a way to enter the house if treated as such.[6] Toward the end of the summer, Þórólfr commences to haunt the district by maddening and killing the cattle of the neighbors. One night the shepherd at Þórólfr's former farmyard disappears. Shortly thereafter, this body is detected, all ravaged and creepy-looking: *var hann allr kolblár ok lamit í hvert bein* (ÍF 4: 93; "he was all coal-blue, and every bone in his body was broken"). In the course of the winter Þórolfr's haunting increases. The undead starts "riding the house," that is, noisily damaging the roof of the haunted place—a typical activity of Norse *draugar* usually performed during the Yuletide period—and terrorizes his widow: *Ok er vetr kom, sýndisk Þórólfr opt heima á bœnum ok sótti mest at húsfreyju; var ok mörgum manni at þessu mein, en henni sjálfri helt við vitfirring. Svá lauk þessu, at húsfreyja lézk af þessum sökum;* . . . . (ÍF 4: 93; "And when the winter came Þórólfr often came home to the farm and plagued the landlady the most. Many people suffered great damage, but she herself was struck by madness. The end of it all was that the landlady died from these attacks.") Several people are killed by Þórólfr. The remaining living flee the haunted place until the entire area becomes desolate. Narrating the story of Þórólfr's hauntings, *Eyrbyggja saga* adds a new feature to *draugr* mythology: *svá var ok mikill gangr at aptrgöngum hans, at hann deyddi suma menn, en sumir stukku undan; en allir menn, þeir er létusk, váru sénir í ferð með Þórólfi* . . . . (ÍF 4: 93–94; "The trouble from his walking became so great that he slew some men, and some fled away; and all those who died were seen in Þórólfr's company thereafter . . . ")

By "infecting" victims, the *draugr* gains the ability of physical reproduction, a trait that popular culture ascribes to vampires, werewolves, and zombies. Thereby, the *draugr* existence transforms from a curse set upon an anti-social or criminal individual to a rapidly spreading epidemic. At last, Arnkell exhumes his father's body to find it *ófúinn* (ÍF 4: 94; "undecayed") und *inn illiligsti* (ÍF 4: 95; "extremely ugly-looking"). The oxen brought along to transport the corpse go mad and perish. Arnkell decides to rebury his father in the wilderness and to seal off the new grave: *Lét Arnkell síðan leggja þar um veran höfðann fyrir ofan dysina svá hávan, at eigi komsk yfir nema fugl fljúgandi . . .* (ÍF 4: 95; "Arnkell had a wall raised across the headland landward of the howe, so high that no-one might ever come thereover except flying birds . . .")

Þórólfr sojourns in the burial site for a couple of years and does not return to the saga's plot until after Arnkell's death. Þórólfr then haunts the two farms of Bólstaðr und Ulfarfell, successively killing cattle and humans likewise. The tenant of Úlfarfell, Þóroddr Þorbrandsson, ultimately exhumes Þórólfr's body a second time and finishes the haunting in the same way as Óláfr did in *Lax-dœla saga*, he burns the walking dead's corpse.

Flóamanna saga ("The Saga of the People of Flói"), dating from early in the 14th century, contains two revenant episodes structuring the biography of the saga's protagonist, Þorgils Þórðarson. The first story focuses on Þorgils' meeting with a *draug, mikinn ok illiligan* (STUANGL 56: 18; "big and evil ghost") during his visit to Björn, a befriended farmer. Face to face with the ghost, Þorgils raises his axe to attack the undead, who retreats and escapades in the direction of his howe. Þorgils tracks down the revenant and annihilates him: *høggr Þorgils þá af honum höfuð ok mælir síðan yfir honum, at hann skuli engum manni at meini verða; var ok aldrigi vart við hann síðan.* (STUANGL 56: 18; "He cuts off his head and conjures him so that he would not be harmful to anyone. Since then he was never seen again.")

Even though being termed *draugr* and, despite his mobility, the undead of this episode is similar to a revenant of the inoffensive *haugbúi*-type rather than to the aggressive vampire-like *draugr* characterized by his uncanny physical and mental powers. The haunting caused by the undead is comparably innocuous insofar as the community of the living is not affected substantially in terms of life and death. Once he encounters resistance, the undead resigns and escapes to his howe where Þorgils is able to destroy him quite smoothly.

An informative feature of this *draugr/haugbúi* episode is the mention of a magical charm spoken by Þorgils and directed to the decapitated corpse to prevent him from haunting once more. The tradition to limit the scope of a suspected undead by putting a spell on him is recorded archaeologically in the form of runic inscriptions from pre-Viking and Viking-age Norway, some of which were scribed inward-facing so the undead would be forced to read it and possibly to obey it (the most famous example being the Eggja stone from Sogn og Fjordane county in Southwest Norway, dating from about 650–700 AD).

A second and much more threatening confrontation of Þorgils with the walking dead is related later on in the saga. Although this second *draugr* episode of *Flóamanna saga* covers merely a page and a half in a printed edition, it is of considerable significance as far as an analysis of the *draugr*'s major traits and his relationship to the medieval and post-medieval vampire myth is concerned. Having converted to Christianity during a sojourn in Norway and returned to Iceland, Þorgils prepares for a voyage to Greenland. The group of travelers consists of Þorgils and his relatives and thralls on one side and of Þorgils' associate Jósteinn, his wife Þorgerðr and 12 followers on the other. In the near-shore area of Greenland's coast the travelers suffer shipwreck. They reach land and make themselves at home in a roughly constructed shack in the nearby bay. Subsequently, the group splits into two parties characterized by antagonistic behavior patterns: *Hann [Þorgils] bað sína menn vera hljóð-láta ok siðsama á kveldum ok halda vel trú sína. . . . Þat er sagt, at Jósteinn ok hans menn gerðu mikit um sik ok höfðu náttleika með háreysti.* (STUAGNL 56: 38–39; "He [Þorgils] ordered his companions to act quiet and behave primly after sunset und to remain loyal to their faith. . . . It is now told that Jósteinn and his people blustered a lot and were very noisy during their night-time games.")

On Christmas morning, splendid weather conditions lure some of the men outside of their habitation. While roaming around in the bay's surroundings, they suddenly hear an *óp mikit í útnorðr* (STUANGL 56: 39; "a loud yell from north-west"), seemingly without attaching much importance to this incident. The day after Christmas Jósteinn's crew returns to their lodge, roisterous as usual. After calm and tranquility have been restored in the interior of the house, the castaways suddenly hear a knock at the door. Because none of them has remained outside, it is clear that the knocking sounds must arise from some alien creature. Nonetheless, one of Jósteinns's mates is bound to be reckless enough to open the door. The consequences of this audacity turn out to be disastrous: *ok hljóp [hann] út, ok varð hann þegar ærr, en um morguninn deyr hann* (STUANGL 56: 39–40; "He ran outside, and raved immediately, and died the next morning"). The following night claims another victim: *maðr æriz, ok kallaz sjá hinn hlaupa at sér, er áðr dó* (STUANGL 56: 40; "Another man raved and claimed seeing the one who had died before running towards him"). The horror continues with a large-scale deadly haunt:

> Eptir þat kom sótt í lið Jósteins ok deyja vi. menn. Þá tekr Jósteinn sótt ok deyr hann. Síðan eru þeir kasaðir í mölinni. . . . Á bak jólum gengu þessir menn allir aptr. Þá tók Þorgerðr sótt ok andaz, ok þar næst hverr at öðrum þeira manna, er með Jósteini höfðu verit. Þórarinn léz síðast. Váru nú allmiklar aptrgöngur, ok sóttu mest Þorgils. . . . Ekki mátti Þorgils ok hans menn í burt færaz meðan

aptrgöngur váru sem master. Í þenna hluta skálans gengu þau mest aptr, er þau höfðu átt. Þorgils lét brenna þau öll á báli, ok var þaðan af ekki mein at aptrgöngum. (STUANGL 56, 40–41)

> Then an epidemic befell Jósteinn's crew, and six men died. Jósteinn, too, was befallen and died. All these dead bodies were buried in the sand. . . . After Yule all these men came walking. Then Þorgerðr was laid low by the epidemic and next one after another of the men who counted among Jósteinn's side. The last one to die was Þórarinn. There were now tremendous haunts, and it was Þorgils who was haunted the most. . . . At the peak of the haunting Þorgils and his men were unable to escape. They walked mostly in the part of the house which had belonged to them. Þorgils had the all burned on a bale and from this moment onwards no damage ever occurred from ghosts.

This episode lays particular emphasis on the transmissibility of draugrism, a trait also mentioned in *Eyrbyggja saga* and paralleled by the corresponding motif of infectiousness in some of the vampire myths: a man who is bitten by a vampire is doomed to turn into a vampire, and a person killed by a *draugr* returns as a *draugr* himself. Hereby the *draugar* are capable of reproducing and multiplying in a way that would ultimately lead to the living being outnumbered by the *draugar* if no counter-measures are taken. In addition to the narrative elements mentioned so far, *Flóamanna saga* documents the motif of a menacing sinister cry at nighttime precluding the events of death. It remains unclear what kind of living or undead entity emits the cry and whether there is any linkage between this person or thing and the appearance of the *draugar*. At any rate, the motif has similarities to the banshee myth known from Celtic (especially Irish), English, and American lore, which is about a feminine spirit whose wailing announces the near-term death of a particular person (for the banshee lore see Briggs 1976: 14–16).

The most comprehensive and probably most noted *draugr* episode is preserved in *Grettis saga Ásmundarsonar* ("The Saga of Grettir Ásmundarson"),[7] which Ármann Jakobsson has studied thoroughly (see Jakobsson 2009: 307–316). *Grettis saga* is a fanciful story based on the life and deeds of the notorious outlaw Grettir. Having spent a homely childhood and youth as a so-called *kolbítr* (literally "coal-biter," that is, the Norse version of the "male Cinderella"-style, unpromising hero), Grettir turns into a gargantuan hero as he reaches adolescence. Grettir is a complex character and by no means an exemplary champion *comme il faut*. He is described as an ugly, irascible, quarrelsome, and rather sociopathic person. His exceptional bodily strength prevents him from being bullied or attacked by his fellow humans, though. The turning point in Grettir's biography is his encounter with the lurid *draugr* Glámr. Long before the decisive showdown between the two, Glámr is introduced earlier in the saga, and at this stage, he is a more or less ordinary living man who is described as tall and sturdy but disliked by the people in the district. Glámr acquires a position as a shepherd on the farm of Þórhallr

Grímsson and soon gets on the farmer's and his wife's bad side due to his unsocial behavior. The narrator brands Glámr *ósöngvinn ok trúlauss, stirfinn ok viðskotaillr* (ÍF 7: 111; "he was a loather of church-song, and godless, surly, and nobody might abide him"). On Christmas Eve morning Glámr requests the farmer's wife to serve his breakfast, rejecting the common custom of fast on that day. Regardless of the snowy and stormy weather conditions Grettir spends the day in the countryside with his sheep; meanwhile, the other people of the farmstead attend church. At nighttime Grettir remains lost without trace, whereupon a search party sets out on Christmas morning. Glámr's dead body is found down in the valley, looking *blár sem hel, en digr sem naut* (ÍF 7: 112; "blue as hell, and as heavy as an ox"). Judging from the giant-size footprints and a nearby pool of blood the searchers conclude that Glámr and a mysterious ghost that had haunted the district for a while have killed each other during a titanic fight. Puzzling enough, no mention as to the identity of this arcane ghost is given throughout the text. The farmers fail to transfer Glámr to the church because the body turns out to be immovable. Finally, Glámr's body is buried under a heap of pebbles. After a while the residents of the district realize that Glámr nocturnally rises from his grave and haunts the living causing fainting fits and frenzy among them: *margir fellu í óvit, ef sá hann, en sumir heldu eigi vitinu* (ÍF 7: 113; "many fell into swoons as they saw him, and some lost their minds"). Glámr starts haunting the former master's farmyard, prompting many dwellers to leave the estate, which sustainably falls into decay. Over the course of the year Glámr kills various animals and humans, among other things the shepherd Þorgautr (Glámr's professional successor) and an unnamed menial whose back Glámr breaks. One day, the saga's title protagonist, Grettir Ásmundarson, arrives at Þórhallsstaðir, Þórhallr's farmyard. Grettir is determined to meet the infamous *draugr*, wherefore he spends three nights all together at the estate. The first night passes by uneventfully. On the second night Glámr appears and kills Grettir's horse without being noticed by any living human. Grettir's eerie third night at Þórhallsstaðir marks a dramatic watershed in Grettir's biography as his confrontation changes his physical and mental constitution cataclysmically. Around midnight, Glámr appears and starts riding the house. A little while later the *draugr* opens the front door and approaches Grettir, who is still lying in his bed. The narrator describes Glámr's physical appearance, notably his head, as *afskræmiliga mikit ok undarliga stórskorit* (ÍF 7: 119; "monstrously big and amazingly thick cut"). The two have an epic fight in the course of which most of the indoor furnishing is shattered to pieces. Despite Glámr's physical advantage, Grettir finally manages to strike down his undead opponent: Glámr falls *öfugr út ór húsunum, en Grettir á hann ofan* (ÍF 7: 121; "head over heels out of the house, and Grettir on top of him"). In the moonlit night Grettir realizes Glámr's abhorrent ugliness even more clearly than before. Overwhelmed by a sudden fatigue and paralysis, Grettir is unable to use his weapons in order to behead the *draugr*. Meanwhile, the narrator ascribes *meiri ófagnaðarkraptr . . . en flestum öðrum aptrgöngumönnum* (ÍF 7: 121; "more malignant power than most other ghosts") to Glámr, a magical force the *draugr* immediately employs to put a hex on Grettir: "*heðan af munu falla til þín sekðir ok vígaferli, en flest öll verk þín snúask þér til ógæfu ok hamingjuleysis. Þú munt vera útlægr görr ok hljóta jafnan úti at búa einn samt. Þá legg ek þat á við þik, at þessi augu sé þér jafnan fyrir sjónum, sem ek ber eptir, ok mun þér þá erfitt þykkja einum at vera, ok at mun þér til dauða draga.*" (ÍF 7: 121; "henceforward shall fall on you exile and man-slayings. Most of your deeds shall turn to your woe, and your guardian spirit will leave you. You will be made an outlaw and it shall be your lot to dwell alone in the wilderness. This I lay upon you that these eyes of mine will always be there before your vision. And you will find it hard to dwell alone, and at last it shall drag you to Death.")

Once the execration has been uttered Grettir regains his strength and destroys the *draugr* by decapitating him. Þórhallr who has been watching the struggle from a safe distance appears and gives profess thanks to Grettir for neutralizing the *óhreina anda* (ÍF 7: 122; "unclean spirit"). Jointly Grettir and his host proceed to the *draugr's* ultimate extermination: *Fóru þeir þá til ok brenndu Glám at köldum kolum. Eptir þat báru þeir ösku hans í eina hít ok grófu þar niðr, sem sízt váru fjárhagar eða mannavegir . . .* (ÍF 7: 122; "Then they set to work and burned Glam to cold coals. Thereafter they bound his ashes in a skin and buried them in far away from the ways of man or beast" . . .)

The Glámr episode concludes with the narrator's telling of the lasting invisible scars the duel with the draugr leave in the hero's psyche: *Á því fann hann mikla muni, at han var orðinn maðr svá myrkfælinn, at hann þorði hvergi at fara einn saman, þegar myrkva tók; sýndisk honum á hvers kyns skrípi . . .* (ÍF 7: 122–123; "Herein he found a great change, in that he had become so afraid of the dark that he dared not go anywhere alone after nightfall. All kinds of apparitions came before him" . . .)

The four *draugar* episodes discussed so far show significant similarities as for the nature and behavior of the Norse undead, allowing the reconstruction of an underlying code of the *draugr* myth. The primary items of this code may be summarized as follows:

- Future *draugar* are depicted as aggressive, sociopathic, and violent persons while alive.
- The main season for the *draugr's* haunting is around midwinter/Yuletide.

- Basic activities of the *draugr* include riding the roofs and the killing of cattle and thralls or other lower-class characters.
- On a more "advanced" stage of his haunting, the *draugr* is able to cause insanity among humans, particularly women.
- The *draugr* is able to recover from a temporary enfeeblement.
- Draugrism is infectious.
- The *draugr* may as well cause epidemic plague outbreaks among humans.
- In addition to superhuman physical force, the *draugr* is equipped with mental powers enabling him not only to drive the living to insanity but also to curse and doom people.
- The *draugr* is capable of sinking into the earth similar to a wraithlike ghost.
- After his death and burial, the *draugr* physically leaves his grave to haunt the living; his body remains undecayed but changes its color to dark blue or black and increases in weight.
- The most promising way to incapacitate a *draugr* is beheading; the *draugr* is ultimately exterminated via cremation.

Obviously, some of the features enumerated here are likely to be older and more authentic Viking age (or even more archaic) than others, whereas some might mirror later developments within the *draugr* myth or influences derived from non-Nordic traditions, especially Celtic lore (cf. the banshee motif in *Flóamanna saga*) and undead stories circulating in Northern England and recorded in the Latin language in *Historia rerum Anglicarum* by William of Newburgh (written ca. 1198). If single Celtic or Anglo-Saxon elements exercised an influence on the Norse perception of the undead, they did not give rise to an extensive ramification of the whole *draugr* matter altogether. Regardless of the philological and folkloristic problems of tracing back each of its features diachronically, the *draugr* myth in saga literature appears as a comparatively invariable cluster of motifs, characters, and settings. It is therefore, from a synchronic viewpoint, possible to refer to the *draugr* myth as a cohesive 13th-century narrative pattern[8] substantially based on older native traditions, the mutability and spry vitality of myths and lore in archaic, widely preliterate societies such as Viking-age Northern Europe notwithstanding.

Nevertheless, the attempt to compare the *draugr* myth recorded in Norse-Old Icelandic saga literature with the "classical" (Eastern) European vampire myth faces two problems. First, the word *vampire* did not enter the English language until 1732,[9] so that applying this term to medieval fiction, strictly speaking, turns out to be anachronistic. Second, the term *vampire* is notoriously difficult to define and to delimit from other forms of undead beings, especially so far as the premodern era is concerned. To find some common ground on which to base this it seems reasonable to use the short definition offered by the *Collins Concise Dictionary* as quoted by Matthew Beresford in his monograph *From Demons to Dracula*: " (in European lore) a corpse that rises nightly from its grave to drink the blood of living people."[10] The centering of blood drinking is somewhat problematic, though, because not all vampire-like creatures necessarily are bloodthirsty; instead, some may suck their victim's vigor by other means as does the German *Nachzehrer* (literally "afterwards devourer")[11] who does not even leave his grave and the Norse draugr who scares his victims to insanity or kills them with brute physical violence.[12] All draugar dealt with in the present study exemplify what Peter Barber has termed "predispistion"[13] for a post-mortal revenant or vampire existence: "people who are different, unpopular, or great sinners are apt to return from the death."[14] This prerequisite clearly applies to the psychograms of Hrappr, Glámr, Þórolfr, and the cheerful ship-wreckers in *Flóamanna saga* likewise. A common feature to both draugar and vampires is the lack of decomposition of their corpses, which is described in the exhumation scenes in *Laxdœla saga* and *Eyrbyggja saga* and in many vampirological testimonies (for the latter cf. Barber 2010: 160–162). The plumpness of the corpse accentuated in *Eyrbyggja saga* and *Grettis saga* is recorded for the Greek *vrykolakas*, a close relative to the South Slavic vampire (cf. Barber 2010: 42, 109). The motif of burying the suspected draugr in a gaunt area or in the wilderness mentioned in *Laxdœla saga*, *Eyrbyggja saga*, and *Grettis saga* is paralleled by corresponding elements in vampire lore.[15] Draugar and European undead including vampires share similarities regarding the strategies used to destroy them; the two preferred methods are decapitating (which is how Count Dracula is annihilated in Stoker's novel) and subsequent cremation, "the once-standard pagan method of disposing of the body."[16] The vampire-killing custom of staking, by contrast, is unknown to Norse *draugr* lore.

Beresford has suggested that "[a]ll the early vampires are perhaps better described as vampiric beings rather than vampires in the true meaning of the word"[17] because "they have some of the qualities of the vampire, but cannot necessarily be identified with the modern vampire."[18] This careful terminological proposal may be adopted for the draugr myth as well, although it should be remarked that besides their vampiric qualities the draugar cover some traits of modern Romero-style zombies as well.

Finally, it is interesting to note that the Norse *draugr* myth shares more common characteristics with the vampire of the nosferatu style as shaped by Friedrich Wilhelm Murnau in his classic 1922 silent horror movie, *Nosferatu: A Symphony of Horror*, rather than with the Stokerian Dracula type and his seductive elegance. Just like the *draugr* in the Old Icelandic sagas, the nosferatu in Murnau's Expressionist film is associated with rashes of frenzy among the living and the outbreak of epidemics. Murnau here draws on the pre-Victorian/Romantic vampire lore and the folkloric vampire (as opposed to the fictional vampire[19]), especially in the "nexus between vampirism and the plague,"[20] which is eminent in the *draugr* myth as well insofar as, like the (folkloric) vampire, the *draugr* both infects his victims with draugrism and acts as a vector for epidemic plagues. The frequently mentioned abhorrent ugliness of the *draugr*'s physical appearance is analogous to the deformed-ness depicted in many vampirological writings and portrayed by Max Schreck wearing the iconic nosferatu mask in Murnau's movie. A fictitious personi-fication of the Old Norse-Icelandic *draugr* then, to finish this with a modest witticism, could lay claim to the honorific name of *Nosferaugr* even more than to the less quirky, but also more inexact portmanteau *Draugula*, the use of which in the title was simply too inviting an eye-catcher to be rejected.

Notes

1. See Brian Frost, *The Monster with a Thousand Faces: Guises of the Vampire in Myth and Literature* (Bowling Green: Bowling Green State University Popular Press, 1989), 3; Matthew Beresford, *From Demons to Dracula: The Creation of the Modern Vampire Myth* (London: Reaktion Books, 2008), 7; Paul Barber, *Vampires, Burial and Death: Folklore and Reality* (New York: Yale University Press, 2010), 1.

2. See Jan de Vries, *Altnordisches etymologisches Wörterbuch* (Leiden: Brill, 1977), 81, s.v. *draugr*.

3. See Hans-Joachim Klare, "Die Toten in der altnordischen Literatur," in *Acta philologica Scandinavica* (1933/34), 39–40; Régis Boyer, *La mort chez les anciens Scan-dinaves* (Paris: Les Belles Lettres, 1994), 34–38.

4. All English translations provided by author.

5. E. O. G. Turville-Petre, *Myth and Religion of the North. The Religion of Ancient Scandinavia* (London: Weidenfeld & Nicolson, 1964), 269–270.

6. Turville-Petre, *Myth and Religion of the North*, 270.

7. *Grettis saga Ásmundarsonar* is often viewed as an analogue to *Beowulf* because it contains a narrative similar to Beowulf's fight against Grendel's mother.

8. See also Turville-Petre, *Myth and Religion of the North*, 623.

9. Beresford, *From Demons to Dracula*, 8.

10. Quoted after Beresford, *From Demons to Dracula*, 7.

11. See Matthew Bunson, *The Vampire Encyclopedia* (London: Thames & Hudson, 1993), 185–186.

12. A (presumably) blood-sucking haugbúi appears in an episode of *Egils saga einhenda ok Ásmundar berserkjabana*, ("The Saga of Egill One-Hand and Asmund Berserkers-Slayer"), a 14th-century *fornaldarsaga*, which is paralleled by a similar story in Saxo Grammaticus *Gesta Danorum* (ca. 1200). In Norse mythology, the motif of blood drinking is represented by Níðhöggr, an eschatological dragon who gnaws

the root of the world ash Yggdrasill and is said to drink the blood of dead people and eat their flesh, thereby uniting modern vampire and (Romeroan) zombie traits. It is probably to Níðhöggr that Matthew Beresford's general statement refers: "There are vampires in Norse mythology" (Beresford, *From Demons to Dracula*, 7).

13. Barber, *Vampires, Burial and Death*, 29.
14. Barber, *Vampires, Burial and Death*, 29.
15. For the latter see Barber, *Vampires, Burial and Death*, 139.
16. Thomas A. DuBois, *Nordic Religions in the Viking Age* (Philadelphia: University of Pennsylvania Press, 1999), 87; for this method applied to revenants and vampires see Barber, 75–78.
17. Beresford, *From Demons to Dracula*, 39.
18. Beresford, *From Demons to Dracula*, 39.
19. See Barber, *Vampires, Burial and Death*, 2–4.
20. Barber, *Vampires, Burial and Death*, 8.

Bibliography

Primary Sources

Eyrbyggja saga. Grœnledninga sögur. Edited by Einar Ólafur Sveinsson and Matthías Þórðarson. Reykjavík: Hið íslenzka Fornritafélag, 1935 = ÍF (Íslenzk Fornrit) 4.
Flóamannasaga. Edited by Finnur Jónsson. Copenhagen: Jørgensen, 1932 = STUA-GNL (Samfund til udgivelse af gammel nordisk litteratur) 56.
Grettis saga Ásmundarsonar. Bandamanna saga. Odds þáttr Ófeigssonar. Edited by Guðni Jónsson. Reykjavík: Hið íslenzka Fornritafélag, 1936 = ÍF (Íslenzk Fornrit) 7.
Laxdœla saga. Halldórs saga Snorrasonar. Stúfs þáttr. Edited by Einar Ólafur Sveinsson. Reykjavík: Hið íslenzka Fornritafélag, 1934 = ÍF (Íslenzk Fornrit) 5.

Secondary Sources

Barber, Paul. *Vampires, Burial and Death. Folklore and Reality*. New York: Yale University Press, 2010.
Beresford, Matthew. *From Demons to Dracula. The Creation of the Modern Vampire Myth*. London: Reaktion Books, 2008.
Boyer, Régis. *La mort chez les anciens Scandinaves*. Paris: Les Belles Lettres, 1994.
Briggs, Katharina Mary. *A Dictionary of Fairies. Hobgoblins, Brownies, Bogies and Other Supernatural Creatures*. London: Lane, 1976.
Bunson, Matthew. *The Vampire Encyclopedia*. London: Thames & Hudson, 1993.
de Vries, Jan. *Altnordisches etymologisches Wörterbuch*. Leiden: Brill, 1977.
DuBois, Thomas A. *Nordic Religions in the Viking Age*. Philadelphia: University of Pennsylvania Press, 1999.
Frost, Brian. *The Monster with a Thousand Faces. Guises of the Vampire in Myth and Literature*. Bowling Green: Bowling Green State University Popular Press, 1989.

Glauser, Jürg. "Supernatural Beings. 2. Draugr and aptrganga." In *Medieval Scandinavia: An Encyclopedia*, edited by Phillip Pulsiano, 623. New York: Garland, 1993.

Jakobsson, Ármann. "The Fearless Vampire Killers: A Note about the Icelandic Draugr and Demonic Contamination in Grettis Saga." *Folklore* 120 (2009): 307–316.

Klare, Hans-Joachim. "Die Toten in der altnordischen Literatur." *Acta philologica Scandinavica* (1933/34): 1–56.

Turville-Petre, E. O. G. *Myth and Religion of the North. The Religion of Ancient Scandinavia.* London: Weidenfeld & Nicolson, 1964.

2

Dracula Anticipated:
The "Undead" in
Anglo-Irish Literature

Paul E. H. Davis

ANGLO-IRISH LITERATURE LARGELY AVOIDS realism. As Terry Eagleton suggests:

> Jonathan Swift's *Gulliver's Travels*, Maria Edgeworth's *Castle Rackrent*, Maturin's *Melmoth*, Le Fanu's *Uncle Silas* and Joyce's *Ulysses* [are part of] 'a literary tradition . . . [of] largely unrealistic works,' with Stoker and Maturin transcending realism altogether. This Irish Protestant Gothic might be dubbed the political unconscious of Anglo-Irish society, the place where its fears and fantasies most definitely emerge.[1]

In the past, Bram Stoker's *Dracula* (1897) was usually seen as a "one-off" work, brilliant and disturbing, but essentially *sui generis* and in a class of its own. Few would deny that *Dracula* has many unique features, yet Eagleton's comments are valuable in that they go some way to placing *Dracula* in the overall context of Anglo-Irish literature. This chapter argues, however, that although Eagleton is undoubtedly right to see links between Stoker and some previous "unrealistic" Irish writers, there are also important connections with writers not usually regarded as "unrealistic" at all. Indeed, it will be suggested that *Dracula* is best regarded as the culmination of *two* distinct, though closely related traditions. In other words, *Dracula* is both the ultimate novel of the "undead" and the ultimate Anglo-Irish Agrarian novel.[2]

The Anglo-Irish writers mentioned by Eagleton could hardly be accused of lacking imagination. Swift's tiny people, giants, airborne islands, and talking horses are manifestly surreal. Yet, as we shall see, even the superficially "realistic" Edgeworth can create some highly unrealistic characters. Violence is, of course, central to most traditions of fiction—mercifully more so than in most people's lives—but Anglo-Irish fiction seems especially to be inclined to the surreal and to the violent and we must ask why this is so.

From the 1760s onward, serious agrarian violence increased across Ireland. The draconian Penal Laws enacted following William III's victories at the Battles of the Boyne (1690) and Aughrim (1691) and the ensuing Treaty of Limerick (1691) kept the Catholic tenantry suppressed. The resentment at loss of land, persecution of Catholics, and betrayal of fair promises by the Ascendancy government in Dublin led to a steady rise in outrages, mainly in the form of the maiming of cattle and rick-burning. Excluded from politics, Catholics joined with Presbyterians and radical Protestants to form the United Irishmen. Their 1798 rising, aided by a half-hearted French Republican invasion (under General Jean Joseph Amable Humbert), was easily defeated and savagely put down by the Irish Government ("Grattan's Parliament") based in Dublin.

Far from freeing the Catholic Irish, the abortive rising led to a full political union between Britain and Ireland under the Act of Union of 1800. The seeds of further turmoil were planted when George III vetoed William Pitt's promise of political rights for the Catholic majority. Once the two Parliaments were merged, both the powerbase and social world of Dublin moved to London and, along with them, went the bulk of the Ascendancy, thus creating the major problem of absenteeism. (In passing, we remember that even Count Dracula was only an occasional visitor to Castle Dracula.) Economic difficulties, ultimately arising from absenteeism, strengthened the demand for Catholic Emancipation—not to be required to take the Test Act in order to enter Parliament or take other public office. In 1823, Daniel O'Connell ("The Liberator") and Richard Lalor Sheil set up the Catholic Association. It was the combination of absenteeism and the desire for emancipation that would dominate the sociopolitical world of Ireland in the first half of the 19th century and which was recorded and reflected first by Edgeworth and later, in a more surreal form, by Joseph Sheridan Le Fanu and Stoker.

In the same year as the Act of Union, Edgeworth published *Castle Rackrent* (1800), her first Anglo-Irish novel, which was also the first regional novel in English. Edgeworth followed up her success with three further Anglo-Irish novels, *Ennui* (1809), *The Absentee* (1812), and *Ormond* (1817), before realizing that she could offer no solution to the underlying problems of Ireland. She admitted, "We are in too perilous a case to laugh, humor [sic] would be out of season, worse than bad taste."[3] Yet throughout these novels, Edgeworth had outlined and analyzed the problems of Ireland as she saw them. Although she finally came to see that there was no way forward, it was an impressive achievement in literary, political, and economic terms. Edgeworth was certainly ahead of her time. *Castle Rackrent*, probably her most success-ful novel, was, like *Dracula*, a unique work and its regional focus certainly influenced Sir Walter Scott and Ivan Turgenev. For our purposes, however, the most striking thing about *Castle Rackrent* is that it is dominated by four totally unrealistic characters, the successive owners of Castle Rackrent itself. The members of the Rackrent family are hedonistic, absentees, drunks, and gamblers, who persecute their tenants mercilessly in order to get ever more money to waste in England.

Beneath the apparently light-hearted banter, Edgeworth reveals the es-sence of Anglo-Irish landlordism, exaggerated no doubt, a caricature indeed, yet strangely ultimately more truthful than any entirely realistic portrayal. Edgeworth identifies the key problem as absenteeism. Landowners leave their estates and employ agents who are often also middlemen, frequently corrupt, to squeeze as much money from the tenants as possible so that the these landowners, now living in London, can try, and fail, to compete socially with the English peerage. Meanwhile, back in Ireland, the Big Houses are falling down, and the abandoned and persecuted tenantry is becoming increasingly resentful.

While Edgeworth, with genuine affection for tenants, does not introduce any acts of agrarian violence into her novels, it is clear that this is what con-cerns her. She had witnessed, first hand, instances of violence in the lead up to the 1798 uprising and the memory stayed with her throughout her life. She once wrote, "All that I crave for my own part is, that if I am to have my throat cut, it may not be by a man with his face blackened with charcoal."[4] Yet Edge-worth was strongly influenced by her father, Richard Lovell Edgeworth, and his Rationalist belief that a simple solution would solve the problem before it was too late.

Edgeworth's solution, founded on the economic principles of Adam Smith and outlined in her Anglo-Irish novels, is to persuade the Ascendancy to see the error of its ways and return to live in Ireland as benevolent landlords—as at the end of *The Absentee* when the elated tenants "had the horses off every carriage entirely, and drew 'em home, with blessings, through the park."[5] There are many twists and turns in Edgeworth's novels but the central mes-sage seeks to promote her long-held though ultimately abandoned Rationalist belief that, despite everything, a solution to the Land Question *is* possible.

Later Anglo-Irish writers—Gerald Griffin (upper class), John and Michael Banim (middle class), and William Carleton ("The Peasant Novelist")—were forced endlessly to re-examine the problems identified by Edgeworth; al-though they brought different perspectives, they too failed to produce any new or convincing solutions. Even when things were taken further, in the wake of the Famine, when Charles Kickham on the one side and Anthony

Trollope on the other, tried to introduce America and England into the equation, still no real answers were discovered. Griffin burned his manuscripts and joined the Christian Brothers before an early death; the Banims became essentially "hack" writers even setting novels in sleepy Eastbourne on the Sussex coast; and Carleton simply put "Black" into the title of some rather feeble later works in the vain hope of repeating the success of his acclaimed Famine novel *The Black Prophet* (1845). Kickham ended up deaf and blind, in a world of his own having alienated most of his friends and colleagues with his fantasy of America saving Ireland; while in *The Landleaguers* (1883), Trollope thought England should step in, suspend *habeas corpus* and read the Riot Act, before turning the clock back to his romanticized vision of the 1840s. Clearly, the chance of finding a solution to the Land Question became increasingly desperate and, above all, ever more gloomy and pessimistic.

So what is an Agrarian novel? These were works written by Anglo-Irish writers of various classes and religions during the course of the 19th century. Owing to lack of serious historians of and in Ireland—there was no Irish Thomas Babington Macaulay—the novelists had to act as historians, sociopolitical commentators, and creative writers. Their subject was what became known as the Irish Land Question. Inevitably and endlessly they use the same basic plot, often with an implied though never realized presence of the supernatural: the Irish-despising son of absentee landowners finds himself in Ireland, sees how his parents' tenants are being mistreated by land agents/middlemen, becomes enlightened, sorts out matters, marries a "true" Irish woman, and returns to live permanently on the family estate. Whether in the socio-realistic novel of Edgeworth at the beginning of the 19th century or in the surreal novel of Stoker at its end, the subject matter remains the same. As Ireland became ever more mired in endless rounds of institutional violence (committed, often technically legally, by landowners) and agrarian violence (committed by tenants), so the analyses became ever darker. Where the agenda espoused by Edgeworth and her followers is essentially positive, especially in the beginning, the alternative agenda followed by Thomas Moore and Stoker was both surreal and much darker in outlook.

Once Anglo-Irish writers had accepted that the land problem in Ireland was probably insoluble, the novels moved from the superficially social-realist (though already containing elements of the unreal) to the overtly surreal. The crucial change was that the problem of Ireland was seen to be eternal and as such it could not "die." We are approaching the world of the undead. The process culminates in vampirism, in *Dracula*. Far from being unique in Anglo-Irish literature, however, Count Dracula had some direct ancestors specifically in Silas Ruthyn in *Uncle Silas* and Carmilla in *Carmilla*—in the 1860s and 1870s—and Dorian Gray in *The Picture of Dorian Gray* in the 1890s. Pre-dating all these, however, is Captain Rock in *Memoirs of Captain Rock* and, to lesser extent, Melmoth in *Melmoth the Wanderer*, both of whom belong to the 1820s.

Charles Maturin was an eccentric Anglo-Irish cleric and writer, who created the first "undead" anti-hero in Anglo-Irish literature with Melmoth. *Melmoth the Wanderer* (1820) is often seen as the first "Irish Gothic" novel and, as Jim Kelly notes, it has only recently been "taken seriously as part of a vigorous and cosmopolitan post-Union literary scene, in which the state of Ireland was raised, portrayed and argued for."[6] The central character of the novel, with its extraordinary and complex narrative, is Melmoth, who wanders the earth after selling his soul in return for 150 years of extra life full of knowledge and power. So, although technically alive, like Dorian Gray later in the century, Melmoth is of the undead—a mixture of pure evil and human form. In this he resembles Count Dracula but, unlike the Count, he can save himself if he can find another person to replace him by making the same Faustian pact. Unfortunately for Melmoth, he can find no one willing to damn himself in this way. His grisly death is not described in detail but, perhaps for that very reason, it is all the more terrifying. Although in some ways *Melmoth* is as original as *Dracula*, its links with Stoker's work are less obvious than is the case with Le Fanu's *Uncle Silas* (1864). In *Melmoth the Wanderer*, the story begins in the 17th century—a key period in Agrarian novels—and begins and ends in Ireland but, as the title suggests, Melmoth wanders abroad. Equally, though he is undead, he is only so for a limited period of time—death for him is postponed rather than beaten. Nonetheless, it is hard to imagine that the well-read Stoker was not aware of the work. One thing we do know: Maturin met Thomas Moore "at a soiree in Lady Morgan's at the end of August 1823,"[7] and that Maturin became more political when writing his *Five Sermons on the Errors of the Catholic Church* [sic] (1824).

Violence between the Protestant Ascendancy and the Catholic tenantry was endemic in 19th-century Ireland. Both sides committed atrocities as violence begat violence. In Anglo-Irish literature perhaps the most powerful motif, implicit or explicit, is the wheel—what Moore, in *Memoirs of Captain Rock* (1824), calls "Ixion's wheel of torture" (Ixion, in classical mythology, was bound to a burning wheel for eternity). Ireland is Ixion, tortured and bound to an ever-rotating wheel: Ascendancy violence begets tenant violence, which begets Ascendancy violence, which begets tenant violence and so on. As Captain Rock insists:

> [W]hile the progress of time produces a change in all nations, the destiny of Ireland remains still the same—that here we still find her, at the end of so many centuries, struggling, like Ixion, on her wheel of torture—never advancing, always suffering—her whole existence one monotonous round of agony.[8]

The inspiration for *Memoirs* came to Moore on a tour of Ireland. He decided to keep a diary which, though containing details of elaborate dinners and social visits, also included reflections on Ireland's past. His original intention was to turn the diary into a purely factual account of his tour. Moore, however, encountered "some real specimens of Irish misery and filth; three or four cottages together exhibiting such a naked swarm of wretchedness as never met my eyes before."[9] The experience so affected Moore that he abandoned his original plan in favor of the "History of Captain Rock and his Ancestors," which may be more livelily [sic] and certainly more easily done."[10] Moore created the persona of Captain Rock, leader of a secret society (known variously as Rockites, Ribbonmen, or Whiteboys), who has been always present in Ireland. Rock exists solely because of the hatred between the Irish tenants and their Anglo-Irish Ascendancy/English masters. In "Captain Rock in London," Moore explicitly states, "For, as long as they flourish, we Rocks cannot die."[11] He recounts Irish "history" from the beginning to the present day [1824]. The dynamics are simple: so long as the English are in Ireland persecuting the tenants, Rock and his followers will attack the Ascendancy—the violence (Rock's lifeblood and what gives him a form of immortality) will continue. So long as the tenants are persecuted, Rock will survive as one of the undead.

Something rather like what historians call the "General Crisis of the 17th Century" seems to have haunted the story of Ireland; she had a bloody and difficult birth into a violent, unsympathetic and evil world. Even today, Oliver Cromwell is still reviled in Ireland, and his name used as an emotive and highly political insult. It remains true that the 17th century is one of the bloodiest on record. It was then that Hibernia's torture really began with essentially the same battles still going on in the 19th century as Ixion's wheel turns once more. In other words, the crisis of the 17th century had not ended when it ended elsewhere. Of course, in the very long run, Edgeworth and her literary followers were right in their analyses and suggested solutions, but it was a lesson learned too late; it was only at the beginning of the 20th century that the Land Question largely settled.

Moore was obviously not a Freudian nor could he have known of later ideas about the "General Crisis of the 17th Century"—though, because Rock claims to be eternal, perhaps we should allow for the possibility that he does know about these things. The essence of Rock's case is that, while other nations change, "the destiny of Ireland remains still the same" (*Memoirs*, p. ix); the same message is repeated time after time and an impressive case is built up. There had been no real change in the system of government:

> So like is one part of the history of Ireland to another that, in reading it, we are
> somewhat in the situation of that absent [minded] man, to whom D'Argeson

lent the same volume of a work four successive times, and who, when asked how he liked the author, answered, '*il me semble qu'il se repete quelquefois.*' The Government of Ireland 'se repete' with a vengeance! (*Memoirs*, p. 108n)

To say that 19th-century Ireland was essentially the same as 17th-century Ireland did not mean that nothing at all had happened: indeed, far too much had happened. Unlike England, Ireland had not enjoyed the benefits of progress but neither had it experienced the quiet and calm of total stagnation. There had been change of a kind, but this had been cyclical rather than linear. It is here that the significance of the image of Ixion's wheel becomes apparent. Ireland never advances and always suffers, "her whole existence one monotonous round of agony" (*Memoirs*, p. ix)—but why does the wheel never stop?

There were several ways in which the wheel might have stopped. It would have stopped if Ireland had been totally destroyed—perhaps sunk, like Atlantis, under the waves of the Atlantic Ocean. Something similar had been proposed, perhaps in jest, by Sir Francis Walsingham, an English Statesmen in Tudor times, and by the Duke of Wellington in the 19th century. Walsingham suggested that the populations of Ireland and the Netherlands be exchanged; the industrious Dutch would transform Ireland into a paradise, while the Irish would neglect the Dutch dykes and all would be drowned. Moore, knowing of Walsingham's proposal, hints that Ireland's suffering had been so great that total extinction might have been preferable.

The wheel might have stopped if one of the contending parties became strong enough to achieve total victory. Perhaps this was the only answer, but the horrors of such victory would eclipse even those of the 17th century. W. F. Trench claims that Moore believed "that Ireland must go through some violent and convulsive process" and "if Separation [sic] was to be the price, it would be well worth paying, however dreadful would be the pain of it."[12] Yet rising after rising had failed and only added to the total of misery: the two sides were too evenly balanced for either to be able to model Ireland entirely in its own image.

Another possibility would be for the parties to compromise, to show goodwill, mutual respect, and tolerance. That was the solution proposed by Edgeworth and her successors. The wheel might have stopped too if the Irish and Anglo-Irish had joined together against the English, which was what nearly happened with the United Irishmen. Moore did toy with this possibility as he reveals in his personal diary:

[W]e cannot possibly judge how far the dawn of independence which rose upon Ireland in '82 might have brightened if it had been overcast by this general convulsion of the whole civilised world.[13]

In *Memoirs*, however, Rock sees no chance of unity or compromise, stressing that for over 200 years both parties have consistently revealed their worst sides in their dealings with each other:

> [I]n this unhappy country it is only the *evil* of each system that is perpetuated—eternal struggles, without one glimpse of freedom, and an unrelaxing pressure of power, without one moment of consolidation or repose. (*Memoirs*, p. ix)

Moore describes the negative side of England at length, associating it with the misdeeds of major historical characters like James I, the Protestant son of the Catholic Mary Queen of Scots, whose reign saw "the first use made of English law . . . to rob thousands of the unfortunate natives of their property" (*Memoirs*, p. 66). It was James who was largely responsible for the "Plantation of Ulster" and the arrival of Protestant settlers into the North of Ireland: "six entire counties of Ulster . . . were forfeited 'at one fell swoop' to the crown."

Perhaps with some regret, Rock admits that, in James's reign "the ROCKS did not flourish" (*Memoirs*, p. 68), though they were still extant. James's successors may have far exceeded his atrocities but Rock is clearly puzzled by the relative indulgence shown to the first of the Stuart Kings of England, perhaps it was because the Irish believed that James was descended from Milesius, the common ancestor of all Celts.[14] Rock seems to endorse this theory when he implies that the Irish are too sentimental and too ready to regard "a prince's promise" as a "kind of convenient talisman, which may be broken over and over, without in the least degree, losing its charm" (*Memoirs*, p. 62). But Rock feels that they are mistaken: no Irishman should trust an English monarch. Yet there are more prosaic explanations. Rock gives more credence to Sir John Davies who explained Irish inaction in the early 17th century as the logical result of military defeat and natural disasters—reinforced by firm English government and law. It was more likely, however, that corruption was the real cause. Rock's theory is that the government of Ireland "*se répète.*"

Captain Rock is the eternal personification of Irish resistance to the English, and *Memoirs* tells the story of the long succession of Irish risings, from the Rebellion of 1641, through 1798, to the Rockite campaign of 1821–24. As with the story of English oppression, little changes in the Irish response. Although contemporary Protestants still regard the Rebellion of 1641 as "an odious and unnatural rebellion," Catholics see this "paroxysm of 'wild justice'" (*Memoirs*, p. 92) as the result of Lord Strafford's policies. So, 1641 is the source of Ireland's ills and the start of the pattern of agrarian violence that—with a brief respite in the first half of the 18th century—still continues in the 1820s. Rock contends that the long-term subjection of the Irish, the allegedly legitimate seizure of their lands, and the persecution of their religion justifies reciprocal agrarian violence. English oppression acts as Rock's recruiting sergeant; they give him "a soul for right, and a soul for riot" (*Memoirs*, p. 106). The process is quite simple:

> [I]n many places where the English had obtained settlements, the natives were *first driven into insurrections by their cruelty, and then punished with double cruelty for their resistance* [sic]. (*Memoirs*, p. 80n)

In short, the situation provides the perfect recipe for endless violence. English oppression makes Rock hard-bitten and cynical. He is an "amateur" (i.e., a "lover") of violence and is grateful to the English because they provide him with his pastime; indeed, he thanks them for creating a "Fund of Discord" upon which he can still draw:

> I am not the less grateful to the 'wisdom of our ancestors' for that inexhaustible Fund of Discord which it has bequeathed to me and my family . . . who contribute weekly, monthly, and annually their quotas to this venerable Fund, and promise to make it as large and lasting a blessing as the Debt of England itself. (*Memoirs*, pp. 106-7)

We have proactive English oppression and essentially reactive Irish resistance and agrarian outrages. This may go some way to explain the motion of the wheel, but we need to consider its operation more minutely. English oppression and Irish resistance are not completely separate forces but are directly linked. Although they may greet examples of Irish resistance with horror and outrage, the English secretly welcome them. In fact, Irish resistance is actually part of their plan, so much so that, when they want more land, they deliberately set out to stir up a rebellion and are utterly unscrupulous in their methods. The role of Orangemen on the wheel is merely that of Government pawns. They are encouraged to provoke the Catholics—and, as ordinary people, they are inevitably exposed to Catholic counter-violence while their masters sit back in safety deciding how to derive maximum advantage for themselves. The pattern is clear: the Government supports landowners, as does the Church of Ireland. A Protestant hegemony uses the law and the military—institutional violence—to maintain order. Once this is achieved, the Government, perhaps with an eye to national or international politics, slightly loosens its grip. Emboldened, the Irish, covertly supported by the Catholic Church, seek to take advantage of this apparent leniency. The Government and the Ascendancy are neither willing nor able to understand the tenants' grievances. Once more they tighten their grip; naturally this elicits an equally violent response—and so the wheel turns again.

It is tacitly admitted in *Memoirs* that Rock and his followers are serving the English purpose, just like the Orangemen. Both groups are fastened to the wheel. Even the British government, in some ways astonishingly naïve, is tied too. Indeed, virtually the full cast list of stereotypical figures is strapped to it as well: Protestant landowners, middlemen/agents, vulnerable ladies, Protestant and Catholic clergy, tenants, and secret societies. The same is true of institutions: the Monarchy, the Government, the Churches, the Military, the Militia, the Judiciary, the Orange Order, and the Nationalists. Names may change but the roles, the places on the wheel, never do. The situation is hopeless and offers neither comfort nor hope except, significantly, to the undead Rock who thrives on the eternal misery. Ireland has become the land of the undead—that is its essential tragedy.

We can now turn to the closest Anglo-Irish literary predecessor to *Dracula*. Appreciation of the influence of the Sensation novels is important to a proper understanding of Stoker's work. As soon as Count Dracula appears, two key elements—vampirism and sexuality—dwarf all others. *Dracula* is not merely a reworking of the Land Question: rather it is a curious blend of the Agrarian novel, the Gothic novel, and the Sensation novel. While some modern critics have identified the novel's Irish parallels, they have missed its links to Agrarian novels and to the circular interpretation of Irish history proposed by Moore. Also, they have not fully appreciated the importance of the Sensation novel exemplified by Le Fanu. Strikingly, the cool reception accorded to *Dracula*—and to other major innovative works of the 1890s, such as Oscar Wilde's *The Picture of Dorian Gray* (1891) and Kate Chopin's *The Awakening* (1899)—echo the equally critical response to Wilkie Collins's *The Woman in White* (1859–60). Both Collins and Stoker reflect changes in society that produced unease in the conservative minded; indeed, "[t]he 1890s has the reputation of being a 'naughty' decade."[15]

Although the Sensation novel was not specifically Irish, one of its greatest exponents, Le Fanu, was Anglo-Irish. Some characteristics of the genre can be traced back to the Gothic novel, exemplified, as we have seen, in the works of Maturin.[16] Stoker was influenced both by the Gothic novel and—to a greater extent—by the Sensation novel.

The Sensation novel was at its height in the 1860s[17] although it had been prefigured in some of the Brontë novels including *Jane Eyre* (1847) and *Wuthering Heights* (1847). Even George Eliot and Charles Dickens indulged in Sensationalism—Eliot in *Adam Bede* (1859) and Dickens in *Great Expectations* (1861). The Sensation novel became a media phenomenon with *The Woman in White* and Mary Elizabeth Braddon's *Lady Audley's Secret* (1862). Sensation novels, often based on reports of real events, set out to shock their predominantly middle-class and female readers. They often involve unjust imprisonment, sealed rooms, secret passages, abductions, murders, hints of the supernatural (real or imagined), and a host of evil characters. A key element is the inversion of the roles of conventional characters. Refined fathers, brothers, and uncles emerge, not as the protectors of vulnerable women but as their persecutors; beautiful, cultured ladies turn into murderers of men; transgression of gender roles becomes the norm.

In Le Fanu's *The House by the Churchyard* (1863), Paul Dangerfield is described as being a vampire, half-alive and half-dead. He glides through corridors rather than walks, as does Silas Ruthyn in *Uncle Silas*; Dangerfield is also described as a "wher-wolf."[18] But it is Le Fanu's *Uncle Silas* that exhibits the most remarkable similarities with *Dracula*. In both, there are female protagonists whose roles differ radically from those found in more conventional novels. Le Fanu's Madame de la Rougierre is a study in transgressive sexuality while Maud Ruthyn fights for survival independent of male support; in *Dracula*, the "New Woman," Mina, is both independent and willful. As some critics saw the Sensation novel as a literary disease that threatened disorder so, in *Dracula*, the Count spreads disorder and disease. In the archetypal Gothic novel, horrors take place in the Appenines or Abruzzi but, in Sensation novels, they occur in the British home. In *Dracula*, the horrors occur both in remote mountains and in the home as the vampire travels from his Transylvanian lair to England. As we know, terror is far greater in a familiar, homely setting.

Dracula is a vampire who, half-dead, must kill and drink blood to be even half-alive. He moves silently, appearing next to his victims without sound or warning. When he arrives at Whitby on the *Demeter*, he changes into a wolf-like dog to escape his pursuers and, later, in the same guise, attempts to enter Lucy's bedroom. Bartram Haugh, like Dracula's Castle, is a semi-derelict Irish Big House. Madame de la Rougierre, like the Brides of Dracula, is herself implicitly vampiric in her apparent ability to lie with the dead before rising again: "Don't you love the dead, Cheaile? I will teach you to love them. You shall see me die here to-day, for half an hour, and be among them. That is what I love."[19]

While the Brides feed off the blood of the young, Madame de la Rougierre feeds off her hatred for Maud. Yet she too meets a suitably vampiric end when she is killed by Dudley Ruthyn, who uses "a longish tapering spike" to dispatch her (*Silas*, p. 415).

In Silas Ruthyn,[20] we see a precursor of Dracula; both are associated with foul weather and wolves. While Dracula controls the wolves and actually becomes one, Maud perceives herself surrounded by wolves and is obsessed by a picture of a girl pursued by "a pack of wolves" (*Silas*, p. 338). Dracula and Silas can enter and leave sealed rooms. Harker sees Dracula "begin to crawl down the castle wall . . . *face down*, with his cloak spreading out around him like great wings" (*Dracula*, p. 47); Silas gets into and out of a sealed room to

murder Charke. Lady Monica Knollys, the force for good in *Uncle Silas*, refers
to Silas as "an old enchanter in his castle" (*Silas*, p. 144), and Maud's own
description of her uncle could apply to Dracula:[21]

> I saw him before me still, in necromantic black, ashy with a pallor on which
> I looked with fear and pain, a face so dazzlingly pale, and those hollow, fiery,
> awful eyes. (*Silas*, p. 194)[22]

A further similarity between *Uncle Silas* and *Dracula* is that Harker, like
Maud, is forced to write letters indicating all is well when, in reality, death is
near; both hear their own graves being dug. While Maud attempts to persuade
Tom Brice to take a note, begging for help, to Lady Knollys, Harker tries to
send a similar note via the Szgany gypsies—but both are betrayed.

Stoker's short story, "Dracula's Guest," is really the "missing chapter" of
Dracula and has taken on a life of its own. It appears that, as a result of a dispute between Stoker and the Estate of J. S. Le Fanu, the chapter was removed
from Stoker's novel shortly before publication because it was "too close" to Le
Fanu's *Carmilla* (1871)—a tale about a lesbian vampire.

Equally, when *Uncle Silas* and *Dracula* are compared with each other, the
similarities, in key parts, are extraordinary; such as Stoker's original plan to set
Dracula in Styria, the setting of *Carmilla*. As Christopher Frayling suggests:

> Stoker seems to have been much taken by the strange and beautiful relationship
> between vampire and victim in *Carmilla*. Lucy and the brides of Dracula court
> their prey in ways which owe much to Le Fanu's listless *femme fatale* . . . *Car-
> milla's* dream-like fantasy about sexually aware, and sexually dominant, women
> . . . would seem to have bitten deep into the psyche of two apparently prosaic,
> not-so-eminent Victorian males: Bram Stoker and his fictional counterpart,
> Jonathan Harker.[23]

Although not a Sensation novel, the influence of Le Fanu's *Carmilla* on
Dracula is significant. The story concerns the lesbian vampire Carmilla's
relentless pursuit of the innocent Laura. Baron Vordenberg, Laura's father,
believes that "[a] suicide, under certain circumstances, becomes a vampire."[24]
In *Carmilla*, Le Fanu seeks to frighten his readers on two levels—also a feature of *Dracula*. First, Carmilla is frightening because she is a woman out of
control both sexually and physically. Secondly, like Dracula, she is a vampire,
a revenant, who returns from the grave to create mayhem. Dracula's diseased
blood infects all those who come into contact with him, but Carmilla's blood
is doubly diseased—it imparts both death and sexual deviance. Carmilla, in
life Countess Mircalla (an anagram of Carmilla), is pursued by a group of men
through Styria and is dispatched by "a sharp stake driven through the heart
of the vampire" and whose "head was struck off" (*Carmilla*, pp. 106–7).[25] In

Dracula, Lucy is dispatched in a similar manner (*Dracula*, pp. 257–8). In short, Stoker appears to look to Ireland's literary past rather than to its future.

Stoker, ever the social climber, married Oscar Wilde's former fiancée,[26] and it is possible that he wrote *Dracula* to compete with Wilde's *The Picture of Dorian Gray* (1891). Like Captain Rock, Dorian Gray lives at the expense of and on the needs of others. Superficially a sophisticated, elegant, intelligent gentleman, he is also violent, evil, and ruthless. He lives on, an immortal, untainted thanks to the portrait, despite his appalling actions; again, he is one of the undead. Like Rock and Carmilla, Gray cannot die—they are all the undead. Gray is a murderer who feeds off the misery, sorrow, and deaths of others. Although, like Dracula, Gray wants to be regarded as a cultured gentleman, as the critic of *The Scots Observer* notes, he is really "a devil."[27] Just as Dracula and the other vampires infect society so, as the critic of *The Daily Chronicle* observes, Dorian "might go on for ever [sic] using his senses with impunity 'to cure his soul,' defiling English society with the moral pestilence which is incarnate in him" (*Gray*, p. 218). When Dorian dies, we encounter a creature, ugly in death, stabbed through the heart:

> Lying on the floor was a dead man, in evening dress, with a knife in his heart. He was withered, wrinkled, and loathsome of visage. (*Gray*, p. 213)

In a curious example of circularity in Anglo-Irish literature and life, Wilde, after his release from jail, used the pseudonym of Sebastian Melmoth (after St. Sebastian and *Melmoth the Wanderer*) while in self-imposed European exile.

Although Moore's *Memoirs of Captain Rock* represents the start of an approach to the Land Question radically different to the one proposed by Edgeworth or even her more Nationalist-inclined successors, Rock's surreal successor was Silas Ruthyn who, 30 years earlier, did what Count Dracula was to do at the end of the 1890s. It is perhaps no coincidence that *Uncle Silas* and *Dracula* appeared in the two decades of the 19th century that were most closely associated with the flowering of sensuality in literature and were notably less prudish than other decades. Ultimately, a rather tedious piece of legislation—the Wyndham Land Acts, which largely handed the land back to the Catholic tenants—finally settled matters in what was eventually to become the Republic of Ireland. Then all the literary discussions that had occurred between the Anglo-Irish novelists during the proceeding century were consigned to the dustbin of history or to the surreal world of film. Dracula made the transition with aplomb, but Silas Ruthyn had less luck, and Captain Rock none at all.

Regardless of who most influenced Stoker in his creation of Dracula, the Count has become synonymous with vampires; but he is also synonymous with Ascendancy landowners. Stoker's tale is the surreal version of what had been recorded over the previous century by his fellow Anglo-Irish writers. Dracula's decaying castle is a decaying Irish Big House and he commits acts of violence on a vast and bloody scale and, quite literally, bleeds both his tenants and his lands dry. As the land of the Ascendancy is gradually removed and their estates become ever smaller, so the Count is reduced to sleeping on all the land he still possesses, the earth in his coffin. As his world collapses behind him and he no longer belongs anywhere, so the Ascendancy landowners witness their world disappearing as Ireland moves toward independence. The Anglo-Irish will have to choose whether to be English or Irish. Unless they can do this they face complete destruction; their natural world suddenly becomes the middle of the Irish Sea and, like the Count, they have nowhere left to run.

Returning to the quotation at the beginning of this chapter, it seems that the tradition of the unreal or the surreal was especially strong in Irish literature—not least because the historical experience of Ireland itself was so extraordinary that it could be better understood in fiction than in history and in surreal fiction than in realist fiction. Of course, Stoker presents Dracula as the last of his line but this was not really the case. The "family tree" that runs from Swift through Maturin, Moore, to Stoker was to grow new branches in the 20th century when James Joyce in *Ulysses* (1922) and *Finnegans Wake* (1939) took the surreal to entirely new and unforeseen heights.

Notes

1. Paul Murray, *From The Shadow of Dracula: A Life of Bram Stoker* (London: Jonathan Cape, 2004), 192, quoting Terry Eagleton.
2. I am deeply grateful to John Clarke, Professor of History at The University of Buckingham, for his help in the preparation of this chapter.
3. Augustus J. C. Hare, *The Life and Letters of Maria Edgeworth*: Volume II [1894] (New York: Books For Libraries Press, 1971), February 1834, 550.
4. Augustus J. C. Hare, *The Life and Letters of Maria Edgeworth*: Volume I (London: Edward Arnold, 1894), 41.
5. Maria Edgeworth, *The Absentee* [1812] (Oxford: Oxford University Press, 1988), 263.
6. Jim Kelly, *Charles Maturin: Authorship, Authenticity and the Nation* (Dublin: Four Courts Press, 2011), 9.
7. Kelly, *Charles Maturin,* 176.
8. Thomas Moore, *Memoirs of Captain Rock &c* (London: Longman, Hurst, Rees, Orme, Brown, and Green, 1824), ix. Further references to this edition are given after quotations in the text and the title shortened to *Memoirs.*

9. Thomas Moore, *Memoirs, Journal and Correspondences of Thomas Moore*: Volume IV (1823), ed. Lord John Russell (London: Longman, Brown, Green, and Longmans, 1853), October 10, 1823, 137.

10. Moore, *Memoirs, Journal and Correspondences of Thomas Moore*, 103.

11. Thomas Moore, *The Poetical Works of Thomas Moore* (London: Bliss Sands & Co., n.d.), 412.

12. W. F. Trench, *Tom Moore* (Dublin: At the Sign of the Three Candles, 1934), 20.

13. Moore, *Memoirs, Journal and Correspondences of Thomas Moore*: Volume IV, 14 April 1823, 57.

14. See John and Michael Banim ["The O'Hara Family"], *The Boyne Water* [1826] (New York: D & J Sadlier & Co., 1869), 24.

15. M. J. Trow, *Vlad The Impaler: In Search Of The Real Dracula* (Stroud: Sutton Publishing, 2003), 31. See Stephen D. Arata, "The Occidental Tourist: *Dracula* and the Anxiety of Reverse Colonisation," in *Dracula*, ed. by Glennis Byron (Basingstoke: Macmillan Press Ltd., 1999), 120; David Glover, *Vampires, Mummies and Liberals* (London: Duke University Press, 1996), 65; Jean-Jacques Lecercle, "The Kitten's Nose," in *The Gothic*, ed. by Fred Botting (Cambridge: D. S. Brewer, 2001), 83.

16. See Margot Gayle Backus, *The Gothic Family Romance* (London: Duke University Press, 1999), 109–112; Roy F. Foster, *Paddy & Mr. Punch* (London: Penguin Books, 1995), 219–220.

17. See Michael Diamond, *Victorian Sensation* (London: Anthem Press, 2003), 189–217.

18. J. Sheridan Le Fanu, *The House by the Churchyard* [1863] (London: Anthony Blond Ltd., 1968), 447.

19. J. Sheridan Le Fanu, *Uncle Silas* [1864] (Oxford: Oxford University Press, 1968), 32. Further references to this novel are in the text.

20. Note the similarity between the name Silas Ruthyn and Lord Ruthven, the vampire in John Polidori's *The Vampyre* (1819).

21. See *Vampires at Midnight*, ed. Peter Haining (London: Warner Books, 1993), 12.

22. Apart from Silas's "awful eyes," we encounter Dracula's "very bright eyes" that "seemed red" (*Dracula*, p. 19) and Rock's "green spectacles" in Thomas Moore, *Memoirs of Captain Rock* (London: Longman, Hurst, Rees, Orme, Brown, and Green, 1824), 5.

23. Christopher Frayling, *Vampyres* (London: Faber and Faber, 1992), 358–359.

24. J. Sheridan Le Fanu, *Carmilla* [1871] (New York: Scholastic Book Services, 1971), 111.

25. The exact origins of staking a corpse are unknown, but it was a widespread practice, especially in Eastern Europe. The belief was that a corpse, pinned to the ground, could not rise to become a revenant and haunt villagers seeking to drag them down to Hell. Similar anti-revenant practices (though not staking) are still pursued in rural parts of Romania.

26. See *The Complete Letters of Oscar Wilde*, eds. Merlin Holland and Rupert Hart-Davis (New York: Henry Holt and Company, 2000), 72n.

27. Oscar Wilde, *The Picture of Dorian Gray* [1891], ed. Robert Mighall (London: Penguin Books, 2003), 218. Further references to this novel are in the text.

3

Retracing the Shambling Steps of the Undead: The Blended Folkloric Elements of Vampirism in Bram Stoker's *Dracula*

Alexis M. Milmine

THE SOMBER EVENTS OF DISEASE AND DEATH affect every society in every generation, but the community's reaction to these events is colored by the particular folklore of the people and region. The genesis of the vampire legend is most likely attributed to these notions on death and dying, giving a familiar face to the pestilence and suffering found within a community. Although the origin of the vampire motif in folklore is unknown, most countries in the world have their own vampire folklore or a borrowed amalgamation of folkways that point to the predominant burial lore surrounding a community's values. Literature often uses the reimagining of the vampire legend and creates a conglomeration of different folklore to create a unique vision of a blood-sucking fiend who emerges from a dun and dank past to stalk the living and pass on the curse of his existence. In Bram Stoker's *Dracula*, the author creates an undead icon of vampirism that transcends time and the ethnic boundaries of folklore, drawing on a multitude of legends about this supernatural being as well as twisting the traditional folklore of Eastern Europe to create the misguided belief in Count Dracula as a typical Transylvanian or Romanian vampire.

The etymology of the term *vampire* has no clear source; and, although many claim the roots of the folkloric figure stems from Greece, "there is evidence which links vampiric beings in prehistory in all corners of the world, from ancient Babylonia to India . . . [and] it is interesting to notice similarities in the vampire myth across differing countries and beliefs."[1] Most folklore scholars agree to the presence of vampires in most parts of the world, but certain researchers, such as Matthew Beresford, incorrectly note the type of folklore as myth instead of legend. Alan Dundes notes that the stories of vampires are not myths or folktales because of the inherent exclusivity of the terms, but instead these stories would be classified as legends, "that is, stories told as true and set in the post-creation world. They might conceivably also be classified as memorates, which are personal narratives of the encounters with a supernatural creature, also told as true."[2] The characterization of vampire stories is crucial to the analysis of Stoker's *Dracula* because of both the use of differing variants of vampire folklore as well as the first-person epistolary form of the events that transpire in the novel mimicking the memorate.

Stoker's choice of format and folklore works on the singular effect of the walking undead on the communities that share this belief, namely fear. The fear of the vampire is attributed to several sources: psychological fear of the dead due to love and guilt toward their relatives,[3] the fear of death,[4] and the fear of violating burial lore among other reasons. The overall reasons for the creation of the vampire legend can be argued as the fears of death and the violation of burial lore because of the preponderance of first-hand accounts that indicate preoccupations with both issues. According to Beresford "the one common element to almost all cases of vampirism is fear. Fear is an important factor in the survival of the vampire because, although the vampire has taken various forms in history, it is difficult to pinpoint one dominant form; fear is the main unifying feature, and therefore can be said to provide the key to the vampire's existence."[5] *Dracula* works on this primal fear and the power it holds over the community because the Transylvanian vampire stalks the night in a civilized world in which the undead should be a figment of an overactive imagination or in the minds of the superstitious; but instead the fear becomes a reality because "whether or not the demonic creature of our worst fears existed in fact, if we only looked into ourselves—and into our society—we should find the demon already there."[6] In this way the figure of Dracula confirms all of different folkloric elements concerning the vampire, but Stoker works with a multiplicity of national folklore that creates an ambiguous and amalgamated *nosferatu* and is now mistakenly taken as a stereotype of any and all of the undead.

While Bram Stoker used some of the traditional folklore of Romania and Transylvania, there are curious overlaps of vampire legends from other areas of Eastern Europe as well as ambiguity that does not fall in line with the geographical and folkloric areas in which Count Dracula originally hails from at the beginning of the book. The very land itself, described by Jonathan Harker at the beginning of the novel, works to create a backward and superstitious land of Eastern Europe that is widely different from the Victorian England that most of the audience of Stoker's time would have been familiar with. One problem with terminology needs to be addressed; and although *vam-*

pire can be used to discuss the blood-drinking fiend found in many tropes in literature as well as the general name for a class of supernatural beings found in folklore, Professor Van Helsing states with certitude that Dracula is a "*nosferatu*,"[7] and this term serves as the proper name for the vampire. While nosferatu exists in Romanian folklore, the term is not generally used; and the most popular terms for the vampire, depending on the state of the vampire, are *siscoi, vârcolaci, pricolici, moroii,* and *strigoii,* and "*nosferatu . . .although* it is sometimes used to describe the Transylvanian vampire, *strigoi* is the much more accepted term."[8] The different terms found in Romanian folklore point to different classes of vampires and each one corresponds to their states of being: with the *strigoii and moroii* used as referents to both living and dead vampires, *vârcolaci* and *pricolici* refer to figures that eat the moon that are sometimes confused with werewolves, and *siscoi* being the Transylvanian term for the vampire and usually refers to a live one.[9] Folklorists have researched the incidence of these terms in the accounts of the undead and have found that in "regards [to] the names used for vampires, dead and alive, *strigoi* (fem. *strigoica*) is the most common Roumanian [*sic*] term, and *moroii* is perhaps the next most usual."[10] Through this examination of the Romanian terms used for vampires, we see that Stoker uses a lesser known term in order to create a unique figure in his fictional realm of the undead; but, in choosing *nosferatu,* he also marginalizes the importance of the native Romanian folklore and this becomes one of the first indicators that Count Dracula is not a typical Romanian *strigoi.* Because the proper terminology has been established for the folkloric portrait of the vampire, an examination of the appearance and actions of Count Dracula and the created vampire figure Lucy Westenra will shed further light on the blending and twisting of the vampire legends in Europe.

Harker learns early on that the ways of Romania and Transylvania are not his own, and he is unbalanced by the both the appearance of Dracula as well as the folklore he finds in this newly introduced country. Count Dracula is described with a singularly peculiar and unusual appearance:

> His face was a strong—a very strong—aquiline . . . with a lofty domed forehead, and hair growing scantily round the temples, but profusely elsewhere. His eyebrows were very massive, almost meeting over the nose, and with bushy hair that seemed to curl in its own profusion. The mouth, so far as I could see it under the heavy moustache, was fixed and rather cruel looking, with peculiarly sharp white teeth; these protruded over the lips, whose remarkable ruddiness showed astonishing vitality in a man of his years. For the rest, his ears were pale and at the tops extremely pointed; the chin was broad and strong, and the cheeks firm though thin. The general effect was one of extraordinary pallor.[11]

At this initial description of Dracula's appearance there are some characteristics that fall in line with the folkloric renditions of the vampire. The ruddy
complexion and extreme pallor are indicated of the vampire across several
countries, not just Romania or the region of Transylvania. Most of the accounts of corpses that are believed to be vampires are noted "as being exceed-
ingly gaunt and lean with a hideous countenance[,] . . . the skin is deathly
pale, but the lips are very full and rich, blub and red."[12] Throughout the folklore of Eastern Europe the corpse is characterized to be alternating pale and
red, depending on whether the vampire has fed. Later on in the novel Harker
also sees Dracula in one of the transport boxes filled with soil:

> looking as if his youth had been half renewed, for the white hair and moustache
> were changed to dark iron-grey; the cheeks were fuller, and the white skin
> seemed ruby-red underneath; the mouth was redder than ever, for on the lips
> were fresh gouts of blood, which trickled from the corners of the mouth and ran
> over the chin and neck. Even the deep, burning eyes seemed set amongst swol-
> len flesh, for the lids and pouches underneath were bloated. It seemed as if the
> whole awful creature were simply gorged with blood; he lay like a filthy leech,
> exhausted with his repletion.[13]

Harker's descriptions of Dracula both fall in line with the first-hand accounts
and folklore surrounding the appearance of suspected vampires down to the
trickles of blood coming from the mouth and the distension. As for Dracula's
hair regaining its original color, there are accounts of vampires in Hungary
in which the vampire's "beard and hair were grown fresh and a new set of
nails had sprung up in the room of the old ones that had fallen off. Under
the former skin, which looked pale and dead, there appeared a new one, of
a natural fresh color."[14] Through the use of folklore from not only Romania,
but also accounts of vampires in Hungary, Stoker cinches the role of Dracula
as a vampire early on in the novel.

    At the surface level of an examination of the Count's appearance, the pre-
ponderance of hair denotes a man whose age is not easily determined, but it
also points to the folklore about the werewolf instead of the vampire, especially with the description of the eyebrows. The influence of werewolf lore is
most likely from Stoker's extensive reading on subjects pertaining to Eastern
Europe, including Sabine Baring-Gould's *The Book of Werewolves* and Emily
de Lazowska Gerard's "Transylvanian Superstitions."[15] The most important
traits to discuss are Count Dracula's mouth and teeth because most modern
audiences and reimagining of vampires in the vein of *Dracula* also portray
the vampire with sharp protruding teeth. In most vampire legends the cursed
undead are relatives in a community retaining their lifelike appearance and
the large teeth of Count Dracula is evidence of fakelore or authorial imagina-

tion. According to many scholars "in folklore it is rare to find examples of the 'long, sharp teeth' common to the literary vampire . . . [and this assumption can be based on] people at the time . . . assum[ing] that sharp teeth would have been a necessity for vampires to be able to bite in order to drink the blood, but this could well have been merely an assumption that vampires drank blood in this manner; in Russian folklore the vampire had a sharp, pointed tongue which lacerated the victim in order to obtain blood."[16] Because the iconic long eyeteeth of the vampire is missing in most accounts of folklore, the argument can be extended that Stoker drew the description of the Count's mouth and teeth from some other source outside of traditional vampire legend. The ambiguous nature of Count Dracula's appearance and actions also causes further speculation on the use of various folklores from Eastern Europe.

Harker further expresses his morbid fascination and discomfort at Dracula's appearance with his description of the man's hands as well as his physical reaction to him. According to Harker's diary he "could not but notice that [the Count's hands] were rather coarse—broad, with squat fingers. Strange to say, there were hairs in the centre of the palm. The nails were long and fine, and cut to a sharp point. As the Count leaned over me and his hands touched me, I could not repress a shudder. It may have been that his breath was rank, but a horrible feeling of nausea came over me."[17] According to Nina Auerbach and David J. Skal "these hairy palms are one of Dracula's few affinities with the werewolf."[18] The blending of werewolf and vampire lore displays Stoker's attempts to create a literary figure that does not clearly fit into any particular country's folklore.

Although we are not given the reasons for Dracula's vampiric state, which would point out the specific folklore that Stoker draws from in terms of these unique characteristics, he does include a possible indicator of the reason for Dracula is one of the number of the undead. In most vampire legends the individuals who are consigned to the fact of vampirism after death are "sorcerers, witches, werewolves, excommunicates, and those who died unnatural deaths (such as suicides and drunkards)."[19] According to the Greek Orthodox ritual of excommunication, the corpses of apostates and excommunicates "generally turned black, swelled out like a drum, and emitted an offensive smell."[20] Although only one of the characteristics of the curse of excommunication is found within Stoker's text, it is enough to postulate on Count Dracula's rejection of Christianity since he has become an abhorrence and affront to the Catholic measures taken later in the novel against him and his ilk. The possibility of excommunication or being rejected by death is also alluded to when Dracula appears in Harker's room and Harker cuts himself shaving because "it amazed me that I had not seen him, since the reflection of the glass covered the whole room behind me."[21] Again he notices this curiosity when Dracula comes closer because "there could be no error, for the man was close to me, and I could see him over my shoulder. But there was no reflection of him in the mirror!"[22] The folklore surrounding death ritual and vampires is clear on the vampire's reflection "because the vampire is 'dead' and soulless, it has no reflection."[23] Although Stoker does not note the way in which Dracula became a vampire, the discrepancies are interesting and cause extreme ambiguity over the type of vampire he is or where the folklore Stoker uses comes from.

Stoker also deviates from the normal vampire lore when he has Dracula sail from Transylvania to England, violating the traditional folkloric belief that vampires preyed on their closest relatives. The only explanation for the violation of the folklore is a Romanian belief that a vampire will begin a reign of terror and death "for a period of seven years, during which it will first kill its relations, then the other residents and animals of its village, then those of every village in its country, after which it will pass into another country where a different language is spoken. There it will become a man again."[24] The only problem with attaching Dracula's movements to this account is that Dracula has no intention of becoming a mortal man and there is no evidence that he has preyed on his family, animals, or destroyed the villages surrounding him in Transylvania. Stoker may have been influenced by this belief, but he rejects a strict adherence to the vampire lore in order to introduce the foreign other into the heart of Victorian England.

The existence of the vampire brides in Dracula's castle, as well as Lucy Westenra's fate as a vampire, is unexplainable by traditional Romanian folklore. According to the folklore "vampires tend to be born rather than made, unlike the examples from vampire literature."[25] Lucy's transformation into a vampire violates most of the folklore in Eastern Europe. The first symptoms of Dracula's attack do highlight the correctness of Stoker's attribution and use of traditional Eastern European vampire lore, not only from Romania but also other countries, because Lucy herself notices "more bad dreams. I wish I could remember them. This morning I am horribly weak. My face is ghastly pale, and my throat pains me. It must be something wrong with my lungs, for I don't seem ever to get air enough."[26] Most people suffering from vampire attacks notice the symptoms of nightmares, but the most often cited symptom is difficulty breathing or feelings of suffocation. Stoker blends the typical symptom of the feelings of anxiety and suffocation with the revenant's need for blood when Lucy exhibits difficulty breathing as well as puncture wounds on her neck.[27] In 1591, in Silesia there is a well-documented case of a suicide that came back as a vampire and "was then buried beneath the gallows, but the apparition still came to the bedsides of the alarmed inhabitants, pinching and suffocating people, and leaving marks of its fingers plainly visible on the flesh."[28] On top of the peculiar symptoms of Lucy, near her death began a transformation into Stoker's version of a vampire because Dr. Seward, Professor Van Helsing, and others notice "her teeth, in the dim, uncertain light, seemed longer and sharper than they had been in the morning. In particular, by some trick of the light, the canine teeth looked longer and sharper than the rest."[29] The folkloric attributes of Lucy's changing teeth cannot be found in any of the accounts of Eastern Europe or any other neighboring regions.

Garlic, one of the apotropaics that most Eastern European folklore argue as a safeguard against vampires, is used in *Dracula* in terms of trying to save Lucy's life. Professor Van Helsing brings garlic flowers to lay around the neck of Lucy as well as going about the windows in the room "first . . . fasten[ing] . . . and latch[ing] them securely; next, taking a handful of the flowers, he rubbed them all over the sashes, as though to ensure that every whiff of air that might get in would be laden with the garlic smell. Then with the wisp he rubbed all over the jamb of the door, above, below, and at each side, and round the fireplace in the same way."[30] The ritual cleansing of the room corresponds to a Romanian belief that on certain days safeguards must be taken "when it is thought evil spirits are abroad [and] garlic is rubbed on windows in the pattern of a cross, placed above the door or rubbed on all means of entry to a building, and sometimes even rubbed on farm animals to protect them against vampires."[31] There is further delineation of Van Helsing's actions because Seward becomes confused by his actions and attributes the use of garlic for the smell,[32] which points to Chinese death rituals in which "'any one who calls at a mortuary house incurs a kind of pollution, especially so if death has been untimely or caused by disease. Some condolers therefore wisely hid a few garlic roots under their garments, convinced that the strong smell will prevent the influences of death from clutching to their bodies.'"[33] Garlic has a strong attribution of Romanian folklore, yet the use of garlic to ward off evil in other countries' folklore suggest that other influences cannot be ruled out in Stoker's choice of herb in warding off Dracula, as well as garlic being a well-known ingredient in folk medicine.

After Lucy's death and transformation into a vampire, the audience would expect, when looking at the traditional Romanian folklore, that Lucy would target her family and friends in her nightly attacks and hunt for bloody sustenance. Stoker deviates from the traditional formula; and Lucy instead targets children, earning the nickname "the Bloofer Lady" among those who had seen her. Lucy's choice of prey can be argued as Stoker's conscious choice to reverse the traditional maternal instincts of a Victorian lady, but vampire attacks on children are present in folklore outside of Romania and other Eastern European countries. Both Lucy and the vampire brides at Dracula's castle exhibit a lust for children's blood as well as seducing young men, which highlights "the similarities between [these characters] and the ancient vampires such as Lilith or the Lamia."[34] Folklore in England and Ireland also stands as influences in the author's creation of vampires in his novel because these vampire legends involve beautiful women who prowl the countryside until they are transfixed in their resting spots.[35] Stoker recasts vampire lore to strike fear in the hearts of his Victorian audience as well as to create an icon of vampirism that would influence subsequent literature on the subject.

The deaths of Lucy and Dracula also illuminate an interesting melding and twisting of vampire lore through the use of garlic, stakes, and knives to dispatch the evil undead. Early after Lucy's death, Van Helsing proposes to dispatch her because of her vampiric state by cutting "off her head and fill[ing] her mouth with garlic, and I shall drive a stake through her body."[36] Cutting off the head or staking the vampire is seen in Romania as ways of dispatching the vampire, but filling the mouth with garlic is prevention against leaving the grave. According to many sources of folklore and folklore scholars "a variety of things may be placed in the mouth (dirt, garlic, a coin) to give the revenant something to chew on or to prevent chewing or blood-sucking entirely."[37] The use of garlic in the mouth, much like placing communion wafers in Dracula's boxes of dirt, does not destroy the vampire, but instead works to keep the revenants from their foul nightly activities. Staking is another peculiar way of destroying the vampire because, even though in some instances it is seen as successful, the only foolproof way of killing the vampire is to burn the corpse entirely. Several Eastern European countries have methods of burning the corpse, with an emphasis that nothing must be left untouched or the vampire will return. Some folk beliefs argue that a moth or a butterfly will escape the body while burning, and it is crucial to catch the insect because "if the butterfly escapes . . . woe to the village, because the vampire wreaks a frightful vengeance, which does not end until finally a period of seven years runs out."[38] The stake is also seen as ineffective in some communities because "the soul, the *vegetative* soul, tied to blood, to the heart, to muscles, and to the intestines, continues to exist until the last part of all this exists, and the vampire will exist up until the least bit of his body exists."[39] Some cultures hold that the stake does not kill the vampire but instead transfixes him to the grave. Stoker deviates from this traditional belief in Eastern Europe, however, and Van Helsing instructs Arthur Holmwood to "take this stake in your left hand, ready to place the point over the heart, and the hammer in your right. Then when we begin our prayer for the dead—I shall read him, I have here the book, and the others shall follow—strike in God's name, that so all may be well with the dead that we love, and that the Un-Dead pass away."[40] Stoker does not note the type of wood the stake is made of and this specificity of the wood is inherent in the vampire lore of Eastern Europe. Distaffs were sometimes used in Romania, whereas in Bosnia and Serbia the stake is made of hawthorn because "the hawthorn is a charm and an antidote . . . they believe in Bosnia that one can catch the devil himself with it."[41] The stake is believed among many to rivet the corpse to the grave to prevent his wandering and to stop the deadly visitations on relatives and other people of the community. In Stoker's work, the unnamed stake is used to kill Lucy completely and release her soul, but the same type of weaponry is not used against Dracula, the stronger vampire, and his method of destruction does not fall in line with problematic vampires in Romania or other regions of Eastern Europe.

Scholars have noted that Dracula's death is replete with ambiguity because he is not dispatched in the normal way that vampire hunters undertake the destruction of a dangerous and powerful revenant. Both Harker and Quincy Morris dispatch an immobilized Dracula with "the sweep and flash of Jonathan's great knife [as] it shear[ed] through the throat; whilst at the same moment Mr. Morris' bowie knife plunged into the heart" and "before our very eyes, and almost in the drawing of a breath, the whole body crumbled into dust and passed from our sight."[42] A pernicious and bloodthirsty vampire such as Dracula would, by folkloric standards, dictate a complete burning of the body, but in Stoker's work knives all too easily dispatch the monster that the protagonists have been valiantly struggling against. Even with this ambiguity surrounding the destruction of Dracula, there is evidence of non-Romanian folklore being employed. In Serbian vampire lore there are many ways to dispatch vampires, including complete burning, decapitation, or supplemental burial (staking of the corpse), but Serbians use a substitution of the ancient forms of neutralizing the vampire, namely "the custom of 'cutting' the corpse, and that most often in the *head* or the *forehead* or the neck."[43] The act of Harker slitting the throat of Dracula can point to the folkloric cutting of the corpse to prevent rising, but there is also the importance of iron in many vampire legends. In Transylvania and other regions of Eastern Europe, a corpse would be buried with sickles "'allegedly in order to prevent the swelling of the body,' [and] 'so that the vampire would cut his throat if he left the grave.'"[44] Analysis into the use of sharp iron objects, including axes, swords, and knives, being placed in the graves also has illuminated the hypothesis that "the deterrent effect of these objects has been attributed to the magical quality of iron."[45] Stoker's use of knives to dispatch Dracula may have arisen from their uses in burial as safeguards against the dead from rising from their grave to haunt and kill the living, but Stoker adapts this folklore in order to create a unique and solitary figure of a terrifying revenant bent on destruction.

Stoker uses folklore from various regions in Europe to create a vampire that violates many of the traditional beliefs about a member of one's own community coming back to wreak vengeance on the living. Stoker subverts Romanian folklore in *Dracula* and melds it with other legends, both werewolf lore and other countries' folk beliefs about the undead, to redefine, albeit incorrectly, the ideas about Transylvanian and Romanian vampires. Society is left with an amalgamation of vampire lore in one package that serves as a unique literary figure but at the same time denigrates the importance of the colorful folklore of various ethnic communities.

Notes

1. Matthew Beresford, *From Demons to Dracula: The Creation of the Modern Vampire Myth* (London: Reaktion Books, 2008), 19.
2. Alan Dundes, "The Vampire as Bloodthirsty Revenant: A Psychoanalytic Post Mortem," in *The Vampire: A Casebook*, ed. Alan Dundes (Madison: University of Wisconsin Press, 1998), 159.
3. Dundes, "The Vampire as Bloodthirsty Revenant," 165.
4. Beresford, *From Demons to Dracula*, 10.
5. Beresford, *From Demons to Dracula*, 10.
6. Beresford, *From Demons to Dracula*, 11.
7. Bram Stoker, *Dracula*, ed. Nina Auerbach and David J. Skal (New York: W. W. Norton and Co., 1997), 209.
8. Beresford, *From Demons to Dracula*, 57.
9. Agnes Murgoci, "The Vampire in Roumania," in *The Vampire: A Casebook*, ed. Alan Dundes (Madison: University of Wisconsin Press, 1998), 14; Beresford, *From Demons to Dracula*, 57.
10. Murgoci, "The Vampire in Roumania," 14.
11. Stoker, *Dracula*, 23–24.
12. Montague Summers, *The Vampire, His Kith and Kin: The History of Vampirism* (Scotts Valley, IAP: 2009), 109–10.
13. Stoker, *Dracula*, 53.
14. Dudley Wright, *Vampires and Vampirism: Legends from Around the World* (Maple Shade, NJ: Lethe Press, 2001), 85.
15. Beresford, *From Demons to Dracula*, 137.
16. Beresford, *From Demons to Dracula*, 103–104.
17. Stoker, *Dracula*, 24.
18. Quoted in Stoker, *Dracula*, 24.
19. Felix Oinas, "East European Vampires," in *The Vampire: A Casebook*, ed. Alan Dundes (Madison: University of Wisconsin Press, 1998), 48
20. Wright, *Vampires and Vampirism*, 20.
21. Stoker, *Dracula*, 30.
22. Stoker, *Dracula*, 30–31.
23. Philip D. Jaffe and Frank DiCataldo, "Clinical Vampirism: Blending Myth and Reality," in *The Vampire: A Casebook*, ed. Alan Dundes (Madison: University of Wisconsin Press, 1998), 145.
24. Beresford, *From Demons to Dracula*, 65.

25. Beresford, *From Demons to Dracula*, 62.
26. Stoker, *Dracula*, 103–104.
27. Stoker, *Dracula*, 134.
28. Wright, *Vampires and Vampirism*, 91–92.
29. Stoker, *Dracula*, 144.
30. Stoker, *Dracula*, 121.
31. Beresford, *From Demons to Dracula*, 66.
32. Stoker, *Dracula*, 121.
33. Paul Barber, "Forensic Pathology and the European Vampire," in *The Vampire: A Casebook*, ed. Alan Dundes (Madison: University of Wisconsin Press, 1998), 129.
34. Beresford, *From Demons to Dracula*, 135
35. Wright, *Vampires and Vampirism*, 50.
36. Stoker, *Dracula*, 179.
37. Paul Barber, *Vampires, Burial, and Death: Folklore and Reality* (New Haven: Yale University Press, 2010), 157.
38. Frederich S. Krauss, "South Slavic Countermeasures against Vampires," in *The Vampire: A Casebook*, ed. Alan Dundes (Madison: University of Wisconsin Press, 1998), 68.
39. Veselin Cajkanovic, "The Killing of a Vampire," in *The Vampire: A Casebook*, ed. Alan Dundes (Madison: University of Wisconsin Press, 1998), 76–77.
40. Stoker, *Dracula*, 191.
41. Cajkanovic, "The Killing of a Vampire," 76.
42. Stoker, *Dracula*, 325.
43. Cajkanovic, "The Killing of a Vampire," 82.
44. Barber, "Forensic Pathology and the European Vampire," 125.
45. Barber, "Forensic Pathology and the European Vampire," 125.

Bibliography

Fine, John V. A. "In Defense of Vampires." In *The Vampire: A Casebook*, edited by Alan Dundes, 57–66. Madison: University of Wisconsin Press, 1998.
Perkowski, Jan Louis. "The Romanian Folkloric Vampire." In *The Vampire: A Casebook*, edited by Alan Dundes, 35–46. Madison: University of Wisconsin Press, 1998.
Funk and Wagnalls Standard Dictionary of Folklore, Mythology, and Legend. Edited by Maria Leach. San Francisco: HarperCollins, 1984.
The Vampire Book: The Encyclopedia of the Undead. Edited by J. Gordon Melton. Detroit: Visible Ink Press, 1999.
Wilson, Katharina M. "The History of the Word *Vampire*." In *The Vampire: A Casebook*, edited by Alan Dundes, 3–11. Madison: University of Wisconsin Press, 1998.

4

Dracula's Kitchen:
A Glossary of Transylvanian Cuisine, Language, and Ethnography

Cristina Artenie

MY FRIEND—Welcome to the Carpathians . . .
I trust that your journey from London has been a happy one,
and that you will enjoy your stay in my beautiful land.
Your friend,

DRACULA[1]

BETWEEN JONATHAN HARKER'S LEAVING Budapest and thereby "entering the Orient" and Dracula's "Welcome to my house," the Occidental tourist discovers the land beyond the forest. Each time a reader opens Bram Stoker's *Dracula*, the Englishman Harker embarks on an incredible adventure filled with mysterious peoples and beliefs, with incomprehensible languages and exotic tastes. The world that lies in front of him, although as fictional as it can be, is built on images and travelers' logs that make up the reified British knowledge of Central Europe[2] and its most vibrant place, Transylvania, the land of vampires. "The impression I had was that we were leaving the West and entering the East; the Western of splendid bridges over the Danube, which is here of noble width and depth, took us among the traditions of Turkish rule."[3]

Crossing the bridge over the Danube in Budapest means crossing into the realm of possibilities where life and death are so intertwined that it becomes hard to discern between the two. Nothing is scarier for the poorly prepared solicitor from London, whose knowledge of the world rests solely on other people's experiences and on the British confidence in railroad efficiency and Baedeker timetables. It is in this gap between real and imaginary, between

Harker's pre-informed representation of Transylvania and his experience of the place that we have to look for clues about his trip and what he saw, heard, or ate in those few days he spent traveling from Budapest to the Borgo Pass. Since the novel's publication in 1897 and up until today, every time an English-speaking reader opens the book and begins their adventure, Transylvania is being reinvented, always the same yet always untrue.

The imperial imagination[4] that first conjured these images of the place has not changed with the passing of the time and with the advance of the Internet. The lack of interest in the real experience Harker might have had at the time but was unable to comprehend, doubled with a passion for exaggeration and misrepresentation of places and people, stems from naiveté and paternalism alike. Never having seen Transylvania, Stoker reconstructed the country in his imagination. He relied on the representations of British travelers, who had already relocated it far away in time and space. Emily Gerard, arguably the most important source both for *Dracula*'s Transylvanian setting and for the theme of the Romanian vampire, speaks of a "secluded land" that she compares to an "island," which has made her forget "the century in which we live."[5] Much like the travelers to the Orient before him, Harker set out for Bistritz to discover Edward Saïd's forlorn *Other*: exotic, erotic, and non-Christian. And although the Orient seeps into Harker's descriptions of the place and its peoples, the balkanist[6] view is the one that shapes this traveler's discourse: East Central Europe is the un-evolved West, frozen in time before the Renaissance and the Reformation. These people are white, yet their features differ from the ones of the English; they are Christian, albeit their Christianity is fraught with superstition; and although they share a common Roman past with the civilized Europe, they are not part of it. Furthermore, in Harker's sympathetic understanding for beliefs and superstitions that the West has long discarded one cannot but notice paternalism and its corollary, superiority. In discussing Harker's Transylvania, contemporary British and North-American literary critics and readers continue to reproduce Stoker's set of attitudes toward East Central Europe and the accompanying representations of Transylvania without much change.

Unfortunately, as Maria Todorova notes, "[i]f Europe has produced not only racism but also anti-racism, not only misogyny but also feminism, not only anti-Semitism but also its repudiation," when it comes to East Central Europe, there is no real attempt to correct the balkanist attitudes and discourse.[7] Perhaps nowhere is this absence of political correctness more visible than in *Dracula*'s case. The fascination the novel holds is best exemplified by the mass production of Dracula apparel, Dracula-spun books, comics, movies, plays, and last but not least, Dracula food, which I will show, is, at best an English version of the real Transylvanian cuisine. The consumerist society produces and devours Dracula paraphernalia at the expense of East Central European peoples and their cultures. It is my intention to discuss some of the most common references to Transylvania and show that critics such as Nina Auerbach, Clive Leatherdale, John Paul Riquelme, Leslie S. Klinger, or Glennis Byron, who work with *Dracula*, have not considered either Stoker's or their own biases toward the region. These biases translate into more than misinformation. Rather, in an attempt to justify Stoker's choice of place and people, they perpetuate a view that is not only outdated but also driven by ideology.

In the confusion of languages, peoples, and beliefs of major or minor aspects of Transylvanian living, it is worth searching for coherence. There is a strong connection between what Harker ate, the people he met, and the places he visited and how they translate into misrepresentation. Looking closely at Transylvanian cuisine, for example, allows us to question Harker's ability to understand where he was, what was happening to him, and whom he met on his journey. At Bistritz, on May 3, Harker is having breakfast at Hotel Royale in Klausenburg, central Transylvania. "I had for breakfast more paprika, and a sort of porridge of maize flour which they said was 'mamaliga' and eggplant stuffed with forcemeat, a very excellent dish, which they call 'impletata.'"[8] Harker notes that he had "paprika, and a sort of porridge of maize flour," which is indicative of the fact that he ate in a Romanian kitchen. *Mămăligă* is indeed corn mush, served as a side dish that is often a stand-in for bread. While Hungarians in Transylvania have adopted the corn mush for their ordinary meals, they would not have served it in a restaurant. For this reason, it is hard to believe that Harker was, indeed, served chicken paprikash with *mămăligă* at all because this mix is a traditional Romanian peasant mix, and the hotels in Klausenburg (at the time the unofficial capital of Transylvania, heavily populated by Hungarians and Saxons[9]) were not managed by and did not employ Romanians. The hierarchy of the province recognized the Saxons, the Hungarians, and the Szeklers as the only three governing nations, while the Romanians were relegated to the margins of society. If Harker dined, indeed, in Klausenburg, he must have had *paprikahendl* with potatoes as a side dish, or with dumplings. It is more likely that he encountered Romanians and Romanian cuisine in Bistritz, a much smaller town, a frontier town with an overwhelmingly Romanian population (all of the statistics give 68 percent and more Romanians in Bistritz and the surrounding area, some Saxons, some Hungarians, and no Slovaks[10]).

If the *paprikahendl* with *mamaliga* is problematic because it raises doubts about Harker's recollections of his trip, the famous stuffed eggplant is a true challenge and highlights Harker's inability with languages. *Impletata* is in fact a mix of two, or even three Romanian words (none of which means eggplant): *împletită*, which is a type of braided bread; *umplută*, an adjective that means stuffed; and *împănată*, another adjective that means half-stuffed, or feathered, meaning that the inside of the "eggplant" (to keep with Harker's menu) is not scooped out, but that the "eggplant" is sliced on the surface and other vegetables are inserted halfway. In fact, there are lots of recipes of vegetables and meats that can either be *umplută* or *împănată*, whereas only the bread is *împletită*.

Without mentioning the fact that *impletata* is not a word in the Romanian lexicon, Klinger notes that "[t]he simplest version of impletata is a scooped-out eggplant with the pulped eggplant, ground meat, breadcrumbs, and butter, and baked. Dozens of recipes are widely available in English, under 'stuffed eggplant.'"[11] Similarly, Leatherdale observes: "'Mamaliga' and 'impletata' come from Johnson (p. 120): 'Egg plant stuffed with chopped meat is National Dish and called 'Ua Impletata.'"[12] Both these descriptions refer to stuffed eggplant, which in Romanian would be *vânătă umplută*. The "Ua" in Johnson's text, reproduced by Leatherdale, could be an attempt to write down the Transylvanian pronunciation of "o," which is the Romanian feminine indefinite article, that is, "a," as in "a[n] impletata." It is even possible that Johnson confused "o" with "una," the Romanian feminine cardinal numeral, that is, "one."

This brief discussion of Harker's Transylvanian meals shows both that his diary entries are not accurate and also that the critics working with the novel have never questioned the information offered by the fictional traveler. Indeed, all the academic work relies on Harker's diary and on a few travelers' logs that Stoker used. Not one critic has really questioned whether the information in these writings is correct. The notes mention Stoker's source for one or another piece of information and they stop at that. And while food could seem a minor entry, it shows *in nuce* that Harker's experience is at best the sum of confusions of tastes, languages, and of peoples and not an accurate portrayal of Transylvania. In an anti-colonial reading, however, it could easily be regarded as a colonial gesture to name, assign meaning, and redraw the map of a newly discovered territory. Yet, nowhere is the discussion of confusion, unchallenged assumption, and (neo)colonial behavior more pertinent than in the case of the calendar.

Chapter 1 of *Dracula* begins with Harker's journal entry: "3 May. Bistritz." The first trick that Stoker attempts to play on the reader is to make them believe that they are going back in time some 10 days. May 3 would be, in Stoker's Transylvania, April 22, the eve of St. George's Day. This way, everything that happens to Harker becomes unclean, un-Christian, as the Greek Orthodox Church is not the good Christian kind of church in the eyes of the Anglican traveler. Not having been influenced and modernized by the

Reformation, goes the Byzantinist discourse,[13] the Greek Orthodox Church is impure, nowadays as much as in Stoker's time. Harker himself is an "English Churchman," a modernized version of Christianity, thus, a better Christian altogether. Harker lives in the future, literally, while Transylvanians live in the past. Interestingly enough, all the main critical editions of *Dracula* play Stoker's game. No edition of the novel makes any mention of this trick. May 3 is just that, May 3, and the reader will find out later, when Harker himself finds out, that it is, apparently, still April. When, on May 4, Harker is leaving Bistritz for the Borgo Pass, the truth comes out and he learns that he has traveled back in time, literally and figuratively, in the time before the new calendar put the West ahead of the "East" with some 10 days.

> 'Do you know what day it is?' I answered that it was the fourth of May. She shook her head as she said again: 'Oh, yes! I know that, I know that! but do you know what day it is?' On my saying that I did not understand, she went on: 'It is the eve of St George's Day.'[14]

Apparently, at the end of the 19th century, Transylvanians lived by two calendars, a religious one and a laic one. On the religious calendar, they were on the eve of St. George's Day, while on the laic one they were well past this terrible date. One of the reasons none of the critics draws attention to this fact in the opening of the novel is because none appear to know that the Austrian-Hungarian Empire had adopted the new calendar long before Harker's visit. Riquelme, for example, writes of the evening

> before May 5 by the Eastern calendar and before April 23, by the Western calendar, which was changed by Pope Gregory XIII in 1582. In Romanian superstition, the eve of St. George's day is linked to occult practices. Stoker's British readers would have known that St. George, the chivalrous dragon slayer, was the patron saint of England (*Enc. Brit.* 11th; Gerard).[15]

Funnily enough, the critic researched when the "Western" calendar was adopted by the Catholic Church but did not check when Austria, or Hungary, had adopted it; similarly, he does not note when the Anglican Church adopted the new calendar, as to give the reader a timeline, thus leaving the impression that the Anglicans adopted the calendar the same day as Rome, maybe?

In turn, Klinger writes that: "The date Harker reckoned as 4 May (presumably using an English, Gregorian calendar) would have been denoted as 22 April on the Julian calendar, still in use in Transylvania at that time."[16] In this note, the new, therefore modern calendar becomes "English," not leaving any room for doubts regarding Transylvanian time; the people here have no idea of the "calendar revolution" in Britain. Furthermore, Klinger, too, assumes too easily that the Julian calendar was still largely in use, and the same mistake is made by Leatherdale: "The reason for the discrepancy is that in 1752 Britain switched from the Julian to the Gregorian Calendar. Russia and Greece did not switch till after World War I. Several countries affiliated with the Greek Orthodox Church still retain the old, Julian Calendar for the celebration of church feasts."[17] The *Dracula* specialists do not question the facts. Instead, they perpetuate Stoker's traveler's discourse, assuming rather than finding out how modern or antiquated Transylvania was in the 1890s. Actually, Austria had switched to the Gregorian calendar in 1583 and Hungary (although under Turkish rule at the time) in 1587, almost two centuries before Britain did. As part of Hungary and later Austria, Transylvania, too, had switched to the Gregorian calendar and the inhabitants were well acquainted with it. Furthermore, following the policy of *magyarization*, an overwhelming number of Romanians converted to Catholicism. They became "United" or "Greek-Catholics," meaning that their dogmas were Catholic while their rituals remained Greek-Orthodox. As Greek-Catholics they followed the same calendar as Rome.

It is, however, important to note that the calendar confusion cannot be entirely cleared. While the Catholic and Protestant Hungarians and Saxons were following the Gregorian calendar in their churches, the segment of Romanians who resisted Hungarian assimilation and remained Greek-Orthodox may have adopted the Gregorian calendar only as a measure of the secular time, while still following the Julian calendar to mark the feasts of the Greek Orthodox Church. In this instance, Stoker's misunderstanding of Transylvanian peoples might have proved inspired. The woman innkeeper in Bistritz, seen by everybody as a Catholic, and therefore Hungarian (because she speaks broken German, something none of the critics are willing to give to a Romanian!), is more likely a Romanian. The description of her attire, "white undergarment with long double apron, front, and back, of coloured stuff fitting"[18] shows that she is a Romanian from Bistritz. The "double apron" is a quintessential Romanian piece of clothing; neither the Hungarian nor the German women wore such aprons. With the innkeeper Romanian, it is easier to understand why she would be so vehemently opposed to Harker's journey to the Borgo Pass and why she would know so well that "it is the eve of St. George's Day." Even more importantly, her being Romanian is the only way to understand why she would be so scared; it is for the Romanians that the eve of St. George's Day is full of dangers, when the *strigoi* can make an appearance and wreak havoc in the community. What threw the critics on the wrong track is the crucifix the woman gives Harker before his departure for Dracula's castle. Indeed, a crucifix is a Catholic symbol; Greek Orthodox followers wear and worship the cross, an empty cross. This confusion of peoples and beliefs, churches and calendars shows that Stoker's image of Transylvania is, at best, distorted and his sources did not help him achieve a more accurate image of the place and of its people.

The misunderstanding of Transylvania and its peoples by Stoker, Harker, travelers such as Gerard, Major Johnson, or Charles Boner, and nowadays by academics favors the skewed interpretations of the land and its culture. In his notes, Harker perpetuates the negative image of the place, reproducing almost verbatim Gerard, when he states that "every known superstition in the world is gathered into the horseshoe of the Carpathians, as if it were the centre of some of sort of imaginative whirlpool; if so my stay may be very interesting."[19] For the Western traveler, whether a fictional character like Harker or actual people who have visited Transylvania in the past 200 years, for literary critics then and now, the "horseshoe of the Carpathians" is a barbaric place. Here, the balkanist[20] view of Transylvania obliterates the truth and sees instead people who believe in everything the West has discarded long ago as foolish, uneducated assumptions. The richness of the folklore, Romanian, Hungarian, and Saxon, is not valued at all; rather, it is used against the people as proof of their backwardness. And while today Irish folklore, for example, is a treasure of the world, Transylvanian folklore is held against the people as a measure of their primitivism, as a means to keep them down, locked in a dark, medieval time. Furthermore, as Harker's notes show, the inability of the British traveler to speak any of the local languages contribute to the confusion of words and beliefs, and in general to the confusion of what is real belief (or superstition) and what is not.

May 5th is the day Harker leaves for the Borgo Pass with a polyglot dictionary in his bag. He has to look up *Ordog* (Satan), *pokol* (hell), *stregoica* (witch), *vrolok*, and *vlkoslak* (either werewolf or vampire, in Slovak and Servian). As the polyglot dictionary of languages of East Central Europe is fictional, the translations that he finds for the various words are sometimes approximate and sometimes altogether wrong. One such approximate translation is the one for the Hungarian word *ördög*, which means simply devil, not Satan. Common expressions in all languages spoken in Europe such as "What the devil . . . ?" occur in Hungarian, too (*"Mi az ördög . . . ?"*) and have little or no religious connotation. The same observation stands for hell, which appears to be a choice word in English to express someone's confusion in a particular situation ("What the hell?") or to show someone being fed up with a particular person or situation ("Go to hell!"). Interestingly enough, *ördög* and *pokol* seem to occur independently from God (*Isten*) or Christian (*Keresztény*), which suggests that these words are used by colorful people who prepare for a long journey, packing, loading, and unloading luggage in a limited space. The fact that "the crowd" looks at Harker should not be so surprising because he is an Englishman and. as such, a curiosity of sorts. "When we started, the crowd round the inn door, which had by this time swelled to a considerable size, all made the sign of the cross and pointed two fingers towards me."[21] It is not uncommon for people today to gather on the shore, for example, and pray, bless the vessel or make the sign of the cross when a ship leaves just as passengers wave goodbye. It would not have been special over a hundred years ago to see the same ritual in any small town in Europe, when a coach crossing the mountains left the station. Harker's note, however, is not to be easily trusted.

As I have shown, at the time of Harker's trip only the followers of the Greek Orthodox Church went by the Julian calendar, and some 99 percent of them were Romanians. When leaving the inn, Harker finds that the crowd in front of the gate is a multiethnic crowd, as attested by the several terrifying words (in at least four languages) that he hears and writes down in his book. These other nationalities had no special beliefs for the day and were living on Gregorian time. It is rather possible that the words he hears, *ördög* (devil), *pokol* (hell), and *vrolok* and *vlkoslak* (werewolf in "Slovak" and "Servian"), have nothing to do with the vampire hiding in the forest, but, as we will see later, with the phases of the moon (still an important time guide for farmers) and with the preparation of the coach for the trip (as talked about previously). Only the *stregoica* makes sense because this is what the biggest fear for the Eve of St. George's Day is: the meeting of a malevolent spirit.

The Romanian word Harker notes in his journal poses a lot more problems than the Hungarian ones. Both the English solicitor and the English-speaking academics writing and annotating the novel are lost as to its meaning in Romanian. Klinger notes that "[t]he translator has misspelt the word, which should read *strigoaica*, the female undead vampire; *strigoi* is the male undead vampire,"[22] and Leatherdale, too: "Stregoica, the feminine of strigoi, is a Wallachian term and comes from Wilkinson, p. 213. It should properly be spelled 'strigoaica.'"[23] Harker himself notes that "stregoica" means "witch," and he is closer somewhat to the definition available at the time. In the *Lexicon from Buda* (*Lesicon romanescu-latinescu-ungurescu-nemtescu*), based on the work of several Romanian linguists from Transylvania, and published in 1825, the words *strigoe* and *strigoiu*, of Latin origin, are translated as "witch" in both Hungarian (*boszorkàny*) and German (*Zauberinn*).[24] It is very likely that this multilingual dictionary was consulted by one or more of the travelers in Transylvania (Gerard, for example, was married to a German-speaking officer stationed for a short while in Transylvania) from where it found its way into Harker's polyglot dictionary. From a dictionary entry to a real practice of beliefs is, however, a long stretch.

If one consults a Romanian dictionary (e.g., the so-called DEX, or *Dicționarul Explicativ al Limbii Române*), one has a slightly different idea of the meaning and use of this word. First, there are two distinct entries: *strigă*, feminine noun, and *strigoi, strigoaie,* masculine and feminine noun. *Strigă,* in superstitions, is an imaginary being, a woman who bothers or tortures little children or takes away the milk from cows. It is also the name of a bird that hunts and eats mice and of a type of butterfly (*Acherontia atropos*), the Death's head moth. The word comes from the Latin *striga* or *strix*, which—in a dictionary that Stoker (or Harker) could have consulted[25]—defines it as either "a screech-owl, which, according to the belief of the ancients, sucked the blood of young children" or "a woman that brings harm to children." According to the DEX, the word *strigoi, strigoaie* (derived with a typically Romanian augmentative suffix), means, in superstitions, the soul of a man (dead or alive) that transforms during the night into an animal or phantom-like apparition that causes misfortune to those it meets. The soul of the dead man comes out of the tomb at night and is causing misfortune to the living. An extended meaning is that of a man born under an unfavorable celestial sign and who, due to a link with the devil, practices magic and sorcery. It is an epithet used for a mean person, a grumpy or morose person, or an odd old man.[26]

Without a doubt, *strigoi* is an interesting word and in Romanian folklore it is quite frequent; something akin to the sorcerer in English or to the leprechaun. The *strigoi* is present in cautionary tales for children living in rural areas who should not, under any circumstance, wander out at night, but rather stay home, say their prayers, and obey their parents. It is used in village parlance to describe the mean or greedy person in the community or the crazy old lady that does not like children playing in her backyard or stealing her fruit. Each community has such characters and lots of stories made up about them. There are no all-encompassing *strigoi* stories that can be found all over the territory inhabited by Romanians, only local stories, with local protagonists. Very often, the *strigoi* is the greedy rich man who abused the farmers and then passed away and his mischievous deeds seem to have never gone away. His prevalence in cautionary tales, comforting tales, and superstitions that make sense and help restore order in the community is very similar to that of the boogeyman. We all know there is no boogeyman yet we fear him nonetheless.

The last two foreign words in Harker's diary entry for May 4th are *vrolok* and *vlkoslak* ("either werewolf or vampire, in Slovak and Servian"), both erroneously spelled. *Vârcolac*, as explained by Romanian dictionaries, is a masculine noun denoting a malevolent spirit responsible for the Moon and Sun eclipses. It comes from the Slavonic word *vlŭkodlakŭ,* itself derived from *vlŭkŭ,* "wolf" (similar versions are the Bulgarian *vrăkolak*, the Serbian *vokodlak*, the Albanian *vurvolak*, and the Modern Greek βουρκόλακας. Even in

French there is the masculine noun *brucolaque*, although *loup-garou*, calqued from the German *Werwolf* is clearly preferred.[27] As mentioned previously, Harker could have heard these words before leaving for the Borgo Pass, and most probably they referred to the phases of the moon, as the coach had to travel at night and the sky map and the light from the moon would have been important.

Nina Auerbach notes that: "Werewolves and vampires are often allied in Romanian folklore. They are natural as well as linguistic kin—both are hybrids, prone to nocturnal transformations into animals—but Dracula, with nineteenth-century faith in his own supremacy, treats wolves merely as his servants."[28] In turn, Klinger comments that: "Montague Summers . . . identifies the *vârcolac* as a mythical being, but he cites Agnes Murgoçi ('The Vampire in Roumania') as the source of the information that the name also applies to 'dead' vampires, distinct from 'live' vampires closely associated with witches."[29] Leatherdale thinks Stoker took the information "[f]rom Baring-Gould, pp. 114–15, though Stoker's 'vrolak' should read 'vrkolak.' This is the first appearance of the word 'vampire' in the novel."[30] As we can see, each critic has a slightly different take on werewolves, spelling, Slavic languages, and how these creatures relate to vampires. The observation clos-est to the truth is the one pertaining to the mythical figure of the *vlŭkodlakŭ*. As a mythological figure in the Slavic cultures, and from there into Romanian culture, the *vlŭkodlakŭ* is capable of swallowing the moon or the sun, as it pleases him. It is not because this figure belongs to mythology that it is hard to accept Auerbach's comment that "[w]erewolves and vampires are often allied in Romanian folklore." They are not of Romanian (Latin or Thracian) origin and, therefore have not entered Romanian folklore in times immemo-rial. Both werewolf and vampire are of Slavic origin, but *vampire* has just recently entered into Romanian vocabulary (the 1825 Transylvanian *Lexicon* does not have an entry for it) while werewolf appears as *vercolaci* in the same 1825 dictionary, with no language of origin and no exact translation into another language. The entry has an explanation that says of these beings that "simple folk believe them to be responsible for the eclipses when all they see are the phases of the moon, *ecclypsis lunae*."[31] We know, today, that werewolf, *vlŭkodlakŭ*, comes from Slavonic and belongs to Slavic mythology. The mod-est entry in the 1825 dictionary shows that Romanians in Transylvania had not yet assimilated the word or the superstition, which contradicts the critic's statement that vampires and werewolves are kindred spirits in Romanian folklore. Furthermore, both the new and old editions of the all-encompassing Romanian language dictionary (DEXRO) explain the vampire as either a "character from popular mythology believed to suck the blood of the living" (DEX 1998) or a "fantastical character believed to suck the blood of the living"

(NODEX 2002).[32] None refer to the vampire as part of Romanian folklore; rather, these definitions show the late import of the word into the language and the little impact it had. At the end of the 19th century the vampire did not exist in the language spoken by Romanians in Transylvania nor in their beliefs, and werewolves were just coming in.

It is obvious now that English travelers through Transylvania, whether Gerard or Harker, were overwhelmed by the multicultural environment in which they found themselves. The peaceful cohabitation of so many nations seemed to have had rather a negative impact on the British subject, not used to seeing so many different ethnicities and religions living side by side. If one considers for a moment that *Dracula* is a classic example of British fear-of-invasion literature, Harker's xenophobia becomes visible. It is the inability to accept Transylvania's complexity that made both the real and the fictitious traveler translate beauty into ugliness, richness into poverty. Unfortunately, the critics working today with Stoker's *Dracula*—some of them travelers through Transylvania, some not—fall into the same trap and rarely question their own assumptions. The more benevolent looks (such as Klinger's) are still incomplete and incorrect, while the more malevolent ones (such as Auerbach's) are just that.

Much like the discussion of the food, the brief discussion of (in)famous words, of backward peoples, and their pagan beliefs and superstitions as they appear to Harker and to the literary critics working on various *Dracula* editions shows how far from the truth each one of them is. It shows, paradoxically, how open-minded people can find themselves so far from understanding Transylvania and its peoples. In her book *Inventing Ruritania*, Vesna Goldsworthy notes that often Westerners today "write about Albanians, Croats, Serbs, Bulgarians and Romanians with the sort of generalised, open condescension which would appal[l] them if applied to Somalis or to the peoples of Zaire."[33] *Dracula* and its critical editions are symptomatic of this type of discourse and for the imagining of Transylvania, both in the 19th and 21st century. The case of *Dracula* is a good example for what Goldsworthy identifies as one of "those marginal and ambiguous areas of the world which have offered refuges to patterns of neo-colonial behaviour no longer acceptable elsewhere."[34] In the battlefield of literature and literary studies, Transylvania is still being colonized.

It has been more than a century since the novel's publication and many of the common errors and misconceptions are still being perpetuated with each new reprint of the novel. One reason why so much erroneous information is possible is simply that: because it is possible. Transylvania does not talk back, or it did not until now. The invention of Transylvania, by British travelers in the 19th century, by Stoker and the academics devoted to his novel *Dracula*, is an overwhelming phenomenon for Transylvanians in particular and Romanians in general. Harker's adventure in the land beyond the forest would be a lot more appealing if the various notes in the critical editions explained the misconceptions and the errors in the text. Rather, these notes gloss over aspects such as the calendar or the shorthand (widely used in Austria-Hungary in the 19th century), to give the Westerner the scientific edge, the moral and religious edge, in short, the high moral ground of civilization. Instead of looking at Harker's fantastic adventure as fostered by a beautiful land rich in culture and in people, today's academics feel that they have to perpetuate an ideological view and construct Transylvania into Europe's heart of darkness, into an Other, into the land of the undead. Nothing could be further from the truth. As I have already mentioned, Harker's adventures can take place in Transylvania and only in Transylvania because this is the land of possibilities.

Notes

1. Bram Stoker, *Dracula* (Peterborough, Ontario: Broadview, 2000), 34. Unless indicated otherwise, all quotes henceforth will be given from this edition.

2. I am using here the more geographically correct notions of Central Europe and East Central Europe rather than Eastern Europe or the Balkans for several reasons: (a) Transylvania is not an Eastern or Oriental place; (b) the terms *Central Europe* and *East Central Europe* are, in my view, the correct ones when it comes to placing the region on the map and lack the obsolete Cold War connotations; and (c) Paul Robert Magocsi makes a strong case in favor of these terms in his *Historical Atlas of East Central Europe*.

3. Stoker, *Dracula*, 31.

4. This term alludes to two book titles: Mary Louise Pratt's *Imperial Eyes: Travel, Writing and Transculturation* (New York: Routledge, 1992) and Vesna Goldsworthy's *Inventing Ruritania* (New Haven: Yale University Press, 1998). It refers both to how travel writing is produced by and, in turn, generates, an ideologically informed discourse and to the power of fiction as part of the colonial enterprise. *Dracula* is the result of the two intertwining discursive traditions.

5. Emily Gerard, *The Land beyond the Forest*, Volume 1, 1–2.

6. The best analysis so far of the balkanist bias is to be found in Todorova's 1997 *Imagining the Balkans* (New York: Oxford University Press, 1997).

7. Maria Todorova, "The Balkans: from Discovery to Invention," *Slavic Review* 53 (1994): 453.

8. Stoker, *Dracula*, 33.

9. The statistics published in the 1938 comprehensive monography *La Transylvanie* by the Romanian Academy show that, while Romanians made up two thirds of the entire population of the province at the turn of the 20th century, 62 percent of the

urban population was Hungarian, followed by Romanian (20 percent), and German 16 percent (804–805).

10. The distribution of the Romanian population in Nasaud county: 34 percent Romanians in urban centers, 72.5 percent in rural areas; 68 percent overall (*La Transylvanie*, 824).

11. Stoker, *The New Annotated Dracula*, ed. Leslie S. Klinger (New York: W. W. Norton, 2008), 19, n. 31.

12. Stoker, *Dracula Unearthed*, ed. Clive Leatherdale (Westcliff-on-Sea, Essex: Desert Island Books, 1998), 30, n. 30.

13. Dimiter G. Angelov, "Byzantinism: the imaginary and real heritage of Byzantium in Southeastern Europe", in *New Approaches to Balkan Studies*, eds. D. Keridis, E. Elias-Bursać, and N. Yatromanolakis (Dulles, VA: Brassey's, 2003), 3.

14. Stoker, *Dracula*, 35.

15. Bram Stoker, *Dracula: A Case Study in Contemporary Criticism*, ed. John Paul Riquelme (New York: Bedford/St. Martin's, 2002), 30.

16. Stoker, *The Annotated*, 33, n. 56.

17. Stoker, *Dracula Unearthed*, 33, n. 56.

18. Stoker, *Dracula*, 34.

19. Stoker, 32.

20. In her book *Imagining the Balkans*, Maria Todorova argues that the West has looked upon East Central Europe as its underdeveloped self from before Reformation and Enlightenment.

21. Stoker, *Dracula*, 36.

22. Stoker, *The New Annotated*, 28, n. 63.

23. Stoker, *Dracula Unearthed*, 35, n. 81.

24. *Lesicon romanescu-latinescu-ungurescu-nemtescu* (Buda: Typographia Regiae Universitatis Hungaricae, 1825), 678.

25. Charlton T. Lewis and Charles Short, *A Latin Dictionary* (Oxford: Clarendon Press, 1879).

26. *Dictionarul Explicativ al Limbii Romane*, s.v. "Strigoi," http://www.webdex.ro/dex/60394/strigoi/, accessed January 9, 2012.

27. *Dictionarul Explicativ al Limbii Romane*, s.v. "Varcolac," http://www.webdex.ro/dex/60394/vârcolac/, accessed January 9, 2012.

28. Bram Stoker, *Dracula*, eds. Nina Auerbach and David Skal (New York: W. W. Norton, 1997), 14, n. 2.

29. Stoker, *The Annotated*, 29, n. 65.

30. Stoker, *Dracula Unearthed*, 36, n. 83.

31. *Lesicon*, 750.

32. *Dicţionarul Explicativ*, http://www.webdex.ro/dex/60300/vampir, accessed January 9, 2012.

33. Goldsworthy, *Inventing*, xi.

34. Goldsworthy, xi.

II

MEDICAL EXPLANATIONS FOR THE VAMPIRE

5

Biomedical Origins of Vampirism

Edward O. Keith

THE VAMPIRE REPRESENTS one of the most enduring, universal, and popular myths of all time, especially in Western civilizations. It has persisted through the centuries and is currently undergoing a resurgence of interest and exploitation.[1] It may be one of the most archaic images that is known.[2] The modern obsession with vampires may be partially attributed to John William Polidori, the author of *The Vampyre*, published in 1819 in *New Monthly Magazine*.[3] The novel *Dracula* (1897) by Bram Stoker masterfully combined all of the European folk beliefs into a single persona.[4] Descriptions of vampires in the novel *Dracula* epitomize their characteristics because the author did extensive folkloric research before writing his masterpiece.

The fascination with vampires and werewolves has continued to grow with movies such as the *Twilight* series and books such as Nancy Garden's *Vampires* (1973) and Anne Rice's *Interview with the Vampire* (1976). Bela Lugosi's 1931 portrayal of *Dracula* is a revered touchstone and Dracula is a favorite Halloween costume.[5] The first feature film to use an anthropomorphic werewolf was *Werewolf of London* (1935), but it was the movie *The Wolf Man* (1941) that catapulted the werewolf, played by Lon Chaney, Jr., into public consciousness.

When the fear of the unknown and of others not like ourselves confronts real or imaginary phenomena that lack apparent explanation, irrationality prevails over rationality.[6] Legends of vampires and werewolves (i.e., hematophages) emerge from this process. The features of vampires and werewolves change depending on the historical period and the culture of reference, but they always oscillate between a diabolic and wicked aura and one of fascination and charisma.[7] Thus, hematophages represent a synthesis of the attitude toward the dualism of life and death.[8] Many cultures have developed myths and legends about hematophages with different features and behaviors, but these tales have in common many elements that lie on the border between life and death and in the search for intelligibility ever coveted by human beings.[9]

Origins

The oldest recorded example of the vampire myth is in a Babylonian prayer thousands of years old.[10] Examples are also present in ancient Greek and Chinese literature.[11] The vampire myth is a variation on zoomorphism, the belief in the capacity of human metamorphosis into animal form. Zoomorphism is prevalent in the myths and legends of many societies.[12] The myths of vampires and were-wolves seem to have a symbiotic associative relationship.[13] There are apparently authentic tales of children reared by wolves or living as wild animals.[14]

Most likely the vampire and werewolf myths developed from mounting fear of a disease a community encountered daily.[15] The vampire myth likely came to Europe from India, via Turkey and the Balkans.[16] According to lore, the vampire is a person whose soul stays in his or her body after death. During the day, the vampire sleeps in a grave, leaving it at night to assault victims. To do this, the vampire must transmogrify into an animal, such as a bat.[17] Like-wise, the metamorphosis of humans into wolves (lycanthropy) is well known in mythology, legend, and scripture and has been extensively surveyed in history, theology, and literature.[18] Lycanthropy likely had its origin in ancient Greek mythology and the Greek god *Zeus Lycaeus*.[19] A relationship between lycanthropy and psychiatric illness was noted in the book of Daniel in the Old Testament where King Nebuchadnezzar is said to have entered a lycan-thropic state after a lengthy depressive episode.[20] In ancient Rome, the wolf was an important symbolic creature, the constant companion of Mars and the protector of Romulus and Remus, the founders of Rome.[21] The werewolf was the subject of accounts by Pliny, Herodotus, and Virgil.[22] The delusional belief in metamorphosis to animal form was termed *Insania Zooanthropica* in the 18th century.[23]

Like all folklore, the legend of the vampire has evolved throughout the centuries. The current image of a vampire has its origin in the folklore and writings of Eastern European countries starting in the early 1700s.[24] The land most associated with vampires is Romania, specifically Transylvania, where the *strigoi morti* (vampires) were kept away with garlic and holy symbols.[25] The peak incidence of lycanthropy occurred in Europe during the 15th and 16th centuries, during the Spanish Inquisition, when the werewolf was a feared satanic representative.[26]

Garlic and crucifixes were ascribed prophylactic protection against vampires, but the only "cure" was to drive a wooden stake through the heart, preferably before burial. If a vampire was suspected of roaming through a village, the churchyard graves would be disinterred and the corpses that appeared to have moved in their graves, were suspiciously well preserved, or that had blood in their mouths were then treated with the stake or decapitated.[27]

One of the best-known epidemics of vampirism occurred in the late 18th century. This was contemporary with the rise of the Age of Enlightenment and marked the shift from witch hunting to vampire hunting.[28] This epidemic provided fertile breeding grounds for the development of vampire literature in the subsequent century, and it also established the typical characteristics of the Western vampire throughout Europe.[29]

Medical Explanations

Because their understanding of medicine included aspects of magic, 18th- and 19th-century villagers used their belief in fables, such as those about vampires and werewolves, to explain the unknown.[30] Werewolf cases attracted the attention of both ancient and modern physicians,[31] and a medical explanation for lycanthropy was given by Paulus Aegineta in the 7th century CE.[32] Such medical explanations for vampirism and lycanthropy became prevalent in the 17th century, when the conditions were described as forms of "madness."[33] However, in the 19th and 20th centuries, case reports became rare and attention turned instead to an examination by psychotherapists of the relevance of dreams and suspicions of vampires and werewolves, drawing heavily from classical and medieval accounts.[34]

Several diseases, including pellagra, porphyria, rabies, and schizophrenia, have been proposed as the genesis of the vampire myth.[35] However, none of these diseases satisfactorily presents clinical signs that would have been required to instigate a widespread European folkloric belief in vampires and werewolves.[36]

Porphyria

The speculated relationship between porphyria and vampirism has received a great deal of media attention.[37] The discoloration of the teeth and urine, bizarre behavior, hypertrichosis, nocturnal wandering, and episodic skin and facial changes suggest that porphyria may have a role in the vampire/werewolf transformation.[38] The strange appearance and behavior of sufferers of porphyria may have led them to be accused as vampires or werewolves during the Middle Ages.[39] It was during this time that the pre-Christian treatment of insanity with isolation in beautiful gardens and sedation using music was replaced with the view that the insane were possessed by evil spirits and were thus to be treated with appropriate inhumanity and savage cruelty.[40] During this period, the belief in werewolves was rife and this could have been exacerbated by the climate of fear and by the convenience of disposing of one's enemies by denouncing them as witches, vampires, or werewolves.[41] Although essentially a pre-Christian belief based on the need to externalize fear, once a story of a vampire or werewolf of sufficient credibility was established, it could persist for several generations and provide a mechanism to explaining other dreadful and otherwise inexplicable happenings.[42]

The photophobia and neurological and psychological sequelae seen in the advanced stages of porphyria are also consistent with the mythical characteristics of werewolves and vampires.[43] The neurological manifestations have not been completely explained but are associated with the urinary excretion of porphyrin precursors.[44] It is easy to imagine how such patients may have attracted suspicion in isolated communities and from the practitioners of the primitive medical arts of the time.[45]

The porphyrias consist of a constellation of syndromes caused by mutations in one of the many enzymes in the synthesis of the heme molecule that is found in the oxygen transport protein hemoglobin and other enzymes. A deficiency of any one of the 7 enzymes required for heme synthesis results in porphyria.[46] The pathway is regulated by end-product inhibition and, because these diseases interrupt the synthesis of heme, it cannot feed back and inhibit the pathway. This results in continued overload synthesis of the intermediates produced in the pathway prior to the defective enzyme. There are 7 types of porphyria, each resulting from the deficiency of a different enzyme, with varying symptoms depending on the location of the defect in the heme synthesis pathway. Defects in enzymes early in the pathway cause accumulation of water-soluble intermediates that are excreted in the urine, while defects in enzymes late in the pathway cause the accumulation of water-insoluble intermediates that are excreted in the feces via the bile.[47]

The most common form worldwide is porphyria cutanea tarda (PCT), with only photosensitive cutaneous symptoms.[48] The biochemical defect causing this disorder is genetic defects (mutations) in the enzyme uroporphyrinogen decarboxylase, which converts uroporphyrinogen to coproporphyrinogen. Uroporphyrinogen thus accumulates in the liver and is eventually excreted in the urine.[49] PCT is inherited in autosomal dominant fashion but only a fraction of those who are genetically afflicted express the classical disease phenotype.[50]

Acute intermittent porphyria (AIP) is common in Sweden and Great Britain.[51] This disorder is caused by mutations in the enzyme uroporphyrinogen

I synthetase and is inherited in autosomal dominant fashion. During acute attacks of the disease porphobilinogen is excreted in large amounts in the urine. AIP famously afflicted King George III of Great Britain, as expressed in the film *The Madness of King George*. This disorder causes no cutaneous symptoms; its most notable symptoms are neurological attacks, such as trances, seizures, and hallucinations.[52] As with PCT, most patients have the latent form of the disease in which they never develop symptoms.[53] Acute attacks are usually precipitated by exposure to exogenous chemicals such as drugs, heavy metals, and toxins that stress the liver.[54]

Congenital erythropoietic porphyria (CEP), also known as Gunter's disease, is inherited in autosomal recessive fashion. This disease is extremely rare, less than 200 cases had been reported prior to 1991.[55] CEP is caused by mutations in the enzyme uroporphyrinogen III synthetase and is characterized by enhanced uroporphyrin formation in erythroid cells in the bone marrow.[56] The uroporphyrins accumulate in the skin, blood, urine, and other body tissues, producing a brown appearance.[57] Accumulation of the uroporphyrins in the teeth also gives them a reddish-brown color. When exposed to ultraviolet light, the uroporphyrins in the skin and teeth fluoresce and appear reddish in color.[58]

The skin in CEP patients is afflicted with vesicle-like lesions when the uroporphyrins are activated by sunlight. This causes appalling photomutilation from the light-activated porphyrin.[59] Photosensitivity is characteristic of patients with CEP and the patient will avoid daylight. They tend to be pale because of the lack of sunlight-stimulated melanin production.[60] Hirsutism may be extensive in patients with porphyria, giving the patient an animal-like appearance. The vesicle-like lesions in the skin will produce an orange or red exudate that also fluoresces in bright moonlight or ultraviolet light. The hands will become scarred and may even take on a claw-like appearance due to loss of the ends of the digits from the photodeterioration of the skin.[61] Bright red urine, resembling blood, is another characteristic feature of CEP.

Symptoms of the severest forms of this disease include accumulation of photosensitive pigments in the skin, leading to photosensitivity, and phosphorescent pigments in the mucus membranes around the mouth and eye, causing them to be red in daylight but to glow at night. In order to obtain the heme porphyrics require to survive, it is possible to imagine them drinking blood, and the metabolism of garlic in the liver would be impaired in such persons because the enzymes that break down the chemicals in garlic depend on heme.

Abdominal pain, an enlarged spleen, psychological symptoms, and seizures also accompany CEP. In the isolated and possibly inbred small villages of Eastern Europe, CEP may have been responsible for the origin of the myths of vampires or werewolves.[62] However, the folkloric vampire is a different creature than the one we are familiar with in the 20th century.[63] One important difference was the belief that it was not uncommon for vampires to be active out-of-doors when the sun shone. In the 18th and 19th centuries there were accounts of vampire sightings occurring during the daylight hours.[64] This challenges the hypothesis that CEP explains the origin of the folkloric vampire but may explain the modern version of the myth. In addition, when exhumed from the grave, the folkloric vampire was always described as looking quite healthy, whereas sufferers of CEP, if they were to be exhumed, would have had a remarkably different appearance.[65] It is also the case that individuals with CEP do not crave blood, the heme necessary to alleviate the symptoms is not absorbed intact on oral ingestion and thus drinking blood would have had no beneficial effect.[66] Finally, CEP is a very rare disease, and it is difficult to imagine that such a rare manifestation of a rare disease could have spurred the rampant reports of vampires that occurred in the 18th century.[67]

Pellagra

First recognized in 1735, during an epidemic of vampire reports, pellagra (a dietary deficiency of the vitamin, niacin, and the amino acid, tryptophan) was the scourge of Europe and the United States in the 18th and 19th centuries.[68] This disease became endemic in Europe as the cultivation of maize (corn) spread from the Iberian Peninsula to the rest of Europe and became the major source of food for poor people. The niacin and tryptophan in corn are bound and have poor bioavailability and thus diets that rely on corn as a staple are predisposed to cause pellagra.

Its impact was especially macabre in Eastern Europe where poverty, culture, and a lack of medical knowledge kept the disease from being diagnosed until 1858.[69] The symptoms of this disease can be subsumed by the "4 Ds": dermatitis, dementia, diarrhea, and death.[70]

Pellagra causes hypersensitivity to sunlight, a main characteristic of vampires and werewolves, who must avoid sunlight to maintain their strength and avoid postmortem decay. Upon initial sun exposure, the skin of a person with pellagra becomes red and thick with hyperkeratosis and scaling. Repeated exposure to sunlight causes inflammation and edema (erythema) that eventually leads to depigmented patches of shiny skin that alternates with rough, brown scaly areas. Repeated episodes of erythema cause the skin to become paper thin and to assume a parchment-like texture.[71] Stoker characterizes Count Dracula, who avoided sunlight and went out only at night, as a man of "extraordinary pallor" without a "speck of color about him" and with a "bloated face." The Count characterizes himself as a "blot on the face of God's sunshine" and notes "I love the shade and the shadow."

Humans suffering from pellagra have a tongue marked by glossitis and excessive redness, causing an intuitive association with blood. Because of the swelling of the tongue, imprints of the teeth are often left on the tongue, suggestive of protuberant teeth or fangs. The lips of pellagra sufferers also become inflamed, reddish, and cracked, reflective of Stoker's description of Count Dracula's lips as having "remarkable redness."

Because of the deficiency of niacin, pellagra causes the neurons in the brain to degenerate, causing dementia with symptoms such as insomnia, anxiety, unjustified aggression, and depression.[72] These are of the manic-depressive type and can become sufficiently severe to require incarceration in a psychiatric hospital.[73] These symptoms parallel those of a folkloric vampire who does not sleep at night and is morose or irritable. An often overlooked aspect of pellagra is pica, the consumption of non-food materials. This may reflect a desperate attempt to include niacin in the diet.[74]

Once vampire or werewolf hysteria spread through a community, it was common for graves to be disinterred to examine the recently buried for evidence of both disorders.[75] Not surprisingly, almost all exhumations yielded perceived evidence of vampirism. Frequently the face of a reputed vampire would be described as being red and marked with fresh blood. Much of this mythology is based on the poor knowledge at the time of the processes of corpse decay.[76] This decay varies with the composition of the soil, the climate, the temperature, and the kind of burial, and it is not uncommon to disinter modern corpses that are still in a good state, even after a long time in the ground.[77] In particular, the absence of oxygen prevents the decay of the tissues while the humidity can, under optimal conditions, saponify the lipids in the skin, making them similar to wax and giving the corpse a "still living" appearance. The production and shifting of gasses produced by putrefaction might be the explanation for the noises and wheezings heard by witnesses of the graves of presumed vampires and werewolves.[78] Ironically, the putrefaction might also explain the presence of "live" blood in the mouth of the corpse of a presumed vampire because body fluids so produced usually emerge from the body openings. Finally, dehydration of the skin would make the hair and nails appear as if they were still growing.[79]

Intriguingly, a second tell-tale sign of vampirism was a ring of cornmeal around the mouth of the deceased. As odd as this association is, perhaps 18th- and 19th-century Eastern European villagers had a better understanding of the link between nutrition, pellagra, and vampirism than they have been credited with having.[80]

Rabies

The desire to bite others purportedly occurring in vampires and werewolves resembles the viral disease rabies, which causes acute encephalitis that leads to psychological disorders in those who become infected.[81] Other symptoms include difficulty swallowing and insatiable thirst. The transmission of the disease from one infected animal to another by biting resembles the presumed ability of vampires and lycanthropes to transmit their disorder to another by the same mechanism.[82] As stated previously, the myths of vampires and werewolves originated in the 18th century in the Carpathian mountains of Eastern Europe, where the occurrence of injuries caused by rabid dogs and wolves was frequently reported.[83]

In this context, some vampire myths relate that the vampire interacted with dogs and wolves both positively and negatively, under different conditions.[84] Additionally, dogs and wolves may help vampires, who can also turn into them, but vampires can also be these animal's worst enemies.[85] Usually the virus of rabies is passed by the bite of an infected animal. The incubation period of several days is accompanied by non-specific symptoms such as elevated body temperature, anxiety, lack of appetite, and fatigue. When the actual disease appears, in some cases there is paralysis, but most often there is an encephalitis accompanied by behavioral disturbances, hypersexuality, a psychotic hyperexitable phase, a generalized sense of dread, the tendency to bite, and hydrophobia.[86] In some cases the symptoms resemble the characteristics of vampires or werewolves; the spasms cause the contraction of the lips and the teeth become more apparent; there may be an emission of blood from the mouth; and the anxiety turns into a fear of water and light.[87]

Psychopathological

Through the centuries, and in many cultures worldwide, persons believed to be werewolves have repeatedly exhibited alterations in consciousness; depersonalization and derealization; acute anxiety and agitation; preoccupation with demonic possession; and compulsive or perseverative behavior, sometimes of a violent, sexually deviant, or impulsive nature.[88] Such features of vampire or werewolf behavior might be explained by ictal and interictal manifestations of complex partial seizures or as symptoms of the episodic discontrol syndrome associated with frontal lobe or limbic system disease or injury.[89]

Although the existence of the vampire myth has remained constant in the history of human societies, countless variations of the myth have emerged down through the centuries.[90] This constant presence in civilization suggests that there is something about the myth that carries great importance and significance to the minds of humans, binding the myth to our history.[91] Its numerous links to other legends and superstitions indicate the existence of a psychic representation.[92] One explanation for the persistence of and fascination with the myth can be provided by the work of psychoanalyst Carl Jung. To Jung, the human psyche contains universal archetypes (images and motifs) that arise from the collective unconscious and originate from an emotion or event that is central to the psychology of all humans. In Jungian terms the vampire is one of the main archetypes of the human psyche[93] and lycanthropy represented the emergence of an archetypal carnivorous beast that engages in sadistic behavior.[94] Jungian analysis suggests that the delusion of lycanthropy was an expression of a primitive identity from which man struggles to free himself.[95] This can be extended to the concept that the werewolf represents a desire for freedom from compulsion, a wish for heightened potency, and an oral-sadistic or cannibalistic impulse rooted in Oedipal conflicts.[96]

Lycanthropy was often considered a manifestation of demonic possession or a consequence or indication of participation in necromancy. Lycanthropes were regarded as heretics up to the beginning of the 17th century.[97] For this reason, self-proclaimed or suspected werewolves were often persecuted, and this persecution may have arisen from a last efflorescence of medieval demonology.[98] It has also been suggested that clinical descriptions of illnesses of diabolical origin, such as vampirism and lycanthropy, played an important role in the transformation of Renaissance medicine from its Galenic (mythological) past to its scientifically based present and future.[99] The metamorphosis into a werewolf occurred by personal intent, the witchcraft of others, the instigation of the devil or evil spirits, and even by the dispensation of saints or other divine agents.[100] Metamorphosis by personal intent could be accomplished by simply donning the skin of the animal into which one wanted to be transformed. The witchcraft of others often involved metamorphosis by incantation or ointments. The King of Wales, Verentricious, was changed into a wolf by St. Patrick, the patron saint of Ireland. Partial transformations have also been recorded.[101]

Another psychological perspective on the myth of the vampire comes from the psychodynamic approach of Sigmund Freud. Freudian psychoanalysis suggests that morbid dread always signifies repressed sexual wishes. In this context the vampire is a phantom projection of the subject's desire to be possessed, controlled, and vampirized.[102] The vampire myth can be approached along various levels of psychosexual development in Oedipal terms: for example, the vampire is often portrayed as an abductor of women, killing and enslaving any men who cross his path.[103]

The sexual nature of the oral aggression of vampires can be understood by an examination of the teeth of a vampire. The teeth represent an obvious sexual image of penetrating others in order to fulfill one's desire for pleasure. Thus, removal of the teeth acts as a type of castration of a vampire, rendering him impotent in his need for oral, and sexual, gratification. This follows Freud's concept of "castration anxiety" and supports the idea that the vampire myth embodies unconscious and unmet sexual desires within human beings.[104]

More obviously, Count Dracula has an undeniable fascination with young women and desires to bite virtuous young women before they are married. In the novel *Dracula*, the Count inflicts his bite, which has already been characterized as having a highly sexual context, upon two young women just prior to their marriage. These episodes portray a crude psychosexual image of virginity-taking.[105] This highly sexual behavior has emerged as a stereotypical image of the male vampire attacking pure young women and, in doing so, removing their purity. As a consequence, vampires were imagined to be unable to function within society, or its regulations and restrictions on human behavior, and this may be contained in the common depiction of vampires being unable to venture out into the light of the sun.[106]

The lycanthropy delusion of being transformed into an animal is often associated with the delusion of growing claws, and often the delusion of growing claws is the first step leading to more complete delusions of lycanthropy.[107] Psychoanalysts see the syndrome of lycanthropy as an expression of primitive id instincts that are being conveyed literally on an animalistic level through a splitting mechanism, thereby avoiding guilty feelings,[108] although a minority of modern reported cases of lycanthropy were directly related to sexual intercourse. Lycanthropy appears to be a non-specific sign of symptom occasionally seen in severe functional psychosis or, less commonly, as a factitious psychological symptom. Because the parietal lobe is the principal sensory area of the cerebral cortex, with the foci of foot and toe sensory interpretation being situated at the superior border of the parietal lobe, it may be that the pathogenesis of somatic delusions, including lycanthropy, is mainly associated with organic lesions of the parietal lobe.[109]

Despite the passage of time and the rationalizing effects of biomedical research, the vampire or werewolf remains a powerful and evocative image. The influence of myth and legend has been filtered and obscured but it is likely that the symptoms of vampirism and lycanthropy and claims of actually being a vampire or a werewolf will continue as long these tales can frighten us.[110]

Notes

1. Steven Kimberly, "A Psychological Analysis of the Vampire Myth," *Estro: Essex Student Research Online* 1 (2010): 38.

2. L. Rodrigues de la Sierra, "Origin of the Myth of Vampirism," *Journal of the Royal Society of Medicine* 91 (1998): 290.

3. Nancy W. Burkhart, "Oh My! Vampires and Werewolves," *Registered Dental Hygienist* 2010" 30(9), http://www.rdhmag.com/index/display/article-display/7620711446/articles/rdh/volume-30/issue-9/columns/oh-my-vampires-and-werewolves.html, accessed January 11, 2012.

4. Jeffrey S. Hampl and William S. Hampl, "Pellagra and the Origin of a Myth: Evidence from European Literature and Folklore," *Journal of the Royal Society of Medicine* 90 (1997): 636.

5. Burkhart, "Oh My!"

6. Moreno Tiziani, "Vampires and Vampirism: Pathological Roots of a Myth," *Antrocom* 5 (2009): 133.

7. Tiziani, "Vampires and Vampirism," 133.

8. Tiziani, "Vampires and Vampirism," 133.

9. Tiziani, "Vampires and Vampirism," 133.

10. Kimberly, "A Psychological Analysis of the Vampire Myth," 38.

11. Kimberly, "A Psychological Analysis of the Vampire Myth," 38.

12. T. A. Fahy, "Lycanthropy, a Review," *Journal of the Royal Society of Medicine* 82 (1909): 37; Hamdy F. Moselhy, "Lycanthropy: New Evidence of its Origin," *Psychopathology* 32(1999): 173.

13. Burkhart, "Oh My!"

14. L. Illis, "On Porphyria and the Aetiology of Werewolves," *Proceedings of the Royal Society of Medicine* 57 (1964): 23.

15. Hampl and Hampl, "Pellagra and the Origin of a Myth," 636.

16. Rodriguez de la Sierra, "Origin of the Myth of Vampirism," 290.

17. Alex Heick, "Prince Dracula, Rabies and the Vampire Legend," *Annals of Internal Medicine* 117 (1992): 172.

18. Miles E. Drake, "Medical and Neuropsychiatric Aspects of Lycanthropy," *Journal of Medical Humanities* 13 (1992): 5.

19. Fahy, "Lycanthropy, a Review," 37.

20. Fahy, "Lycanthropy, a Review," 38.

21. Fahy, "Lycanthropy, a Review," 37.

22. Illis, "On Porphyria and the Aetiology of Werewolves," 23.

23. Fahy, "Lycanthropy, a Review," 37.

24. Hampl and Hampl, "Pellagra and the Origin of a Myth," 636.

25. Burkhart, "Oh My!"

26. Fahy, "Lycanthropy, a Review," 37.

27. Heick, "Prince Dracula, Rabies and the Vampire Legend," 172.

28. Tiziani, "Vampires and Vampirism," 134.

29. Tiziani, "Vampires and Vampirism," 134.

30. Hampl and Hampl, "Pellagra and the Origin of a Myth," 636.

31. Drake, "Medical and Neuropsychiatric Aspects of Lycanthropy," 5.

32. Fahy, "Lycanthropy, a Review," 37.

33. Fahy, "Lycanthropy, a Review," 37.

34. Fahy, "Lycanthropy, a Review," 38.

35. Hampl and Hampl, "Pellagra and the Origin of a Myth," 636.

36. Hampl and Hampl, "Pellagra and the Origin of a Myth," 636.

37. Hampl and Hampl, "Pellagra and the Origin of a Myth," 636.

38. Illis, "On Porphyria and the Aetiology of Werewolves," 25; Drake, "Medical and Neuropsychiatric Aspects of Lycanthropy," 5.

39. Illis, "On Porphyria and the Aetiology of Werewolves," 23.

40. Illis, "On Porphyria and the Aetiology of Werewolves," 24.

41. Illis, "On Porphyria and the Aetiology of Werewolves," 25.

42. Illis, "On Porphyria and the Aetiology of Werewolves," 25.

43. Fahy, "Lycanthropy, a Review," 38.

44. James P. Kushner, "Laboratory Diagnosis of the Porphyrias," *New England Journal of Medicine* 334 (1991): 1432.

45. Moselhy, 'Lycanthropy," 175.

46. Kushner, "Laboratory Diagnosis of the Porphyrias," 1432; Burkhart, "Oh My!"

47. Burkhart, "Oh My!"

48. Kushner, "Laboratory Diagnosis of the Porphyrias,"1432.

49. Kushner, "Laboratory Diagnosis of the Porphyrias," 1433.

50. Kushner, "Laboratory Diagnosis of the Porphyrias," 1433.

51. Burkhart, "Oh My!"

52. Kushner, "Laboratory Diagnosis of the Porphyrias," 1433.

53. Kushner, "Laboratory Diagnosis of the Porphyrias," 1433; Nick Lane, "Born to Purple: The Story of Porphyria. *Scientific American Online.* (2002). Available at http://www.scientificamerican.com/article.cfm?id=born-to-the-purple-the-st, accessed January 12, 2012.

54. Kushner, "Laboratory Diagnosis of the Porphyrias," 1433.

55. Kushner, "Laboratory Diagnosis of the Porphyrias," 1434.

56. Kushner, "Laboratory Diagnosis of the Porphyrias," 1434.

57. Burkhart, "Oh My!"

58. Burkhart, "Oh My!"

59. Lane, "Born to Purple."

60. Burkhart, "Oh My!"

61. Burkhart, "Oh My!"

62. Burkhart, "Oh My!"

63. Ann M. Cox, "Porphyria and Vampirism: Another Myth in the Making," *Postgraduate Medical Journal* 71 (1995): 644.

64. Cox, "Porphyria and Vampirism," 644.

65. Cox, "Porphyria and Vampirism," 644.

66. Cox, "Porphyria and Vampirism," 644.

67. Cox, "Porphyria and Vampirism," 644.

68. Tiziani, "Vampires and Vampirism," 136.

69. Hampl and Hampl, "Pellagra and the Origin of a Myth," 636.

70. Hampl and Hampl, "Pellagra and the Origin of a Myth a," 636.

71. Hampl and Hampl, "Pellagra and the Origin of a Myth," 636.

72. Hampl and Hampl, "Pellagra and the Origin of a Myth," 636.

73. Hampl and Hampl, "Pellagra and the Origin of a Myth," 636.

74. Hampl and Hampl, "Pellagra and the Origin of a Myth," 636.

75. Hampl and Hampl, "Pellagra and the Origin of a Myth," 636; Tiziani, "Vampires and Vampirism," 134.

76. Tiziani, "Vampires and Vampirism," 135.

77. Tiziani, "Vampires and Vampirism," 135.

78. Tiziani, "Vampires and Vampirism," 135.

79. Tiziani, "Vampires and Vampirism," 135.
80. Hampl and Hampl, "Pellagra and the Origin of a Myth," 638.
81. J. Theodorides, "Origin of the Myth of Vampirism," *Journal of the Royal Society of Medicine* 91(1998): 114; Tiziani, "Vampires and Vampirism," 136.
82. Theodorides, "Origin of the Myth of Vampirism," 114.
83. Theodorides, "Origin of the Myth of Vampirism," 114.
84. Tiziani, "Vampires and Vampirism," 136.
85. Tiziani, "Vampires and Vampirism," 136.
86. Heick, "Prince Dracula, Rabies and the Vampire Legend," 172; Tiziani, "Vampires and Vampirism," 136.
87. Tiziani, "Vampires and Vampirism," 136.
88. Drake, "Medical and Neuropsychiatric Aspects of Lycanthropy," 5.
89. Drake, "Medical and Neuropsychiatric Aspects of Lycanthropy," 5.
90. Kimberly, "A Psychological Analysis of the Vampire Myth," 38.
91. Kimberly, "A Psychological Analysis of the Vampire Myth," 39.
92. Rodriguez de la Sierra, "Origin of the Myth of Vampirism," 290.
93. Kimberly, "A Psychological Analysis of the Vampire Myth," 39.
94. Fahy, "Lycanthropy, a Review," 38.
95. Fahy, "Lycanthropy, a Review," 38.
96. Fahy, "Lycanthropy, a Review," 38.
97. Illis, "On Porphyria and the Aetiology of Werewolves," 24.
98. Drake, "Medical and Neuropsychiatric Aspects of Lycanthropy," 5.
99. Drake, "Medical and Neuropsychiatric Aspects of Lycanthropy," 5.
100. Illis, "On Porphyria and the Aetiology of Werewolves," 23.
101. Illis, "On Porphyria and the Aetiology of Werewolves," 23.
102. Kimberly, "A Psychological Analysis of the Vampire Myth," 40.
103. Rodriguez de la Sierra, "Origin of the Myth of Vampirism," 290.
104. Kimberly, "A Psychological Analysis of the Vampire Myth," 41.
105. Kimberly, "A Psychological Analysis of the Vampire Myth," 41.
106. Kimberly, "A Psychological Analysis of the Vampire Myth," 42.
107. Moselhy, "Lycanthropy," 175.
108. Moselhy, "Lycanthropy," 175.
109. Moselhy, "Lycanthropy," 175.
110. Fahy, "Lycanthropy, a Review," 38.

6

Evidence for the Undead:
The Role of Medical Investigation in
the 18th-Century Vampire Epidemic

Leo Ruickbie

R EADERS IN LONDON OPENED THE MARCH 1732 EDITION of *The Gentle-man's Magazine* to learn "that certain dead Bodies called Vampyres, had kill'd several Persons by sucking out all their Blood." The same story was carried by newspapers and periodicals across Europe. In Paris, Voltaire remembered the moment: "Nothing was spoken of but vampires, from 1730 to 1735." It was more than just talk. Jean-Jacques Rousseau wrote to the Archbishop of Paris, saying "If there is in the world one attested story it is that of the Vampires. Nothing is missing: proces-verbaux, certificates from Notabilities, Surgeons, Priests, Magistrates. The juridical proof is most complete."[1] Counter-intuitively, it was the Enlightenment, the Age of Reason that provided the best evidence for the existence of the vampire.

Voltaire was right to say that the first half of the 1730s was abuzz with talk of vampires, but the public debate and flurry of publications across Europe began earlier and lasted longer. Picking up on an earlier discussion in the late 17th century on the *Nachzehrer* (literally "after devourer" or commonly "shroud-eater"), from 1732 to 1733 some 20 books, dissertations, and articles appeared in the first year of this latest craze. Most of these were scholarly, academic texts, despite some lurid titles, such as *Dissertatio de Cadaveribus Sanguisugis* ("On the Blood-Sucking Cadavers"). By 1734 Michael Ranft remarked that during Leipzig's last Easter fair "it was impossible to enter a bookshop without seeing something about bloodsuckers." He had written one of them himself—on the "chewing dead"—which was then being published in a new German edition. The debate would eventually reach the Vatican and the royal courts of Europe.[2]

Voltaire's source, and quite possibly Rousseau's as well, was the biblical scholar and leading Catholic theologian Dom Augustin Calmet (1672–1757).[3] Calmet's reputation rested on a 20-volume exegesis of the Bible, but he had also alarmed French readers in 1746 by announcing that:

> In this age, a new scene presents itself to our eyes, and has done for about sixty years in Hungary, Moravia, Silesia, and Poland: they see, it is said, men who have been dead for several months, come back to earth, talk, walk, infest villages, ill use both men and beasts, suck the blood of their near relations, make them ill, and finally cause their death. . . . These *revenans* are called by the name of oupires or vampires, that is to say, leeches; and such particulars are related of them, so singular, so detailed, and invested with such probable circumstances and such judicial information, that one can hardly refuse to credit the belief which is held in those countries.[4]

What was important about the 1730s was the amount of new evidence that was forthcoming, its widespread promulgation and this new word *vampire*.[5] Calmet had scooped much of the evidence together for his book, which Voltaire had certainly read.[6] Calmet began with one of the earliest accounts, perhaps the first of Rousseau's "certificates from Notabilities."

Case Number 1: Kisolova

Sometime earlier that year a man called Frombald, holding the important post of Imperial Provisor at Gradisk (Veliko Gradište) on the Habsburgs' Military Frontier, had received a deputation of villagers from "Kisolova," thought to be modern Kisiljevo in what is now the Republic of Serbia. The villagers were in a state of great alarm. One of their neighbors, a man by the name of Peter Plogojoviz, had died 10 weeks before and been buried according to local custom. However, Peter had come back.[7]

According to his wife, he had knocked on the door and demanded his *opanki*, the traditional peasant footwear of the region. After she fled the village, other people started saying that they had seen Peter, too. But not just seen him. They said Peter visited them in the night and lay upon them with such force that they felt the life being squeezed out of them. In 24 hours, they were dead. Within the space of 8 days, 9 people had died from Peter's nightly visits. The villagers knew exactly what he was: one of the "Vampyri," as Frombald carefully noted. To make sure, they wanted to exhume the body and look for the tell-tale signs—the body undecomposed and the hair, beard and nails still growing—and they wanted the Imperial Provisor and a priest to be present. Frombald told them they would have to wait while he sent a request to his superiors in Belgrade. The villagers refused to wait, threatening to leave the village *en masse* before the vampire could kill everyone, as had happened, they said, sometime before. Frombald explained the necessity of waiting to them. Frombald ordered them to wait. Frombald no doubt shouted at them. The Kisolovans were adamant. Frombald must have mulled the situation over carefully. Serbia had been recently snatched out of the jaws of the Ottoman Turks and the region remained politically tense. A deserted village in the Military Frontier could have repercussions, not least with his superiors. So it was that he found himself taking the road to Kisolova with the priest and an escort of villagers.

As they entered the village, they found—no doubt to their surprise—that the body had already been dug up. Frombald lost no time in inspecting it:

> First, from the body and its grave there was not the slightest smell of death. The body, except the nose, which was fallen in, was very fresh. The hair and beard, also the nails, the old ones having fallen away, had grown on him. The old skin, which was somewhat whitish, had peeled off and a fresh new one had come out under it. The face, hands and also feet, and the whole body, were so recreated that they, in his lifetime, could not have been more complete. In his mouth, not without surprise, did I see fresh blood, which, after the general opinion, he had sucked from those killed by him. In sum, all the indications were presented which these people (as already noted above) should themselves have.[8]

As Frombald and the priest observed the scene—the fresh earth around the grave and the extraordinary condition of the body—the villagers were already busy sharpening a stake. The wood of the white-thorn was said to be preferred.[9] Forthwith, they drove it through the heart of the corpse. Frombald was aghast as fresh blood spurted from the corpse's ears and mouth, and the priest must have blushed at the "other wild signs" that Frombald declined to describe in his letter "out of high respect." The body was then burnt to ashes. Frombald was careful to point out that if any mistake had been made in this matter—the desecration of a grave and the summary execution of someone who may not have been quite dead, come to mind—then all blame should rest squarely on the fear-crazed peasants.

On July 21, 1725, the people of Vienna opened the *Wienerisches Diarium* to find an account of Frombald's report. It must have raised a few eyebrows, but the impact of this astonishing story was circumspect. There was one exception. Michael Ranft had just passed the *Magister* degree at Leipzig University and was only 25 years old when he published his first book, *Dissertation historico-critica de masticatione mortuorum in tumulis* ("Historico-Critical Dissertation on the Chewing Dead in their Graves"). It is a short text in Latin, running only 28 pages, and reproduced an account of Frombald's report in full. Ranft scoffed at the suggestion that vampires truly sucked the blood of the living, but he conceded that their victims were real enough, carried away, he argued, by the magical effects of their own imaginations and that of Plogojoviz mysteriously still functioning after his death.[10]

Ranft, in a sense, was only contributing to the tail-end of a discussion that began in the late 17th century, despite his up-to-date example, and would only become influential during the debates of the 1730s when he included astonishing new stories. For his part, Frombald's official and impartial testimony carried weight, but it was not the most important of the vampire reports.

Case Number 2: Medveđa

When a peasant fell off a hay wagon and broke his neck in 1727, it was not just another agricultural accident. It was the beginning of a vampire epidemic that would bring the small village of Medveđa in Serbia to the notice of the world. Variously called Metwett, Medwedia, and Medwegya in the sources, this is probably the village of Medveđa lying near Trstenik on the banks of the Zapadna Morava river about 200 km south of Kisiljevo.[11] The peasant in question was a local *hajduk* (militiaman) named Arnond Paole. Paole had returned to Medveđa from Turkish-controlled Serbia with strange stories of being attacked by a vampire near "Gassowa" (possibly Kosovo), but he calmed his neighbors by telling them that he had eaten earth from the vampire's grave and smeared himself with its blood as an antidote. Serbian folklore contained no notion of vampirism being transmitted through the blood. About 20 or 30 days after his death, the villagers discovered that the antidote had not worked.[12]

People started complaining that Paole had returned from the grave to torment them. Four people subsequently died. The local headman, who had experience of these matters, ordered them to dig up Paole. His body had not decomposed and fresh blood was seen to come out of eyes, nose, and ears, and his nails and skin had fallen off to be replaced by new growth. According to local custom, they pierced his heart with a stake whereupon he uttered a loud cry. They burnt the remains to ashes. Because they believed that his victims would also become vampires, they similarly disposed of the bodies of his victims.

Despite the destruction of Paole's corpse, vampirism returned to the village in the winter of 1731. In the short space of 6 weeks, 13 people had died. This time the matter was reported and, fearing plague or something like it, a specialist in contagious medicine called Glaser was dispatched from "Parakin" (Paraćin) to investigate. Traveling southwest for about 60 km—perhaps a 2 days' ride, depending on conditions—Glaser arrived on December 12 and conducted a house-to-house search. Although he found no evidence of infectious disease, he did find several of what he was told were vampires. In the graveyard, locals showed him the bodies of dead people who appeared fatter, younger, and fresher than when they had been alive. He documented their name, ages, length of time since death, and the general opinion of the villagers. Glaser reported back to the commander at Jagodina, further down the Morava.[13]

In consequence another commission was formed comprising Johannes Flückinger, regimental surgeon to Baron Fürstenbusch's Infantry Regiment, J. H. Siegel, field surgeon to the "Morallischen Regiment," and Johann Friedrich Baumgarten, also of Fürstenbusch's Regiment.[14] Traveling to Medveđa in early January they met Captain Groschitz of the local militia (the Stallater hajduk company) and Hadnack (headman) of the village who explained the current situation.

Although Paole was now quite dead, some people had eaten the meat of livestock that he had attacked as a vampire. Within three months 17 died, some without any apparent disease, in the short space of 2 to 3 days. The officers marched down to the cemetery and ordered the graves of the victims to be opened. Flückinger spread out his instruments and conducted a series of autopsies, which he carefully documented as follows:

1. Stana, female, 20, died in childbirth 2 months previously, found to be "complete and undecayed." After opening the body, fresh extravascular blood was found in the cavitate pectoris. The arteries and veins were filled with fluid blood and the inner organs appeared fresh and healthy. New nails were observed on one of her hands. The child had been carelessly interred and consequently half-eaten by dogs but was also considered to be a vampire.
2. Miliza, female, 60, buried 90 days previously, was found to be fat and healthy looking, more so, said those who had known her, than she had been in life. She had eaten the meat of sheep killed by vampires and was suspected of spreading the contagion further.
3. An unnamed child, 8 days old, buried 90 days earlier, also vampiric.
4. An unnamed boy, 16, buried 9 weeks earlier, in the vampiric condition.
5. Joachim, male, 17, buried 8 weeks earlier, dissected and found to be vampiric.
6. Ruscha, female, age not recorded, buried 8 weeks previously, found to be full of fresh blood. Also her child, 18 days old, not listed separately.
7. An unnamed girl, 10, died 2 months previously, again "complete and undecayed" with much fresh blood.

8. An unnamed woman, age not recorded, died 7 weeks previously, and her 8-week-old child both found to be decomposed. It was noted that the earth and grave were like those of the vampires interred nearby.
9. Rhade, male, 21 (or 23), a servant to a hajduk corporal, died 5 weeks previously, completely decomposed.
10. An unnamed woman, identified as the wife of the Bariactar, and her child, dead 5 weeks, similarly decomposed.
11. Stanche (or Stancko), male, 60, a hajduk, dead 6 weeks, a profusion of liquid blood in the chest and heart, and similarly vampiric in other regards.
12. Milloe (or Millove), male, 25, a hajduk, and a vampire.
13. Stanoicka (or Stanvicka), female, 22, daughter-in-law of the hajduk Joviza, was still florid and healthy looking with fresh blood coming out of her nose. A great quantity of fresh blood was found in the chest and stomach. The body was not in the least decomposed. A bruise was noted under her ear, one finger long. It was said that, while still alive, she had awoken one night with screams and in great anguish, saying that Joviza's dead son Milloe had returned from the grave and tried to strangle her. Within days she was dead.

The attacks had been indiscriminate: 7 women; 5 men; and 5 infants of unspecified sex. Several of them held positions of local importance or were connected to those who did. Significantly, not all of the dead had become vampires themselves. Five of those disinterred were found to be in the expected state of decomposition.

Tradition was adhered to: no samples could be taken. Local gypsies were given the unenviable task of decapitating the bodies and burning the remains. The ashes were then scattered in the Morava River. The decomposed and hence non-vampiric bodies were reburied.

Flückinger's report, called *Visum et Repertum* ("Seen and Reported," probably a generic rubric), was dated January 7, 1732. On January 26, 1732, it was counter-signed by Lieutenant Colonel (*Oberstleutnant*) Büttener and J. H. von Lindenfels of the Prinz Alexander Regiment in Belgrade as being in all regards truthful and accurate.

Flückinger's report was published in Nuremberg a few months after being submitted to the Belgrade authorities. German periodicals, such as the scientific *Commercium litterarium*, quickly picked up the story, but so too did the *London Journal*, *The Gentleman's Magazine*, and *The Grub Street Journal* in Britain, *Le Glaneur* in Holland, and the *Mercure* in France. In Vienna the French and Prussian ambassadors relayed the news to their respective governments, leading King Frederick Wilhelm I of Prussia to order an investigation by the Royal Society of Science. *Visum et Repertum* became a bestseller.[15]

Case Number 3: de Cabrera

Calmet related another case of about 1730 or before, located at what he called "the house of a Haidamaque peasant" somewhere vaguely "on the frontiers of Hungary."[16] This story was attributed to a certain "Comte de Cabreras," a captain in the "Alandetti regiment." However, there was no Cabreras of the Alandetti, although an identification with Juan de Cabrera i Perellós of the Spanish noble family of Cabrera, serving in Anton Diego, Marquis D'Alcaudete's regiment seems likely.[17]

According to an unnamed source of Calmet's, who had apparently heard it directly from de Cabrera in Freiburg im Breisgau in Germany in 1730, the captain had been detailed to investigate a report from a soldier billeted with a local family. The soldier had informed his superiors that his host had died suddenly after the arrival at dinner of the host's father who had been dead and buried for the last 10 years. Taking along some of his brother officers, a surgeon, and an auditor, Cabrera verified the soldier's tale and consequently had the body of the supposed revenant exhumed. It was, in Calmet's words, "found to be like that of a man who has just expired, and his blood like that of a living man." Cabrera had the corpse decapitated and re-interred. Information regarding two more cases was forthcoming: a corpse laid in the ground for 30 years past had returned three times to suck the blood from his brother, one of his sons, and a servant, all of whom subsequently died; another, dead for 16 years, had sucked the blood of two of his sons, causing death. Cabrera had these bodies exhumed also. The first was again found with "blood in a fluid state, like that of a living person"; the condition of the second was not described. He ordered that a nail be driven through the temple of the first and that the second should be burnt. Cabrera made his report and was dispatched to carry it to Emperor Charles VI himself. The involvement of military personnel, including legal and medical officers, gives the story apparent authority, but at the present time it is unsubstantiated.[18]

Further Evidence

The success of Flückinger caused subsequent writers to trawl their history books and adduce more examples of the chewing dead, murderous revenants, and blood-sucking corpses. Calmet was expansive on the subject. Quoting extensively from recent literature, such as the *Lettres Juives* ("Jewish Letters") and notably the events documented by Karl Ferdinand von Schertz in *Magia Posthuma*, he built up a picture of a widespread supernatural contagion stretching across Eastern Europe from Russia to the Balkans.[19]

Later writers would rediscover the case of Michael Kasperek (also Casparek) from 1718. Here was a classic example of an old-fashioned

Wiedergänger redefined as one of the new *Blutsauger*. Kasperek allegedly returned from the dead to molest the people of Lublau. Forty days after his internment, his corpse was still found to be undecayed. Even after the destruction of the corpse, during which the blood was seen to flow as if he had been alive, Kasperek continued to play havoc. The explanation shifted to the supposed possession of a magic ring and involvement in witchcraft, and the clergy attempted an exorcism. This also failed and Kasperek was blamed for an outbreak of fires, as well as being held responsible for getting his wife and a number of serving-maids pregnant. The case was published in 1718 and 1719, and included in Hauber's 1738 *Biblioteca* as a ghost story. While contemporaries counted him a *Wiedgergänger*, *Schimmelreiter*, and poltergeist animated by the Devil, by 1825 he had become "the oldest Vampyr . . . in Hungary." Certainly he had in common some of the vampiric elements, such as incorruptibility and flowing blood, and had been dealt with by the traditional methods of decapitation, heart removal, and burning but uncharacteristically he survived destruction of the body.[20]

The great debate of the 1730s also resurrected an early work by Pitton de Tournefort. De Tournefort's *Voyage into the Levant* was commissioned by Louis XIV and concerns natural history and cultural observations. Buried among them is de Tournefort's lively account of a Greek *vrykolakas*: "a Specter [sic] consisting of a dead Body and a Demon."[21] The *vrykolakas* exhibited all the symptoms of the Serbian vampiric corpse. Between 1732 and 1741 there were 4 new French editions and 2 in English.[22]

The evidence was piling up. The vampire seemed incontrovertible. However, despite his initial credulity, Calmet ultimately came down on the side of skepticism, even if this was not always clear. He was not unusual in this: de Boyers and Harenberg, for example, were also skeptical. This did little to abate the popular panic—"nothing was spoken of but vampires." By publishing so much, Calmet and the rest were fueling the fire, and, as we have just seen, this would in time consume earlier stories. As a reviewer of the 1759 English translation of Calmet remarked "we are at a loss to say, whether his book is most likely to do good or harm among the ignorant and superstitious."[23]

Discussions between Cardinal Schrattembach, Bishop of Olmutz, and the Archbishop of Trani, later Cardinal, Giuseppe Davanzati (1665–1755), led to the latter's own dissertation on the subject—*I Vampiri*—written between 1738 and 1744. Widely circulated in manuscript, Davanzati's work was read and praised by Pope Benedict XIV, swaying the pontiff's to condemn the belief in vampires when he published on the matter some years later. The pope was particularly concerned by the vampiric body's incursion on the sphere of the saintly through incorruptibility.[24]

Calmet had corresponded with Maria Theresa (1717–1780), Empress of the Holy Roman Empire, who was concerned enough by the epidemic to have her personal physician Gerard van Swieten investigate the matter. An incident in Hermersdorf near the Silesian–Moravian border had just been reported. Van Swieten deputed two court doctors, Johannes Gasser and Christian Vabst, to investigate. The body of Rosina Polakin, being exhumed in January 1755 and found to be vampiric—undecomposed and with fluid blood in the veins—had been subjected to the traditional treatment with the added proviso of first being dragged through a hole in the cemetery wall. The Empress issued a proclamation (*Rescriptum*) in March that year prohibiting the staking and burning of corpses.[25]

The vampire had left the misty realms of folklore and entered scientific, legal, and theological discourse. Independently reported, these cases unnervingly agreed upon the vampiric condition. Taken together they became an epidemic. The juridical proof was, as Rousseau said, complete. But nobody wanted to believe it was true. Not Rousseau and certainly not the Church for whom the undead were an affront to the resurrection, corporeal incorruptibility an intrusion on sainthood,[26] and blood drinking a dangerous trespass on the Holy Sacraments.[27] However, they could not escape the facts. But what were the facts?

"A Man Can Die But Once"[28]

Frombald, Glaser, Flückinger, and de Cabrera (if we can include him) all reported an uncorrupted body apparently filled with fluid blood, sometimes looking "healthier" than when alive, and described as fresh with "new" skin and nails, which attacks the living, draining their vitality to the point of death. These were presented as the facts; but is it possible that things were not as they seemed?

Most early modern and modern commentators have rejected the folk explanations and over the years a number of theories have been advanced to account for vampirism. Seeking to locate the condition in the diseased body, several medical specialists have forwarded diverse pathologies as the origin of vampire beliefs. All of these cluster around the supposed symptoms of the vampire itself.

Photosensitivity and anemia have led many to porphyria, especially as blood drinking has sometimes been prescribed as a cure. First proposed as an explanation for lycanthropy by L. Illis of Guy's Hospital in 1964, this rare, mostly inherited, genetic disorder also became associated with vampirism, mostly notably by biochemist Dr. David Dolphin in 1985. Speaking before the American Association for the Advancement of Science he claimed that, not only werewolves, but also vampires were simply sufferers of a disease that disfigured them, possibly causing the teeth to protrude in a fang-like manner, made it possible for them only to come out at night, and gave them a thirst for blood. Dolphin also claimed that the condition was exacerbated by garlic. The extreme form of porphyria that Dolphin was referring to (congenital erythropoietic porphyria) is so rare that only about 200 cases have ever been diagnosed. It does not lead to a craving for blood, indeed blood drinking as a medical treatment in the case of porphyria is ineffective, and there is no evidence for garlic's negative effect.[29]

In 1997, Drs. Jeffrey and William Hampl postulated a link between vampirism and pellagra. Identified in 1735, pellagra (from the Italian *pelle agra*, meaning "rough skin") is an acute condition caused by nutritional deficiency (of niacin and tryptophan), usually resulting from dietary dependence on corn. Following its export from the New World, corn was sown across Southern and Eastern Europe where warmer conditions were conducive to its growth. Pellegra followed in its wake. Symptoms include hypersensitivity to sunlight, skin inflammation, and scaling (whence the rough skin appellation), dementia from brain deterioration, and resulting unpredictable behavior, diarrhea, anorexia, and gastrointestinal bleeding. Left untreated the patient wastes away to death. The Hampls additionally made a connection between this wasting away and the supposed actions of vampires upon their victims and noted that where pellegra was endemic, vampirism was, too.[30]

Thinking that there might be more than coincidence behind the timing of severe rabies outbreaks in southeastern Europe from 1721 and 1728 and the subsequent vampire epidemic rabies, the Spanish neurologist Dr. Juan Gomez-Alonso proposed in 1998 that vampirism was a folk explanation for rabies in humans. He noted several supposed similarities between the two conditions: biting as a means of transmission; hypersensitivity that could lead to an aversion to sunlight or strong odors such as garlic; facial spasm that could produce an aversion to mirrors; and increased sex drive.[31]

While these conditions might resemble folk ideas of vampirism they cannot explain them because these folk beliefs are specifically concerned with the problem of the returning dead, not with human illness. They focus on the appearance and behavior of the presumed vampire, whereas even the least-educated peasant knew that vampires were already dead before they exhibited such signs. In the cases documented by Frombald, Glaser, Flückinger, and de Cabrera (if we can still include him) there is no mention of the vampire's reaction to garlic, sunlight intolerance, mirror avoidance, unhealthy appearance (quite the opposite), or increased sex drive (the *Wiedergänger* Kasperek excepted). None of these explanations address the problem of the vampiric body.

The condition of Plogojoviz's body seemed abnormal—paranormal—to the villagers, even to the Imperial Provisor and the regimental surgeon, but modern medicine has discovered that many of the traditional signs of vampirism are in fact part of the natural process of decomposition. When Frombald and Flückinger saw that the "old" skin of the vampires had fallen away and had been replaced by a "new" one, they were not entirely wrong. They had only incorrectly interpreted what we today know is skin slippage, the process by which the epidermis comes away from the dermis. The "new" nails observed were probably simply the nailbeds themselves. The full and "healthy" appearance was caused by gases released during decomposition which bloat the body, hence the old woman who looked better fed than when alive. The florid or ruddy appearance can result from livor mortis (lividity) as the tissues become saturated with blood. The presence of "fresh," that is, liquid blood is also possible; although blood normally coagulates at death, decomposition can cause it to liquefy again. The presence of blood in and around the mouth, taken as a sign of the vampire having sucked blood from the living, is caused by gas putting pressure on the lungs so forcing blood from the lungs up into the mouth and nose. The terrible cry of agony uttered by the vampire Paole upon staking is likewise explained by gases formed by decomposition. The impact of the stake on the chest cavity forces these gases up the throat and past the glottis to make a surprisingly lifelike sound. In fact, the Prussian Royal Society of Science had already pointed some of these issues out within a month of being commissioned to investigate in 1732, but Europe ignored their reasoning in favor of sensationalism.[32]

The investigations considered here, through the use of the language of officialdom—neutral, bureaucratic, signed, and dated—created the sort of expert testimony that seemed to verify the folklore. The vampiric body had been witnessed, medically examined, and concluded to be real. The scientific proof was apparently there. The debate was widened by scholarly discussion that refused to allow the "facts" to speak for themselves.

At the outset there always were two camps for and against vampirism. Medically trained military personnel coming face to face with the vampiric body *in situ* reported vampirism as a factual condition. The intellectual elite, on the other hand, had no first-hand experience and being in the vanguard of scientific progress had a vested interest in preserving the status quo.[33] In an age when the only reliable indicators for death were considered to be either rigor mortis or putrefaction,[34] deviations from these norms proved a troubling problem, resulting in knee-jerk skepticism. Calmet, like many other writers, resorted to cataloging the many anomalies reported of the deviant dead—incorruptibility, return, and even childbirth—as a means of normalizing the vampire. The condition of the vampiric body could be explained as natural because there were so many oddities in nature or so the reasoning went. It would require the development of forensic medicine to scientifically verify that the vampiric body was, after all, a natural one. Everybody, in a sense, is vampiric because the body, in the absence of its former owner, continues a strange "afterlife" of decomposition that was more varied than earlier realized and that can be, and was, mistaken for something else entirely.

Notes

1. Voltaire, *Dictionnaire Philosophique* [1764], in *Oeuvres Complétes de Voltaire*, vol. 32 (Paris: P. F. Dupont Fils, 1819), 756; Jean-Jacques Rousseau, Letter to Christophe de Beaumont, Archbishop of Paris, 1763, in *The Oxford Book of the Supernatural*, ed. Enright (Oxford: Oxford University Press, 1995), 220.

2. Michael Ranft, *De Masticatione Mortuorum in Tumulis* (Leipzig: August Martin, 1725, expanded edition 1728), with a German edition in 1734, quotation 178; Johann Christian Stock, *Dissertatio de Cadaveribus Sanguisugis* (Jena: Litteris Hornianis, 1732); also to be mentioned are W. S. G. E., *Curieuse und sehr wunderbare Relation, von denen sich neuer Dingen in Servien erzeigenden Blut-Saugern oder Vampyrs* (n.p.: n.p., 1732); Gottlob Heinrich Vogt, *Kurtzes Bedencken Von denen Acten-maeßigen Relationen Wegen derer Vampiren, Oder Menschen- Und Vieh-Aussaugern* (Leipzig: August Martin, 1732); Christian Frideric van Dalen, *Dissertatio de Vamypris Serviensibus* (Duisburg: Johannes Sas, 1733). The most important extracts are reproduced in Klaus Hamberger (ed.), *Mortuus non mordet: Kommentierte Dokumentation zum Vampirismus 1689–1791* (Vienna: Turia and Kant, 1992).

3. Voltaire had met Calmet in 1754 when he visited the library of the Abbey of Senones where Calmet was its abbot and would later caricature him as a superstitious bigot. See Massimo Introvigne, "Antoine Faivre: Father of Contemporary Vampire Studies," in *Ésotérisme, Gnoses et Imaginaire Symbolique*, ed. Richard Caron et al. (Leuven: Peeters, 2001), 605.

4. Augustine Calmet, *Dissertations sur les Apparitions des Anges, des Démons et des Esprits* (Paris: de Bure, 1746), 249–250; quotation from the English translation, *The Phantom World*, trans. Henry Christmas (Philadelphia: A. Hart, 1850), 233–234.

5. Calmet, *Dissertations*, 249, spoke of "Oupires, ou Vampires." As Koen Vermeir, "Vampires as Creatures of the Imagination: Theories of Body, Soul and Imagination in Early Modern Vampire Tracts (1659–1755)." 2011. HAL : halshs-00609387, version 1, http://halshs.archives-ouvertes.fr/docs/00/60/93/87/PDF/Vermeir-Vampires_as_creatures_of_the_imagination.pdf, 5, points out there were early occurrences of the Polish cognate words *upierz* in 1693 and *upior* in 1695 in French, but it is the transliteration of the Serbian word that now enters wider use. For the etymology see Katharina M. Wilson, "The History of the Word Vampire," in *The Vampire: A Casebook*, ed. Alan Dundes (Wisconsin: University of Wisconsin Press, 1998), 3–11, especially for 17th-century occurrences of the word in English.

6. Calmet's source was Jean-Baptiste de Boyer, Marquis d'Argens, *Lettres Juives*, vol. 5 (Lausanne and Geneva: Marc-Michel Bousquet & Co., 1738). Montague Summers, *The Vampire in Europe* (London: Kegan Paul, 1929), 149, claimed that this had been translated into English as *The Jewish Spy* in 1729, but the earliest edition of the 5-volume set is dated 1739 (Bodleian Library), which, of course, makes more sense.

7. Frombald, "Copia eines Schreibens aus dem Gradisker District," *Wienerisches Diarium*, 58 (July 21, 1725): 11–12. The *Wienerisches Diarium* locates the village in Hungary. Frombald signed himself "Kaiserl. Provisor in Gradisker District." At the time this was within the short-lived Kingdom of Serbia (1718–1739), then a Habsburg possession. "Kisolova" is used in the original text, but many later accounts use "Kisilova." "Plogojowitz" is often given, as well as "Plogojovic," but "Plogojoviz" is the form as first published in 1725. Antoine Faivre, *Les Vampires* (Paris: Le Terrain vague, 1962), 49–50, argued that "Frombald" was actually "Fromann." Calmet's source was *Lettres Juives*, 1738, letter 137, and not the original document. See also Jutta Nowosadtko, "Der "Vampyrus Serviensis" und Sein Habitat: Impressionen von der österreichischen Militärgrenze," *Militär und Gesellschaft in der Frühen Neuzeit* 8 (2004): 151–167.

8. Frombald, my translation.

9. Leopold von Ranke, *The History of Servia* (London: Henry G. Bohn, 1853), 46.

10. Michael Ranft, *Dissertatio historico-critica de masticatione mortuorum in tumulis* (Leipzig: Breitkopf, 1725); Franz Schnorr von Carolsfeld, "Ranft, Michael," in *Allgemeine Deutsche Biographie*, vol. 27 (Leipzig: Duncker & Humblot, 1888), 228f. See the account in Vermeir, "Vampires," 23–28.

11. There is another Medveđa further south near Pristina, but the greater distance from other geographical features mentioned in the sources (the town of Paracin and the Morava river) make this village a less likely candidate.

12. *Visum et Repertum über die sogenannten Vampirs oder Blut-Aussauger* (Nürnberg: Schmidt, 1732); also published in Anon., *Acten-mäßige und Umständliche Relation von denen Vampiren oder Menschen-Saugern, Welche sich in diesem und vorigen Jahren, im Königreich Servien herfürgethan* (Leipzig: August Martin, 1732), 9–15; W. S. G. E., Curieuse; and Johann Christoph Harenberg, *Vernünftige und Christliche Gedancken über die Vampirs* (Wolfenbüttel: Johann Christoph Meißner, 1733), 27–35. A number of variations between these are to be noted. The author is Fluchinger in the Schmidt publication, Flückinger in Anon., and Flickinger in both W. S. G. E. and Harenberg. Both Barber and Jenkins, and most other modern authors, prefer Flückinger, although from what I have seen of the original manuscript it is "Fluckinger." We find "Arnod Paole" in W. S. G. E., "Arnond Parle" in Harenberg, but "Arnond Paole" in the original manuscript and Schmidt's edition; modern accounts often give "Arnold Paule." The village is Medvegia in Schmidt's edition, Medwedia in W. S. G. E., and Meduegia in Harenberg. Harenberg adds a number of other details which appear to be mere embellishments. See also Hamberger, Mortuus, 49–54.

13. Introvigne, "Antoine Faivre," 601, states that Glaser wrote his report for the Marquis Botta d'Adorno, the "Austrian administrator of Serbia." Serbia was at this time governed by Carl Alexander von Württemberg (1684–1737). See *Commercium*

litterarium ad rei medicae et scientiae naturalis . . ., Nuremberg: Societas Litteris Jo. Ernest Adelbulneri, 1732, 82–83; also reproduced in Hamberger, *Mortuus*, 46–49.

14. "Morallischen" is found in Schmidt's edition; identified incompletely as the "Maragl. Regiment" in W. S. G. E., *Curieuse*; possibly the Marulli Regiment is meant.

15. *Commercium litterarium ad rei medicae et scientiae naturalis* . . . , 1732 (XII, March), 90–92, and (XVIII, April), 141–44; *London Journal* for March 11, 1732; *The Gentleman's Magazine* 2 (March, 1732), 681, and discussion in (May, 1732), 750f and 755f; *The Grub Street Journal,* March 10, 1732; *Le Glaneur,* identified as No. XVIII by Calmet, *Phantom World,* 36; Introvigne, "Antoine Faivre," 602; Summers, *Vampire,* 132.

16. Calmet, *Dissertations,* 277, and Calmet, *Phantom World,* 33–34, whence Summers, *Vampire,* 147–149, but dating it 1720 and locating it in a village he called "Haidam." In a footnote on p. 37 Calmet connects this case with that of "Arnald Paul," although this appears to be based on his confusion over the location and the similarity with the story he tells about Paole, which is not the same one related by Frombald.

17. Javier Arries, "El comte de Cabrera: Un caçador de vampirs valnecià a l'Hongria del segle XVIII," *L'Upir* 3 (July–September, 2009): 4–49. Michael Ranft calls him "Anton Didacus, Graf von Alcandette," which is a little closer to "Alandetti" in *Der genealogische Archivarius,* vol. 8 (Leipzig: Heinsius, 1733), 335; but certainly not "Alexandetti" as in Colin Wilson, *The Occult* (London: Random House, 1971), 446.

18. Calmet, *Phantom World,* 34. Summers, *Vampire,* 147, was entirely convinced; Introvigne, "Antoine Faivre," 599, dismissed it; and both Paul Barber, *Vampires, Burial and Death* (Yale: Yale University Press, 2010) and Mark Collins Jenkins, *Vampire Forensics* (Washington, D.C.: National Geographic Society, 2011) ignored it. Lionel and Patricia Fanthorpe, *The Big Book of Mysteries* (Toronto: Dundurn Press, 2010), 269, added a wealth of new details including reference to "the notorious *Cadreras* [sic] *Manuscript*" without citing any sources.

19. Calmet, *Phantom World,* 29–32, on Karl Ferdinand de Schertz, *Magia Posthuma,* (Olmutz, 1706). Schertz's book has long baffled those who have tried to find it. I have checked the holdings of the major British and German libraries and found no trace of it, but there is card index in the library of the National Museum of Prague, shelfmark 48 G 11, for Car. Ferd. de Schertz, "Magia Posthuma [etc.], Olomuccii, 1706," http://nris.nkp.cz/Katalog.aspx?sigla=ABA010&katkey=KNMKCT, tab number 457; and another is listed in the Bibliothèque Municipale, Nancy, shelfmark 303 675, giving Rosenburg and 1704 as the publisher and date, see http://bookline.nancy.fr/catalogue_enligne_nancy.htm. However, I have not been able to inspect either of these copies.

20. For a discussion see Introvigne, "Antoine Faivre," 599, and Thomas M. Bohn, "Das Gespenst von Lublau: Michael Kaspereks/Kaspareks Verwandlung vom Wiedergänger zum Blutsauger," in *Vampirismus und magia posthuma im Diskurs der Habsburgermonarchie,* ed. Christoph Augustynowicz and Ursula Reber (Munich: LIT Verlag, 2009). For the sources see *Litterae ex Comitatu Liptoviensi superiori Hungaria 1718, mense Julio* (1718); *Das Europäische Niemand: Gespräche von neuen und alten Staats-Angelegenbeiten,* 2 (1719), 972–980; Eberhard David Hauber, *Biblioteca sive Acta et Scripta Magica* (Lemgovia: Meyer, 1738), 709–714; Georg Conrad Horst, *Zauber-Bibliothek,* vol. 5 (Mainz: Kupferberg, 1825), 387–390. The case is, however, curiously absent from Barber, *Vampires,* and Jenkins, *Forensics.*

21. Pitton de Tournefort, *Voyage into the Levant* (London: D. Midwinter et al., 1741), 142.

22. Stu Burns, "And With All That, Who Believes in Vampires? Undead Legends and Enlightenment Culture," in *European Studies Conference Selected Proceedings* (University of Nebraska at Omaha, 2007), http://www.unomaha.edu/esc/2007Proceedings/Burns_vampirespaper.pdf, 3-4.

23. *The Monthly Review* 20 (London: R. Griffiths, 1759), 564.

24. Davanzati, *Dissertazione sopra I Vampiri*, Naples, MS of 1744, published 1774; Benedict XIV, *De servorum Dei beatificatione et Beatorum canonizatione*, 2nd ed. (Patavii: Manfré, 1749); Introvigne, "Antoine Faivre," 600; Vermeir, "Vampires," 29.

25. Gerard van Swieten, "Remarques sur le Vampyrisme de Sylesie de l'an 1755," ONB Vienna, 7237 PI, with a later German publication, *Abhandlung des Daseyns der Gespenster, nebst einem Anhange vom Vampyrismus*, trans. Andreas Ulrich Mayer (Augsburg: n.p., 1768), from which I cite the Polakin case, p. 192; Introvigne, "Antoine Faivre," 599-600, 608; Jenkins, *Forensics*, 117; Roy Porter, "Witchcraft and Magic in Enlightenment, Romantic and Liberal Thought," in *Witchcraft and Magic in Europe: The Eighteenth and Nineteenth Centuries*, ed. Bengt Akarloo and Stuart Clark (University of Pennsylvania Press, 1999), 214-216; Gabor Klaniczay, "The Decline of Witches and the Rise of Vampires," in *The Witchcraft Reader*, ed. Darren Oldridge (London: Routledge, 2002), 387-388. For a political interpretation of this development, see Michael Pickering, "Attitudes toward the Destruction of Vampire Bodies in the Habsburg Empire," in *Inside and Outside of the Law: Perspectives on Evil, Law and the State*, ed. Shubhankar Dam and Jonathan Hall (Oxford: Inter-Disciplinary Press, 2009), 119-131.

26. Ranft, *De Masticatione* (1728), 2, §4, was early to grapple with this.

27. It is not just the vampire who drinks blood; Calmet noted that vampire blood mixed in bread was taken as an antidote in Russia. This and the general point is also discussed by Marie-Hélène Huet, "Deadly Fears: Dom Augustin Calmet's Vampires and the Rule Over Death," *Eighteenth Century Life* 21 (1997): 222-232.

28. *Shakespeare, Henry IV, Part 2* (1597), act 3, sc. 2, l. 253.

29. L. Illis, "On Porphyria and the Aetiology of Werwolves," *Proceedings of the Royal Society of Medicine* 57 (1964): 23-26; Dolphin's paper was not published but was reported by Philip M. Boffey, "Rare Disease Proposed as Cause for 'Vampires,'" *New York Times*, May 31, 1985. Dolphin's theory was succinctly debunked by Ann Cox, "Porphyria and Vampirism: Another Myth in the Making," *Postgraduate Medical Journal* 71 (1995): 643-644. See also Barber, *Vampires*, 161.

30. Jeffrey and William Hampl, "Pellagra and the Origin of a Myth: Evidence from European Literature and Folklore," *Journal of the Royal Society for Medicine* 90 (1997): 636-639; Jenkins, *Forensics*, 15-18.

31. Juan Gómez-Alonso, "Rabies: A Possible Explanation for the Vampire Legend," *Neurology* 51 (1998): 856-859.

32. Barber, *Vampires*, 161; Introvigne, 602.

33. Thomas Kuhn, *The Structure of Scientific Revolutions* (Chicago: University of Chicago Press, 1962), is the classic analysis of this situation, although in this case the "evidence" did not lead to a paradigm shift.

34. Pickering, "Attitudes," 125.

7

Undead Feedback: Adaptations and Echoes of Johann Flückinger's Report, *Visum et Repertum* (1732), until the Millennium

Clemens Ruthner

V AMPIRES ARE PERFECT EXAMPLES of fantastic liminality and transgression.[1] Originating from Slavic borderlands in a quasi-colonial setting, they invaded Central and Western Europe as a cultural topic in the days of early Enlightenment, when reason and the laws of nature as the new basis of knowledge (épistèmé[2]) were under construction.[3] Here the vampires provided for considerable confusion and textual production,[4] as they mark a serious ontological trespass; as deconstructivists *avant la lettre*, they question not only the central human binary of life and death in times of secularization, but they also challenge the cultural boundaries between nutrition and procreation, along with the body/soul divide on which Christianity is founded. They are *undead* and still no immaterial ghosts, but revenants with a disturbingly bodily presence, as can be read, for example, in a definition given in the anthology *Zauberbibliothek* ["Magical Library", 1821-] by Georg Conrad Horst. It is quoted by Herbert Mayo, one of the later protagonists of the essay presented here, in 1846: "A Vampyre is a dead body which continues to live in the grave; which it leaves, however, by night, for the purpose of sucking the blood of the living, whereby it is nourished and preserved in good condition, instead of becoming decomposed like other dead bodies."[5]

Definitions of this kind, which tend to distinguish between the bloodsucking Slavic vampires and their less biting colleagues in folklore, such as the Germanic *Wiedergänger* (who is just a nuisance by his mere presence),[6] raise the question of whether they are adequate or do such typological distinctions only apply to *belles lettres*?

But the vampires of Southeast European folklore[7] are also an epitome of *cultural transfer*. It is important to know that on the basis of their haunting lies the fundamental experience of *foreignness* between cultures, which probably led in the 1730s to a serious misinterpretation of the essence of Balkan vampirism in Central and Western Europe.[8] Even the term *vampire* itself seems to be the result of a miscomprehension by foreigners.[9]

The examination of the conditions for this culturally highly *productive* misunderstanding, however, should be left to other scholars with more expertise in the fields of anthropology and linguistics.[10] Instead, this chapter,[11] which situates itself in the field of literary and cultural studies, will deal with the ways in which the vampires, those immigrants from the "superstitious" peripheries to the imperial centers of "enlightened" "civilization," have established themselves in Western cultures through narration or narrativization,[12] respectively; thereby I will focus on the significance imparted to literary procedures when it comes to the strategic filling the gaps of the first narratives, their *Leerstellen* as it were.

Previous research has focused predominantly on the *shape-shifting* of the vampire in literature and film, in particular on the historical metamorphosis from the distended peasant corpse found in South Slavic folklore to the pale, distinguished figure of Count Dracula.[13] In contrast, it will be pointed out here how the historical sources of vampirism dating from the 18th century were contaminated later on by the motif stock of the emergent genre of *Gothic*[14] literature. As we know, vampirism is driven by a principle of *contagion*, the domino effect of "passing it on"—and, as will be shown, texts can have a similarly undead quality and give "feedback" to each other, and even cross-fertilize each other as it were.

What needs to be examined, however, is not only intertextuality[15] *per se*, but also the cultural "grammar" of narrative *reworking* that is operative behind a text when it is re-told in new versions over and over again. Vampirism has namely become a modern myth[16] in the same way as, for instance, the grand narratives of Antiquity, the songs of the *Guslars*, or the urban legends of our time are being constantly modified, extended, and thus further elaborated. In this respect, the reception of these tales always means production at the same time. "Every telling of that myth is a part of that myth; there is no *Ur*-version, no authentic prototype, no true account," as Marina Warner states.[17]

As has become commonplace, this principle of narrative reworking governs all literary texts or films following Bram Stoker's *Dracula*: what is new, however, is that it also affects other genres of writing. Thus, in an almost postmodern sense, the aesthetic difference between fiction and non-fiction seems to blur here already—in a similar process that can be also observed between literary ghost stories and spiritualist case studies. Here a sort of chicken-and-egg problem seems to exist, namely: does the observer of a "genuine" ghostly apparition really describe what he or she sees or rather "see" what is already written, that is, what he or she has read? So, consequently, it may be asked in our case: does a cultural narrative arise from vampirism whose effects, in turn, influence, inform or even "edit," so to speak, its own "folklore" origins?[18]

Part I

A prime example of the narrative metastasis of vampire texts is the uncanny incident that took place in Medveđa (Медвеђа), Serbia, during the winter of 1731–1732. The locals felt haunted by their dead who kept allegedly returning from their graves; the following mass mortality in their village was attributed to those "vampyres" (and not to an anthrax epidemic as we tend to think nowadays[19]). The resulting social turmoil caught the attention of the Austrian military, which kept occupying the former enemy territory after the end of the Turkish Wars. As a consequence, a sort of fact-finding mission was carried out twice, and the events were reported for posterity by the Austrian epidemiologist ("Contagions-Medicus") Glaser, and later by his compatriot, the military doctor Johann Flückinger. Thus, the well-documented case was destined to become one of the *X-Files* of the early Enlightenment period, triggering a discussion about the nature of death and the afterlife in medicine, philosophy, and theology.[20]

A first case of that kind had already taken place in the village of Kisolova (probably today's Kisiljevo/Кисиљево) in 1725; however, it took the Medveđa incident to make vampirism a common topic and then revisit the facts provided before. Thus, among all the other contemporary documents of vampirism, Flückinger's report, usually cited under its Latin title *Visum et Repertum,* is probably "the very core text,"[21] or at least the one which has been reprinted most often. However, along with editorial changes (which can be easily excused given the strange spelling of the original), various divergences, mistaken interpretations, and fictitious additions can be noticed in later publications of this report. In order to make these amendments visible, it makes sense to begin with the two original documents of the Medveđa incident.[22]

Glaser's report only mentions briefly the disturbing phenomenon of mass mortality in the village and its attribution to vampires by the local population, ending with a list of fatalities. The author had 10 graves opened up and, according to his notes, identified 2 women as the epicenter of the vampire attack; one of the suspects, Miliza, was a newcomer to the village, and the other, Stanno, had died in childbed. Their accusation does not come as a surprise because from an anthropological perspective both women are in principle

what is called "dangerous dead"[23] given the social circumstances of their de-
mise; also the gender assigned to the vampire in its earliest phase should be
noted here and in what follows.

Six weeks after Glaser, the other Austrian doctor Flückinger and his army
colleagues arrived on the scene and investigated the same events. They also
had graves opened up, and included lists of the bodies they exhumed and examined, among which those of Miliza and Stana. Subsequently, all suspicious
corpses were beheaded and burnt by local gypsies. But in contrast to Glaser,
Flückinger did not limit himself to a simple examination of the corpses but
carried out a full autopsy. He also offers an alternative etiology of the events
and works it up into a narrative centered on a *man*, which stretches further
back into the past.

What we see here is in fact a *double* contact with cultural foreignness, first
of the local Serbs with their formerly Turkish environment and then between
Serbs and Austrians. The villagers claim unanimously that

> Approximately 5 years ago a certain *hajduk* [peasant farmer] by the name of
> Arnont Paule broke his neck after having fallen from a hay wagon; while alive,
> he frequently said that he had been tormented by a Turkish vampire in Kosovo;
> therefore he had eaten soil from the vampire's grave and anointed himself with
> the latter's blood in order to get rid of that plague. 20–30 days after his death
> some people complained that they were tormented by the very same Arnont; as
> then 4 people actually got killed by him.[24]

Apart from the alternative chain of events Flückinger proposes, it is interesting that something akin to narrative—and epistemological—"uncertainty"
("*hésitation*") is formulated here which, according to Tzvetan Todorov,[25]
was to become *the* structural pattern of the fictional genre of the Fantastic in
the 18th and 19th centuries. First, Flückinger reports from hearsay and then
refers to the returning Arnod Paole[26] as an imagined ("gedachte") haunting,
whereas the author's concluding use of the word *würcklich* ("actually") confirms the explanation of the events in which he could not believe initially.

In the months following the reports by Glaser and Flückinger, other texts
appeared, which were, together with theirs, soon to form the "core canon" of
historical documents on vampirism,[27] albeit not all of them were published
and rather disappeared into the archives. These additional sources are of
interest as they add other stories derived from popular belief to Flückinger's
central narrative, sometimes with robust sexual elements.

In a letter of January 26, 1732, the Cadet ("Fähnrich") von Kottwitz, for instance, reports not only the Medveđa incident but also occurrences in another
village by the name of Kucklina:

> And, what is even more appalling, a *hajduk* who had been interred yesterday
> came back to his wife to lie with her. The following day she told the lieutenant

of the village that her husband had done his thing as well as in the days when he was still alive, except for the fact that his semen had been really cold.[28]

In the (unpublished?) *Relationis Historicae Semestralis Autumnalis Continuatio* of 1732, the inhabitants of Possega are visited by a "Vampyr" "in the shape of a well-known serpent" ("*in Gestalt einer dort sehr bekannten Schlange*").[29] Some years later, around 1740, the report of a certain Captain von Beloz emphasizes that the vampires "commonly prey on their own relatives" ("*gemeiniglich nur ihren eigenen Verwandten nachstellen*").[30]

Thus, eventually, in the numerous connections made between the occurrences in Serbia through a certain (mis-?)interpretation[31] of the local belief systems, the central narrative—and concomitant discourse—of vampirism had been established in Western cultures when they were stricken by similar events in Moravia, Silesia, and other Habsburg peripheries around 1750.[32] These new incidents, however, were not used to prove the "backwardness" of the colonized Balkans again, but rather—from an enlightened/Protestant/Prussian perspective—of the Catholic Austrian Empire as a whole.[33] The contagion through superstition had been passed on, as it were; on the other hand, any plausible scholarly theory of vampirism had been dismissed by then, and so enlightened science closed one of its weirdest case studies.

This rational closure already becomes apparent in the *Lettres juives* (*Jewish Lettres*, 1738) by the Marquis d'Argens. After having recounted the stories of Kisiljevo and Medveđa in Letter 137, the enlightened Frenchman attributes vampirism to a pathologically "disturbed" imagination. However, in his account, the alleged vampire does not suck the victim's blood either—he rather strangles her:

> In examining the Circumstances of the Death of these Victims to *Vampirism*, I plainly discover all the Symptoms of an epidemick Fanaticism, and am convinced, that the Impression which Fear had made on their Minds was the true Cause of their Destruction. Do but mark the Story of *Stanoska, She goes to bed well, awakes in the Middle of the Night, and cries out in a Fright, that one of her Acquaintances, lately dead, had attempted to strangle her in her Sleep: In this Condition she languished for a few Days, and then died.*
>
> Now, is there any Man so blind as not to see, that the *Vampirism*, in this Case, is not more than a disturbed Imagination?[34]

Part II

After this brief sketch of the core texts on the vampire "epidemic" of 1732, we shall now move forward more than 100 years, thereby jumping the temporal gap that opens up between the historic reports plus the contemporary journalistic

and academic texts[35] on the one hand, and the emerging literary genre of vampire fiction[36] on the other.

One example must be selected from all the numerous quotations and
adaptations of Glaser's and Flückinger's texts, on account of its unmistakable literary ambition, which offers convincing evidence of the way the basic
vampire model is increasingly reworked and expanded. It is a publication
titled *On the Truths Contained in Popular Superstitions*, written in 1846 by
Mayo, first appearing in *Blackwood's Magazine* in 1849 and then in a book
version. Dr. Mayo was a former Senior Surgeon at the Middlesex Hospital
and also Professor of Anatomy and Physiology at King's College, London.
He uses vampirism along with water divining, mesmerism, and other paranormal phenomena in order to discuss what the "soul" is and whether these
phenomena can be explained by electricity or another "life force." However,
the major hypothesis of this text only marginally concerns us here: what is of
greater interest is which use the author makes of Flückinger's text.

Mayo's book might best be described as popular scientific fiction. Its beginning is already very instructive as the author describes his own fascination for
ghost stories as a child and then the disillusionment that follows:[37]

> Vain were all my efforts to revive the pleasant horrors of earlier years: it was as
> if I had planned going to a play to enjoy again the full gusto of scenic illusion,
> and, through absence of mind, was attending a morning rehearsal only; when,
> instead of what I had anticipated, great-coats, hats, umbrellas, and ordinary men
> and women, masks, tinsel, trap-doors, pulleys, and a world of intricate machin-
> ery, lit by a partial gleam of sunshine, had met my view. The enchantment was
> no longer there—the spell was broken.[38]

However, in his own book Mayo employs methods that resemble the stage
machinery with which he compares the (dis)illusion felt in the face of the
supposed supernatural. There are no trap doors and other special effects from
the theatre trick box, but indeed a set of literary strategies, *topoi*, tropes and
intertextual references used to turn the uncanny into a narrative.

The text uses clearly fictionalized case studies to which popular scientific
reflections are added, thereby following the old pattern of the so-called
"explained supernatural" from the Enlightenment period,[39] albeit in a post-
Romantic version. In this context Mayo comes to the topic of the Medvedja
vampires, the narration of which he starts using the modern *topos* of Eastern
Europe as a place of non-civilization and superstition:

> This is no romancer's dream. It is a succinct account of a superstition which to
> this day survives in the east of Europe, where little more than a century ago it was
> frightfully prevalent. At that period Vampyrism spread like a pestilence through

Servia and Wallachia, causing numerous deaths, and disturbing all the land with fear of the mysterious visitation, against which no one felt himself secure.[40]

In what follows, Mayo elaborates the story of Paole, visibly giving his imagination free rein; or, to formulate it in a less author-centred way, the stock of existing literary conventions stemming from the times between the Serbian peasant and the British doctor affects the narration of the latter and leads to further emplotment.[41] Mayo introduces a female co-protagonist into the text, who is nowhere to be found in Flückinger's report. On the other hand, the crude sexual elements inherent in some other historical documents are repressed and replaced by a chaste and finally tragic love story.

So in Mayo's revised account, the *hajduk* (i.e., peasant soldier) Paole returns from the war in early 1727, acquires a small property in Medveda "near Belgrade" (here the author clearly misjudges the real geographical distances), manages his estate, and attains a certain prosperity.[42] Irreproachable in his manners, he nevertheless appears oddly concerned, yet even tormented by something, and he thus avoids his beautiful neighbor Nina, who, as a result, becomes even more interested in him; at this point Mayo inserts the following dialogue started by Nina:

> "What is it, dear Arnod, that makes you sad? It cannot be on my account, I know, for you were sad before you ever noticed me; and that, I think," (and you should have seen the deepening rose upon her cheeks), "surely first made me notice you."
>
> "Nina," he answered, "I have done, I fear, a great wrong in trying to gain your affections. Nina, I have a fixed impression that I shall not live; yet, knowing this, I have selfishly made my existence necessary to your happiness."
>
> "How strangely you talk, dear Arnod. Who in the village is stronger and healthier than you? You feared no danger when you were a soldier. What danger do you fear as a villager of Meduegna?"
>
> "It haunts me, Nina."
>
> "But, Arnod, you were sad before you thought of me. Did you then fear to die?"
>
> "Ah, Nina, it is something worse than death." And his vigorous frame shook with agony.
>
> "Arnod, I conjure you, tell me."
>
> "It was in Cossova this fate befell me. Here you have hitherto escaped the terrible scourge. But there they died, and the dead visited the living. I experienced the first frightful visitation, and I fled; but not till I had sought his grave, and exacted the dread expiation from the Vampyr."
>
> Nina's blood ran cold. She stood horror-stricken. But her young heart soon mastered her first despair. With a touching voice she spoke—"Fear not, dear Arnod; fear not now. I will be your shield, or I will die with you!"

And she encircled his neck with her gentle arms, and returning hope shone, Iris-like, amid her falling tears. . . . It is a strange world. The ills we fear are commonly not those which overwhelm us. The blows that reach us are for the most part unforeseen. One day, about a week after this conversation, Arnod missed his footing when on the top of a loaded hay-waggon, and fell from it to the ground. He was picked up insensible, and carried home, where, after lingering a short time, he died.[43]

What is evident here is the dramatization of the material by means of inserting a dialogue between the sombre Arnod and the devoted Nina who seeks to rescue him. There is a faint shimmer of romantic hope (a narrative strategy creating suspense), before Arnod is carried off by a sudden and banal death, as reported in Flückinger: he becomes the victim of a farming accident and falls off the hay wagon.

This dramatic dialogue of the potential lovers that Mayo has added to his version of the story is obviously informed by the literary vampire narrative that already existed in the first half of the 19th century, in the wake of Polidori's *The Vampire* (1819) that soon circulated in dramatized versions.[44] Along with the dialogical form and the melodramatic body language of the characters, the motif of the gentleman driven by a dark secret (into whom Mayo has turned his Arnod) lends weight to this suspicion. Eventually, this gloomy hero is unable to free himself from the curse, not even when he is facing the innocent beauty of the maiden—a constellation that can be found in Polidori's sequel to Gothic romance (in the figure of Aubrey and his sister in *The Vampyre*) and in other texts.[45]

In this respect, it might also be significant that at the beginning of his book, Mayo refers respectfully to Walter Scott as "the Scottish Shakspeare" (sic).[46] Scrutiny shows here that the literarily ambitious doctor seems to have been deeply influenced in particular by the format of Scott's *Letters on Demonology and Witchcraft* (1830) insofar as Mayo's text is pseudo-epistolary as well, speaking to a fictitious addressee ("Dear Archy") in a half-narrative (or dramatized) and half-argumentative (essayistic) form.

After that invented dialogue between the lovers, however, Mayo largely follows again the narrative pattern set by Flückinger's report, albeit with minor aberrations, as well. When the inhabitants of Medveđa are afflicted by vampirism, the decision is taken to exhume Arnod's corpse in the presence of two military surgeons from Belgrade accompanied by a drummer boy, who then faints on seeing the corpse.[47] This motif is clearly being used solely to increase the sense of horror, for it in no way matches the historical background: why would two army doctors on a forensic fact-finding mission need a drummer—unless possible borrowings from fiction are assumed here as well?

An almost self-reflexive indicator of Mayo's intertextual kinship can be seen in the fact that one of the graves visited is provided with a quite inappropriate decoration:[48]

> It was on a gray morning in early August that the commission visited the quiet cemetery of Meduegna. . . . Here and there a stone had been raised. On a considerable height, a single narrow slab, ornamented with grotesque Gothic carvings, dominated over the rest. Near this lay the grave of Arnod Paole, to which the party moved.[49]

These Gothic carvings appear displaced—if not grotesque—in Orthodox Serbia, but actually, they might be just meant as a narrative device to create a certain "Gothic" atmosphere of imminent horror. Moreover, the opening lines are rather reminiscent of Poe's *The Fall of the House of Usher* (1839/40) than of Flückinger (apart from the fact that Mayo gives the wrong time frame, August instead of January[50]).

From this moment on, Mayo's account seems to be unaltered again. After the exhumation, Arnod's undecayed corpse gives the impression of being astonishingly alive—a constant motif in the historic vampirism documents— before it is burnt as a consequence.[51] However, the visitation does not stop and there are further deaths, which are recorded in the text with the same list of fatalities given by Glaser and Flückinger.[52]

Here it is worth noting that almost all the later text versions display the same obsession with inventorying the dead that features in Glaser and Flückinger's reports. This might have less to do with the fact that the authors of vampire texts were often bureaucrats, than that the cataloging, which is blunt and pedantic at the same time, is retained as a narrative signal to suggest that the events have been officially authenticated.

A further point of interest is the way in which Mayo removes all traces of Habsburg occupation and the quasi-colonial cultural contact between the officers and the villagers from his story: nothing about the two army doctors indicates that they are Austrians. And eventually, even the episode with Nina remains only a romantic addition, a sort of "blind" motif, given that the beautiful neighbor is never mentioned again in the rest of the text, nor does she appear among the counted dead.

Part III

If Nina is clearly an entirely fictional creation on Mayo's part, then a more modern literary transcription of Flückinger's report has resurrected another corpse on his list of the dead for the sake of emplotment:

Slowly the reddish pale sun is sinking behind the hills. The people rush to their homes. . . . Who now still knocks, to whom the door won't be opened. While the young farmer's wife Stanacka is warming herself by the fire and eating her supper, her father speaks softly about the strange occurrences that are the only topic on these December days in Medvedja-upon-Morava.[53]

Under the chapter heading, "A Gruesome Look into the Grave," Flückinger's report is here once again brought back to an undead life in 1998 by the author and artist Hauke Kock who has illustrated his own text. The sensationalist book title *Vampire, Fürsten der Finsternis: Wahrheit und Legende* (*Rulers of Darkness: Truth and Legend*) indicates that Kock is less a seeker of the former and more a purveyor of the latter; his approach is semi-fictional in a way that is typical of "specialist" vampire literature published around the millennium. However, the author does not elaborate the story of the "protagonist" Paole itself but fills out the empty spaces of a subplot with narrative *topoi* (or clichés?) drawn from the genre of fantastic literature to create a different focus and to intensify the narrative background for the vampire's appearance.

In Flückinger's account, the woman in question is mentioned twice, once in the wake of the central narrative of Paole's death, and then again on the list of the dead:

Hereby the hayduck Joviza reports that his daughter-in-law by the name of Stanoika lay down to rest in a fresh and healthy state; around midnight she would rudely wake up screaming and shivering terribly and complaining that she had been strangled by the 9-weeks-dead hayduck's son Milloe; from now on she would feel great pain in her chest and do worse and worse until she eventually died on the third day.[54]

In Kock's version, the same facts are narrated as follows:

Around the hour of midnight, a terrible cry suddenly cuts the silence. Everyone in the house awakes with a shock; there are shouts: what happened? get some light! They find Stanacka, sitting up in bed, touching her neck and shaking all over. The young woman gasps, all color drained from her face. . . . Breathlessly she haws that a man had come and lain down on her and choked her by the neck. She had recognized this man: it was Milloe.[55]

Not only Stanacka, but also the army doctor—who bears the name Fluchinger here—is given a micro-biography with the clichéd psychological traits that go with it:

Johannes Fluchinger is not a superstitious man. In his profession as doctor of the regiment he is used to the harsh tone of soldiers, and through his medical experience he thinks he is prepared for all terrors of the world. . . . When with a dull pounding the shovel hits the coffin lid, the talk of the bystanders ends abruptly. Eagerly Fluchinger awaits the opening of the coffin, but the sight of dead Miliza makes him shiver. He has seen many corpses, but never anything like this. Until now, he has considered the descriptions of Arnod Paole as hyperbolic, a product of overwrought nerves, but what lies here in front of him, in the pale winter sunlight is extraordinary and apparently unnatural.[56]

What is encountered here are the stock-in-trade procedures of the Fantastic in literature: even the way the opening scene is set at an open fire during an eerie winter night creates the familiar atmosphere of horror literature. Stanacka evokes the female victims of vampire films, and Fluchinger himself is turned into a sort of Dr. Van Helsing projected back into the past, a hero of enlightened science. As is often the case in neo-Gothic literature, his intellectual authority is used to raise the possibility that vampires might after all really exist. However, what Fluchinger sees in the grave is less the vampire of Enlightenment, but more the hyperbolic rhetoric and *topos* of inexpressibility found in horror literature after H. P. Lovecraft.

Thanks to this intertextual *pot pourri*, Paole finally becomes a literary character in a text that aims to thrill rather than to account. But already from Sheridan Le Fanu and Bram Stoker on, almost no piece of vampire fiction can do without an exhumation scene,[57] which goes hand-in-hand with the intertextual disinterment of stock motifs stemming from the great traditions of Gothic fiction and later the horror film. Eventually this undead recycling can also be seen in H. C. Artmann's playful short prose text, "Dracula Dracula" (1966), which is a parodistic repertory of standard situations of the vampire narrative and, at the same time, its obituary—ending with a list of vampires that is clearly meant as a tribute to Flückinger and the long history of fiends in literature and film:

> Gathering of the most prominent enemies of Count *Dracula* stemming from the dynasty of the leftist *Nosferatus*:[58]
> Ancclam the Sucker, bischof
> von Szüthváry
> Tyrann Kallimachus von Brod
> Frederick of Draquenstin
> Erzritter Görödömffyi
> Mordazla, fee der mongolen
> Aksu der protosibirier . . .[59]

Some remarks in conclusion: This chapter has sought to show how *topoi* and other narrative patterns of the Fantastic in literature can slip into a "historical" case report and fictionalize it,[60] and how an "undead feedback" of motifs from classical Gothic literature must be assumed here. Thus, the vampire material—strangely resembling a half-empty grave—is repeatedly refilled with contemporary fantasies and themes "exhumed" from popular literature; it is bloated like the Serbian corpses and turned into a literary legend, even when it defiantly lays claim to historicity. Mayo is thus mistaken in his introduction: is he not a "romancer" indeed—or even a *Necromancer*?

In texts such as his, the effects of popular mythologizing processes can be observed *in actu*—as an infection, as it were, of the fleetingly "authentic" by narrative logic, as the dressing-up of a particular material in form of elaboration and emplotment. It thus seems very probable that any kind of writing about vampires sooner or later becomes fiction, which feeds on the fiends as they do on the living. Thus, in many respects, literature is the *most* undead thing there is, which through the power of words conjures up the presence of something that is absent. However, this only partly excuses the various popular scientific "non-fiction" vampire books of our own time, which seek to make a quick and dishonest profit from their fascinatingly gruesome subject. But this is another story.

Notes

1. For the notion of liminality in the context of horror literature, see Clemens Ruthner, "Fantastic Liminality: A Theory Sketch," in *Collisions of Reality: Establishing Research on the Fantastic in Europe*, ed. Lars Schmeink and Astrid Böger (Berlin, New York: de Gruyter, 2012), 35–49.

2. See Michel Foucault, *The Order of Things: An Archaeology of Human Sciences* (London: Tavistock, 1966).

3. See Milan V. Dimic, "Vampiromania in the 18th Century: The Other Side of the Enlightenment," in *Man and Nature/L'Homme et la Nature*, ed. Robert J. Merrett (Edmonton: Academic Printing, 1984), 1–22; Gábor Klaniczay, *Heilige, Hexen, Vampire: Vom Nutzen des Übernatürlichen*, trans. Hanni Ehlers and Sylvia Höfer (Berlin: Wagenbach, 1991), 73–97.

4. For a survey of the cultural history of vampirism in Europe, see, for example, Massimo Introvigne, *La stirpe di Dracula: Indagine sul vampirismo dall'antichità ai nostri giorni* (Milan: Mondadori, 1997); Clemens Ruthner, "*Untote Verzahnungen: Prolegomena zu einer Literaturgeschichte des Vampirismus*," in *Poetische Wiedergänger: Deutschsprachige Vampirismus-Diskurse vom Mittelalter bis zur Gegenwart*, ed. Julia Bertschik and Christa A. Tuczay (Tübingen: Francke, 2005), 11–41; Erik Butler, *Metamorphosis of the Vampire in Literature and Film: Cultural Transformations in Europe, 1732–1933* (Rochester: Camden House, 2010).

5. Herbert Mayo, *On the Truths Contained in Popular Superstitions: With an Account of Mesmerism* (Edinburgh, London: W. Blackwood, 1851), 22.

6. See Claude Lecouteux, *Die Geschichte der Vampire: Metamorphose eines Mythos*, trans. Harald Ehrhardt (Munich: Artemis & Winkler, 2001), 74–101; *Geschichte der Gespenster und Wiedergänger im Mittelalter* (Vienna, Cologne: Böhlau, 1987).

7. The best survey of vampirism in folklore is probably Peter Mario Kreuter, *Der Vampirglaube in Südosteuropa: Studien zur Genese, Bedeutung und Funktion* (Berlin: Weidler, 2001).

8. See Vlado Vlačić, "Militärberichte und Vampirmythos," in *Kakanien revisted*, www.kakanien.ac.at/beitr/vamp/VVlacic1.pdf, accessed November 24, 2009.

9. On the word *vampire*, see Katharina M. Wilson, "The History of the Word 'Vampire,'" *Journal of the History of Ideas* (1985), 577–583; Peter Mario Kreuter, "The Name of the Vampire: Some Reflections on Current Linguistic Theories," in *Vampires: Myths and Metaphors of Enduring Evil*, ed. Peter Day (Amsterdam: Rodopi, 2006), 57–63.

10. See notes 7 and 8.

11. Special thanks to Malcolm Spencer (Birmingham), Andrew Cusack (Dublin), and Marco Frenschkowski (Hofheim/Ts.) for linguistic and vampirological assistance.

12. See Wolfgang Müller-Funk, *Die Kultur und ihre Narrative: eine Einführung* (2nd ed. Vienna, New York: Springer, 2007).

13. See Paul Barber, Vampires, Burial, and Death: Folklore and Reality (New Haven: Yale University Press, 1988), 2 et passim; Hans Richard Brittnacher, Ästhetik des Horrors: Gespenster, Vampire, Monster, Teufel und künstliche Menschen in der phantastischen Literatur (Frankfurt/M.: Suhrkamp, 1994), 125 et passim; Clemens Ruthner, "*Süd/Osteuropäer als Vampire: Draculas Karriere vom blutrünstigen Tyrannen zum mythischen Blutsauger (Prolegomena zu einer Literaturgeschichte des Vampirismus II)*," in Kakanien revisited, www.kakanien.ac.at/beitr/fallstudie/CRuthner3.pdf, accessed February 25, 2003; Butler, *Metamorphosis of the Vampire in Literature and Film*.

14. Among the numerous surveys of the subject, see, for example, Fred Botting, *Gothic* (London, New York: Routledge, 1996); David Punter, *The Literature of Terror: A History of Gothic Fictions from 1765 to the Present Day* (London: Longman, 1996); Jerrold E. Hogle, ed., *The Cambridge Companion to Gothic Fiction* (Cambridge: Cambridge University Press, 2002).

15. For the purpose of this article, a rather pragmatic notion of intertextuality will be applied. See Graham Allan: *Intertextuality* (London: Routledge, 2000), 1: "Texts, whether they be literary or non-literary, are viewed by modern theorists as lacking any kind of independent meaning. They are what theorists call intertextual. The act of reading, theorists claim, plunges us into a network of textual relations. To interpret a text, to discover its meaning, or meanings, is to trace those relations. Reading thus becomes a process of moving between texts. Meaning becomes something which exists between a text and all the other texts to which it refers and relates, moving out from the independent text into a network of textual relation. The text becomes the intertext."

16. See Laurence Coupe, *Myth*, 2nd ed. (London: Routledge 2009).

17. Marina Warner, *Managing Monsters: Six Myths of Our Time* (London: Vintage, 1994), 8.

18. This process of mythological "feedback" between "folklore" (or "history," respectively) and "literature" might go much further than can shown in the context of this chapter. It remains rather unclear if Romanian villagers believed in the vampires of their tradition or in what they retrieved from more powerful sources of cultural memory, namely Hollywood films and popular fiction, when the last reported case of

"vampirism" in Romania took place in 2004: see Timothy Taylor, "The Real Vampire Slayers," *Independent* (London), October 28, 2007.

19. See Christian Reiter, *"Der Vampyr-Aberglaube und die Militärärzte,"* *Kakanien Revisited*, www.kakanien.ac.at/beitr/vamp/CReiter1.pdf, accessed on August 17, 2009.

20. See Klaus Hamberger, *Mortuus non mordet: Dokumente zum Vampirismus 1689–1791* (Vienna: Turia & Kant, 1992).

21. Hamberger, *Mortuus non mordet*, 57.

22. The texts are taken from Hamberger's annotated reader *Mortuus non mordet*—now unfortunately out of print—which remains up to the present day the only reliable (German) edition of vampire source materials from the 18th century.

23. See Lecouteux, Geschichte der Gespenster und Wiedergänger, 32–36.

24. All translations provided by the author—C. R. Quoted from Hamberger, *Mortuus non mordet*, 49–50 (spelling as in original): "vor ongefehr 5 Jahren ein hiesiger Heyduckh, nahmens Arnont Paule, sich durch einen Fahl von einem Heüwag den Hals gebrochen; dieser hat bey seinen Lebzeiten sich öfters verlauten lassen, dass er bei Cossowa in dem Türckischen Servien von einem Vampyren geplagt worden sey, dahero er von der Erden des Vampyrgrab gegessen, und sich mit dessen Blut geschmieret habe, umb von der erlittenen Plag entledigt zu werden. In 20 oder 30 Täg nach seinem Todtfahl haben sich einige Leüth geklaget, daß sie von dem gedachten Arnont geplaget würden; wie dan auch würcklich 4 Persohnen von ihme umbgebracht worden."

25. See Tzvetan Todorov, *The Fantastic: A Structural Approach to a Literary Genre*, trans. Richard Howard (Ithaca: Cornell University Press, 1975), 25.

26. I am using the common spelling of the name here; it probably was Arnaut Pavle (Арнаут Павле) originally.

27. Hamberger, *Mortuus non mordet*, 57.

28. Quoted from Hamberger, *Mortuus non mordet*, 56: "und was noch abscheulicher, so ist ein gestern beerdigter Heyducke folgende Nacht zu seinem Weibe gekommen und solcher ordentlich beygewohnet, welche solches gleich Tages darauff dem Hadnack selbigen Ortes angedeutet, mit Vermelden, daß er seine Sache so wohl, als bey Lebzeiten verrichtet, ausser dass der Samen gantz kalt gewesen."

29. Hamberger, *Mortuus non mordet*, 57–58.

30. Hamberger, *Mortuus non mordet*, 58.

31. Whereas the local population obviously found occurrences during the life and the wake of a deceased person decisive on who was going to be a vampire, the Austrian doctors were looking for forensic evidence on/in the dead bodies; moreover, there is not much indication that the vampires from the Balkans actually sucked blood; they were rather said to torment and kill their relatives and fellow villagers. See Vlačić, *"Militärberichte und Vampirmythos."*

32. See Hamberger, *Mortuus non mordet*, 76–96.

33. See Bernhard Unterholzner, *"Vampire im Habsburgerreich, Schlagzeilen in Preußen: Zum Nutzen des Vampirs für politische Schmähungen,"* *Kakanien revisited*, www.kakanien.ac.at/beitr/vamp/BUnterholzner1.pdf, accessed August 25, 2009.

34. Jean Babtiste de Boyer Marquis d'Argens, *Jewish letters*, trans. Anonymous (Newcastle: J. Fleming, 1739–44), vol. 3, 243. The author's knowledge of the Medveđa

incident was based on a report in the *Mercure Historique*, a periodical published in The Hague.

35. Barber calls the spectacular spreading of vampirism in Europe around 1732 an "early media event" (*Vampires, Burial, and Death*, 5).

36. The first known vampire poem in world literature, *Mein liebes Mägdchen glaubet* by Heinrich August Ossenfelder, was published in 1748 by Lessing's brother-in-law Mylius. It was followed by several decades of silence until the era of German and English Romanticism around 1800.

37. See Mayo, *On the Truths Contained in Popular Superstitions*, 1–2.

38. Mayo, *On the Truths Contained in Popular Superstitions*.

39. This genre included non-fictitious collections of ghost stories that were used by the popular philosophers and pastors of Enlightenment to fight "superstition": see Clemens Ruthner, *Am Rande: Kanon, Kulturökonomie und die Intertextualität des Marginalen am Beispiel der (österr.) Phantastik im 20. Jahrhundert* (Tübingen, Basle: Francke 2004), 73–75.

40. Mayo, *On the Truths Contained in Popular Superstitions*, 23–24.

41. On narration and emplotment, see, for example, Hayden White, *Metahistory: The Historical Imagination in Nineteenth-Century Europe* (Baltimore: Johns Hopkins University Press, 1973) and Wolfgang Müller-Funk, *Die Kultur und ihre Narrative*.

42. Mayo, *On the Truths Contained in Popular Superstitions*, 25.

43. Mayo, *On the Truths Contained in Popular Superstitions*, 25–27.

44. In French, for example, by Charles Nodier (*Le Vampire*), or in English by James R. Planché (*The Vampire and the Bride of the Isles*), both dating from 1820. The opera *Der Vampyr* of 1828 by Heinrich Marschner and Wilhelm Wohlbrück was based on these predecessors.

45. See Ann Tracy, *The Gothic Novel, 1790–1830: Plot Summaries and Index of Motifs* (University of Kentucky Press, 1981). On romance as one of the basic forms of narrative, cf. White, *Metahistory*.

46. Mayo, *On the Truths Contained in Popular Superstitions*, 2.

47. Mayo, *On the Truths Contained in Popular Superstitions*, 28

48. Mayo, *On the Truths Contained in Popular Superstitions*, 27.

49. Mayo, *On the Truths Contained in Popular Superstitions*, 22.

50. Mayo, *On the Truths Contained in Popular Superstitions*.

51. Mayo, *On the Truths Contained in Popular Superstitions*, 28.

52. Mayo, *On the Truths Contained in Popular Superstitions*, 29–31.

53. Hauke Kock, *Vampire, Fürsten der Finsternis: Wahrheit und Legende* (Hamburg: Carlsen, 1998), 8: "Langsam versinkt die rotblasse Sonne hinter den Hügeln. Die Menschen eilen in ihre Häuser. . . . Wer nun noch anklopft, dem wird nicht geöffnet. Während sich die junge Bäuerin Stanacka am Feuer wärmt und ihr Abendmahl verzehrt, spricht ihr Schwiegervater leise über diese merkwürdigen Vorkommnisse, die das einzige Thema sind in den Dezembertagen in Medvegia an der Morava."

54. Hamberger, *Mortuus non mordet*, 50–51, see 53: "Darbey meldt der Heydukh Joviza, daß seine Schwiegertochter nahmens Stanoika vor 15 Tag frisch und gesund sich schlafen geleget; umb Mitternacht aber ist sie mit einem entsetzlich Geschrey, Forcht und Zittern aus dem Schlaf aufgefahren, und geklaget, daß von einem vor 9

Wochen verstorbenen Heydukhenssohn nahmens Milloe sey umb den Hals gewürget worden, worauf sie große Schmertzen auf der Brust empfunden und von Stund zu Stund sich schlechter befunden, bis sie endlich den 3ten Tag gestorben."

55. Kock, *Vampire*, 9: "Um die Stunde der Mitternacht durchschneidet plötzlich ein entsetzlicher Schrei die Stille. Alle im Haus sind mit einem Schlag wach; Rufe: Was ist passiert?—Mach doch einer Licht.

Sie finden Stanacka, aufrecht im Bett sitzend, sie betastet ihren Hals und zittert am ganzen Leib. Die junge Frau ringt nach Luft, alle Farbe ist aus ihrem Gesicht gewichen. . . .

Atemlos und stockend klagt sie, ein Mann sei gekommen, der sich auf sie gelegt und am Hals gewürgt habe. Sie hat diesen Mann erkannt, er heißt Milloe."

56. Kock, 9 and 12: "Johannes Fluchinger ist kein abergläubischer Mensch. In seinem Beruf als Regimentsarzt ist er den rauhen Umgangston unter Soldaten gewöhnt, und mit seiner medizinischen Erfahrung glaubt er, allen Schrecknissen der Welt gewappnet zu sein. . . .

Als die Schaufel mit einem dumpfen Pochen auf den Sargdeckel stößt, endet das Gespräch der Umstehenden abrupt. Mit Spannung erwartet Fluchinger die Öffnung des Sarges, doch der Anblick der toten Miliza lässt ihn frösteln. Er hat schon viele Leichen gesehen, aber niemals zuvor etwas Derartiges. Bis eben hielt er die Beschreibungen vom Fall Arnod Paole für Übertreibungen, ein Produkt überreizter Nerven, doch was hier vor ihm liegt, im winterfahlen Tageslicht, ist außergewöhnlich und offensichtlich unnatürlich."

57. See [J. T.] Sheridan Le Fanu, "Carmilla," *In a Glass Darkly*, ed. Robert Tracy (London, New York: Oxford's World Classics, 2008); Bram Stoker, *Dracula*, ed. Maurice Hindle (London: Penguin Classics, 2003), 228 (chapter xvi).

58. Translation: "Versammlung der hauptsächlichsten feinde des grafen *Dracula* aus dem geschlecht der linken *Nosferatu*."

59. H.C. Artmann, *"Dracula Dracula: Ein transsylvanisches Abenteuer,"* in *The Best of H. C. Artmann*, ed. Klaus Reichert (Frankfurt/M.: Suhrkamp, 1975), 300–310, qtd. 310. Words in italics are in Cyrillic letters originally.

60. The fact that the fantastic in literature generally fictionalizes the epistemological conflict of "Enlightenment vs. superstition" in a way corresponds with the metamorphosis of this particular work of non-fiction into a literary text here.

III

THE FEMALE VAMPIRE IN
WORLD MYTH AND THE ARTS

8

Women with Bite: Tracing Vampire Women from Lilith to *Twilight*

Nancy Schumann

A T THE BEGINNING OF THE 21ST CENTURY, women finally have the right to vote, hold jobs, earn more money than their husbands, and wear short skirts. Even the veiled Muslim women that we ignorant Westerners like to view as several centuries behind women's liberation are more likely than not to have university degrees, jobs, and an attitude. Nobody even needs to change their name when getting married anymore. Yet, not all that glitters is gold, and these appearances are somewhat deceiving.

Of course, the women's liberation movement and the sexual revolution have achieved great things in many aspects, but inequalities still persist. It remains the exception rather than a normal occurrence for women to earn more than men and even equal pay is not yet the norm. And yes, there is still such a thing as "a typical male domain." Films in general and the horror genre in particular are two of these "typical male domains." In 2009 only 17 percent of British films were directed by women and only 16 percent credited female screen writers.[1] The numbers are even lower when looking at horror films of any description.

This very real life fact finds its way into the realms of the fantastic where there is even less reason for inequality between the sexes. There are very few female directors or screenwriters, and thus there are very few heroines saving their co-protagonists from evil. Women in horror are predestined to be the victims: victims of violence, psychological terror, and supernatural seductions. In any case, they are damsels in distress to be rescued by some hero: Byronic, in shining armor, or otherwise. They are far less likely to be either the story's heroine or the perpetrator of violence.

This, however, is surprising for a variety of reasons. First of all, there is most definitely an audience demand for strong female leads in the genre. The long-running and vastly successful series, *Xena: Warrior Princess* and *Buffy the Vampire Slayer*, attest to that. Secondly, the horror and fantasy genres offer a chance to explore alternative worlds and ways of life by their very nature. There is no need for the same physical limitations that hold true in the real world to apply.

Let's look at the fabulous fiend that is the vampire, for example. Vampires are beautiful, strong, and immortal. They possess various supernatural powers. They thirst for human blood. There are various defensive methods that will protect humans from vampire attacks, such as the well-know garlic, wooden stake or, more recently, verveine. All of these things apply to male and female vampires alike. Yet, when most people are asked to think of a vampire they will think of Dracula, rather than his brides, or, in case of the *Twilight* generation, they'll think of Edward rather than Alice or Victoria.

Women in 21st-century vampire literature are Bellas (from *Twilight*), Sookies (from *True Blood* and the Charlaine Harris novels), or Elenas (from *Vampire Diaries*) and, for the most part, they are not even vampires themselves, but a vampire's girlfriend. However, these women can look back on a rich history of fanged ladies who haunted their victims before the high-school beauties were born. Before male domination put women and vampiresses on the side lines, vampire ladies ruled both literature and folklore all over the world. In cultures older than our Western civilization, religious practice starts with belief in the primal goddess. The social order was matriarchal: "The family was ruled by the mother, the people by queens, and the heavens by goddesses."[2]

It was common to worship the female in agricultural societies, as women were the first to cultivate plants, which led to adoration of Mother Earth. Humans of both sexes had an innate respect for the primal goddess and all things female were mysterious, even sacred, to them. Naturally, their monsters were female, too. The reasons for any unusual occurrence could be traced to a female fiend: the vampiress of folklore and legend. Every civilization around the world has vampire-like characters in its legends and mythology. They have different names and varying abilities, but all drain their victims, either of blood or life energy.

Vampires in general are used to explain adverse events during childbirth and sudden or violent deaths. A sudden or violent death could of course befall anybody. So, the resulting vampire could be male or female of any age or social status. However, people would more commonly encounter pregnancies and births and all the things that can go wrong along the way. Thus, it makes perfect sense to have more female vampires in old folkloric reports.

First of all, there was the real and present danger that women would die giving birth. This is something that changed only relatively recently and only in Western society. Certainly our great-grandmothers were still as likely as not to survive having children. Women who died in childbirth could turn into vampires. Their restless spirits would haunt the living and endanger other women during their pregnancies.

Secondly, children might die during birth and their mothers might turn into vampires out of grief. These creatures would then attack other women's babies in their sleep, draining them of life blood and energy so the children slowly withered away. These two types are the more ordinary vampiresses. They seem somewhat reactionary characters, taking revenge for the pain they've experienced in life.

In later folkloric reports the main feature becomes the vampiress's beauty, which enables her to attract young men in order to drink their blood. People feared the succubus in general and the figure of Lilith in particular. The succubus is a more active vamp character who attacked men as well as children. She is a divine being rather than a vampiress that used to be a human woman, and she is the very embodiment of male supremacy at risk.

These features symbolize two things: motherhood is the fulfillment of womanhood. Consequently, a woman without children seeks revenge for her loss. In addition to this, the vampiress lives beyond social borders. This automatically makes her a sexual woman, which is a threat to young, potent men.

Lilith

The artists of the Western world have adopted Lilith from ancient traditions focusing on her man-eating characteristics. Lilith is commonly known as a figure from Hebrew legends, though she is curiously not found in the Bible. There is, of course, a discrepancy in the creation myth found in Genesis:

> Genesis I: 27 reads: "So God created man in his own image, in the image of God he created him; male and female he created them."
> Genesis II: 18 and 22 read: "The LORD God said, 'It is not good for the man to be alone. I will make a helper suitable for him.' Then the LORD God made a woman from the rib he had taken out of the man, and he brought her to the man."[3]

Scientifically, this discrepancy is quickly explained. Researchers found out that the gap derives from the fact that these are two creation stories. Genesis I was written by Hebrew priests about 700 BCE, while Genesis II is far older, perhaps based on a Sumerian story.

Still, the contradiction had to be accounted for when people understood the Bible literally and two different theories developed: the first one states that Adam was initially perfect, just like God who himself is nonphysical and combines male and female gender features. Therefore, Adam must have possessed male and female characteristics to be perfectly balanced and faultless like God. Later, God turned Adam into the first human by separating the male from the female part; Eve was created. The human beings were both imperfect and needed each other to be complete.

The second theory brings Lilith into existence as first wife to Adam. She was his helper in Eden, formed, like Adam, out of dust. Yet, while Adam considered her one of the beasts, and, therefore, inferior, Lilith regarded herself equal to him. Lilith demanded equal rights that Adam was not willing to give:

> Adam and Lilith never found peace together; for when he wished to lie with her, she took offence at the recumbent posture he demanded. "Why must I lie beneath you?" she asked. "I also was made from dust, and am therefore your equal." Because Adam tried to compel her obedience by force, Lilith, in rage, uttered the magic name of God, rose into the air and left him.[4]

Lilith becomes the mother of succubus and incubus creatures after her flight from the Garden of Eden. Some writings speak of Lilith herself becoming a succubus. A succubus is a demon who attacks men in their sleep, forcing them to have sex. The male counterpart is the incubus who attacks women in the same manner. This version of Lilith is described in the Babylonian *Talmud*. The *Talmud* itself speaks of a beautiful, nymphomaniac woman called Lilith. This work led rabbis to prohibit young men from sleeping alone in the house for fear that Lilith might harm them.

A slight confusion is caused by the fact that Lilith is described as a succubus and as draining young men's blood. The succubus attacks at night and leaves the victim exhausted but is not normally associated with blood. Lilith, however, is a succubus-like creature that sucks young men's blood during the attack, giving us one of the earliest combinations of vampirism and sexuality.

Men attacked by Lilith lose semen and blood, which leaves them twice as exhausted. Lilith as a promiscuous woman is a danger in more than one respect. She seduces men to immorality and sin and drains them of their life energy. She takes her revenge on men while they are asleep, when the subconscious dominates their dreams because deep down in the subconscious lives a secret yearning for a passionate woman. Lilith can easily enter this secret place and cause men to father demon children; children that will be like their mother, succubus-like. She is a major threat to patriarchy but also an excuse for it. The succubus attack frees men of responsibility for their nightly fantasies. Being under Lilith's attack they cannot be blamed for immoral dreams and nocturnal emissions.

All of this made Lilith a key figure for Jewish and other feminists in the 20th century: "[M]ay the Lilith, who has been obscured by the mists of demonology these thousands of years, be revealed as the first woman on earth, equal to man and a free spirit."[5] Feminist de-demonizing of Lilith has been heavily debated among scholars on this subject. It has most notably been argued that doing so totally ignores the evil side of Lilith, which cannot be denied.

Lilith is not just an independent woman and she is not just a male fantasy. Lilith is a monstrous vampire but she is so for a reason. In a world where both sexes actually have equal rights, a being like Lilith might not even exist.

Contemporary Vampire Women

What remains of the monstrous, beautiful, uncompromising vampiress of folklore in 21st-century fiction?

First of all, let's go back a few decades in vampire fiction to when Anne Rice's *Vampire Chronicles* entered the stage. Everybody knows Lestat, Louis, and Armand, of course, but there are also the female vampires in their lives: Akasha, Gabrielle, and Claudia. They are the personified three aspects of the primal goddess: Claudia, the demonic child is the virgin; Gabrielle, the cold mother, is just that; and Akasha, the feminist mother of all vampires, is the witch. All three of them are women of a new millennium. All three of them are strong women that rule their own worlds. The restrictions of the eras into which they were born do not apply to them. Role models, such as daughter, mother, or queen, do not define any of them.

For Claudia, the vampire child, vampirism enforces an eternal victim role upon her. No matter how experienced and strong-willed she becomes, she will always look like a doll and be treated as such. Furthermore, she has no voice of her own; the reader sees her through Louis' and Lestat's eyes.[6] But she does not picture herself a victim, only humans can be victims to Claudia. She may look like a "Botticelli angel," yet she is more frightful than the devil. Claudia doesn't remember ever being human. Vampirism is her very nature. She never questions it and uncompromisingly demands her place in the world.

Claudia shows her ancestry in her choice of victims; like Lilith she prefers to drain women and children. The beautiful child is also a seductress but she doesn't hunt human men. She only accepts vampires as equals and therefore works her charms on Louis, who is hopelessly devoted to her. Yet, Louis, like the world in general, cannot accept this independent woman over whom he has no control. The patriarchal society Louis represents fears her uncompromising nature. Claudia is not allowed to change the world to suit her needs. She is not allowed to live.

Claudia shows her power twice: once in killing Lestat and then by making Madeline her new companion to replace Louis. Despite her physical form she is perfectly capable of killing an adult male vampire and does so without remorse. Later, Madeleine, the doll maker, helps Claudia to create surroundings to match her size so the little woman doesn't look out of place anymore. Yet the precise moment when Claudia's world changes shape to fit her, when she is at her most content, is the moment adult male vampires condemn her to burn in the sun. The beautiful Botticelli angel is too frightful a vampiress to be allowed to live.

Gabrielle, Lestat's human mother, is essentially a grow-up version of Claudia. Not only are their looks described pretty much alike, but they also share the natural attitude towards vampirism. While all the male vampires in the *Vampire Chronicles* long for their human pasts, these women are liberated by vampirism. They shed their old human lives the moment they are turned. Gabrielle is as independent and uncompromising as Claudia and kills her human victims methodically, without remorse. Yet, Gabrielle is allowed to stay alive.

The reason is simple: Gabrielle doesn't interfere with worldly affairs. She chooses to live in the eternal surroundings of nature where humans do not venture. Thus she is no threat, although her fellow vampires certainly fear her. The price of her eternal independence is giving up a major role. Strong, beautiful, and frightening, Gabrielle becomes a background figure. Her self-willed isolation allows her control over her own life but she is not allowed to change the world.

Changing the world is exactly what Akasha, the mother of all vampires, attempts to do. Akasha is like Lilith, the mother of demons that plague humanity. The source of vampirism in the *Vampire Chronicles* abandoned her children several millennia ago but when she returns she does so to take over the world. The vampire queen is the most uncompromising feminist. Her deadly power is to be used to kill human men on a massive scale to allow the world that women would build to flourish.

She silently waited for thousands of years for the world to be ready to be run exclusively by women. Akasha plans to keep only a few males to ensure future generations of humans and envisions a less violent society as a result. Only when men can no longer remember violence and are incapable of grasping the concept of rape and all the other crimes committed against women over the centuries, shall the number slowly be allowed to increase. Akasha works with a natural example, demonstrating that is exactly how bees survive, and with a supernatural one, showing off Lestat as the very embodiment of male violence. This goal can only be achieved by killing thousands of men.

The vampiress is divinely monstrous[7]; having outgrown even the need for blood, she is truly immortal, not even sunlight can burn her. Humanity would not stand a chance against her rule. Yet, the vampires that fear her as much as humans fear vampires will not let her rise and rule again. It takes several ancient vampires, some barely younger than Akasha, to work together but they finally succeed in destroying her. The only feminist feature of their victory is that Akasha is destroyed by another vampiress.

Despite all her power, the weakness lies in Akasha herself: she claims a male consort for herself; she needs Lestat. Although he is unable to influence her and she says she would rather kill him than give up her purpose, it is this very weakness that brings her own destruction, allowing her destroyer to catch her by surprise. Because of this weakness Akasha is destroyed by the women that fear her most: female vampires protecting their human family. Like Lilith of legend. Akasha is a threat to the human children of a vampiress who found fulfillment in motherhood. It is the mother, not the vampiress, that opposes the divine rule.

The mighty Queen of Heaven is stopped by the most traditional of gender roles: the mother, the Victorian "angel of the house,"[8] living forever to care for her children. The limitless fantastic is reined in by the limitations of family and the reader never learns what this feminist world would look like. Women and vampires who would change the world are not allowed to survive in it.

The concept of family that is the destruction of Akasha plays an even more prominent role in more recent vampire stories, such as the *Vampire Diaries, Twilight,* and *True Blood* sagas. It's safe to say that Anne Rice started a trend for modern vampire literature in humanizing vampires. They are part of human society: different but not so very unlike their human neighbors.

Authors have come up with a variety of solutions to enable their vampires to join mainstream living. Vampires are hunters, no more cannibalistic than the average human, stalking wild animals for their blood. There is also the occasional willing donor or the option of synthetic blood, the scientific advance solving at least one big vampiric problem. Without the need to kill for survival vampires don't necessarily have to stay in the dark, keeping their existence a secret.

In the late 20th- and early 21st-century more vampire literature is produced by women than by men. The point of view of the narrative changes to a human perspective. The narrators in all these stories are women, sharing their view of the world and their places in it. Significantly, all narrators are human at the beginning of the stories. However, although two of the three female protagonists are transformed into vampires as the story progresses and all of them get bitten at some point, they are far from being victims.

All of these stories share characteristics with the classic Gothic novel and all of them are typical female vampire stories in so far as they are without doubt "tales of seduction."⁹ It is, however, not the vampires who seduce, but the heroines.

Elena, Bella, and Sookie are modern-age superwomen. They are as far removed from their vampiric ancestry as possible. Rather than being a threat to children, as Lilith was, they are in fact "übermothers," protecting their human and vampire families alike.

Bella actually becomes a mother naturally, having a child with Edward. Bella starts protecting her child from day one and is quite literally willing to die for her. These maternal instincts don't change in the slightest once Bella becomes a vampire, despite the fact that the birth means her human death. Unlike the vampiress of folklore, Bella holds no grudge against the child that killed her. She feels nothing but love for her daughter. She never even entertains the idea of ending Renesmee's life, neither before nor after the birth.

Even before that Bella takes care of both her parents as well as protecting the Cullens (Edward's "family"). Elena protects her friends from evil vampires and becomes the entire town's mother protector when she turns into a ghost after her death as a vampire. Finally, Sookie is the good, Southern girl with natural maternal instincts toward all her friends, who yearns to have a normal family life herself one day, though that might involve vampires.

All three of these women are examples of modern-day, independent women who can apparently do everything and all at the same time, too. They have jobs or school responsibilities, families to take care of, vampire boyfriends, vampire vendettas to sort out, and despite all this they are beautiful, pleasant people, perfect hostesses who can cook.

Elena is very much a modern woman who has successfully killed her inner angel to achieve the feminist ideal of female independence.¹⁰ Smart, pretty, and used to getting what she wants, the teenage girl is queen of her high school "released into full use of her power."¹¹ In fact she is a scheming, calculating, selfish girl when she is first introduced. She doesn't shy away from spreading vicious rumors and using her friends to get Stefan's attention. In contrast, the vampire is presented as her savior as far as her character goes. Out of love for him she is suddenly willing to change her behavior, to be a better person, and recognize how fantastically loyal her friends are. The vampire's love transforms Elena into an angel.

However, the transformation is not complete: Elena encounters the dark side of vampirism in Damon and keeps this a secret from Stefan. She is an unwilling victim to Damon but she still doesn't want to get the help that could save her. The old "social division of women into either pure and chaste, or as impure and corrupt"¹² encountered in classic Gothic novels does not apply to this heroine. Smith as the author and Elena as the protagonist both accept "the cruel as a normal, almost an invigorating component of human life."[13] Thus, the rounded character of the story's heroine is a good person with a dark side.

Only as a vampire does Elena rise to moral heights, protecting the Salvatore brothers and her human friends from her own evil twin, Katherine. When this "good" vampiress is killed she ascents to sainthood and continues as a ghost to keep her hometown safe.

Bella, as a human, is not unlike the *femme fatale* vampiress in older works. She plays the active role in her relationship with Edward from the start. Irritated by Edward's reaction to her, she pushes for an explanation. Where Edward is passive and seeks isolation to escape the temptation that is Bella, she won't let him get away without answers. Even when the answer is his nature as a vampire, combined with her quality as the perfect victim for him ("you are exactly my brand of heroin"[14]), Bella does not retreat. Having forced Edward to admit his feelings for her, their love for each other becomes the only fact that matters to her. Bella, the woman, is defined by action, while Edward, the vampire, is an observer.[15]

Sookie is a modern woman taking care of herself, paying her own bills and content with her place in the world. Her character carefully balances female independence with the search for Mr. Right. While Sookie is not a career woman she manages her own life without male protection or financial support. The payments she accepts from various vampires in the course of the stories might be generous, but they are always earned by her unique abilities to care for people and vampires alike.

The world that would so easily be destroyed by male vampire battles is kept safe by these women. At the same time they are strong, independent women who get what they want. The only example to the contrary is Bella finally agreeing to marry Edward before having sex. Apart from this one instance, the ladies demand and don't take *no* for an answer. In fact, even that example becomes a tool for Bella in achieving her goal of becoming a vampire herself.

Edward, who is an old-fashioned patriarch in many respects, tries everything to prevent Bella from turning into a vampire, while the change is the most natural thing to Bella, far more natural than getting married and, initially, having children. The vampire motif is clearly used to suggest a sexually aggressive woman in the very traditional sense of the Gothic novel[16]; as soon as Bella's wish for sexuality is fulfilled, there is no stopping her transformation into a vampire. The human girl was the virgin victim, but the sexual woman is automatically a vampire.

Family, rather than being the instrument of oppression, becomes the sphere these women control. They keep order within the family unit and protect it against external threats. They don't need to venture into the outside world for adventures and they don't need to isolate themselves to have control over their lives. Their families not only provide them with purpose: they give them control too.

The Cullens in the *Twilight* saga present a prime example of real-life equality between the sexes. Reassuringly heterosexual, the extended family unit is made up of four functioning couples, decisions are made by committee and any victory is a group effort. They are only ever referred to as "the Cullens," not "Carlisle's family" or anything similar, that would imply that he was actually their leader.

The family unit that is each individual couple and the larger Cullen clan are the all-important fundamental component of their society to protect. Each member of that family has the same value and is protected by every other member of that family, regardless of individual feelings or opinions. On account of this, Bella, Alice, Rosalie, and Esme have the same status as the male vampires and none of them strives for power beyond that.

The vampire women of the 21st century are strong, independent characters. They rule their own worlds, be these domestic or territorial. Many motifs of older vampire stories and Gothic novels in general can be found in these contemporary works. There is a return to the vampiress who rules by love and whose actions are defined by love.[17]

However, love and life happen on more equal terms now. The vampiresses are as devoted to their partners as these are to them. The couples are mostly presented as literally made for each other; the vampiric partner has defied the laws of time with his own immortality to find the one person in the world he is finally destined to spend eternity with. Only Sookie appears as a "normal" modern woman experiencing several relationships. Although not all love stories have a happy ending, all of these loves are sincere and immortal in their own right.

On the surface the heroines appear reactionary characters, yet another reincarnation of the Victorian "angel of the house," dreaming of undying love. It is true that they don't affect global matters, nor do they ever attempt to and that is rather disappointing.

Yet, the new vampiress is uncompromising in her own way. She is finally a woman who doesn't have to choose between family and independence. She can do both and do both well; Elena, Bella and Sookie fight relentlessly to defend their loved ones and still don't allow their vampire boyfriends to pay the bill after a night out. They are sexual women, fought over by several supernatural males, who are still good mothers. They are not limitless, fantastical creatures. Then, again, they lead near-human lives that seem to require superhuman skill to maintain.

So is there a world-changing, earth-shattering vampire queen in today's literature? No, unfortunately the limitless opportunities of the fantastic remain unexplored in that respect. Has today's literature produced a strong, independent heroine women can be proud of? Yes, insofar as the modern, humanized vampiress has become a more active, self-rescuing heroine that is also a domestic goddess. She does not need a male companion, neither for approval nor for protection any more, but equally she does not reject companionship for the sake of appearing independent. Her actions ensure that she has nothing to prove to anybody.

Female vampires have gained prominence in vampire stories and female writers have more than infiltrated the genre. However, it does seem that readers would much rather drool over gorgeous vampire heroes than see a vampire queen take over the world and change its order.

Tellingly, the continued threat of HIV in modern society brought a revival of vampire interest with it just as the spread of syphilis did in the 19th century. This indicates that humanity is still answering similar events with similar explanations. For this reason, if nothing else, vampire stories will continue to be written. Consequently, there is a chance that one day a vampiress will, literarily if not literally, succeed in changing the world order.

Notes

1. Kev Geoghegan, "Damsels in Distress," http://www.bbc.co.uk/news/entertainment-arts-12665443, accessed March 10, 2011.

2. Raphael Patai, *The Hebrew Goddess* (Detroit: Wayne State University Press, 1990), 24.

3. http://www.biblegateway.com, accessed October 24, 2003.

4. http://www.webcom.com/~gnosis/Lilith.html, accessed June 30, 2003; quoting Robert Graves and Raphael Patai, *Hebrew Myths: The Book of Genesis* (New York: Doubleday, 1964), 65–69.

5. http://www.lilithmag.com/resources/lilithsources.shtml, accessed July 4, 2003.

6. Nina Auerbach, *Our Vampires, Ourselves* (Chicago: University of Chicago Press, 1995), 154–155.

7. Barbara Creed, *The Monstrous-Feminine: Film, Feminism, Psychoanalysis* (London: Routledge 1993).

8. Nina Auerbach, *Woman and the Demon: The Life of a Victorian Myth* (Cambridge, MA and London: Harvard University Press, 1982).

9. James Twitchell, *The Living Dead: A Study of the Vampire in Romantic Literature* (Durham, N.C.: Duke University Press, 1997), 39.

10. Auerbach, *Our Vampires, Ourselves.*

11. Auerbach, *Our Vampires, Ourselves.*

12. Juliann Fleenor, *The Female Gothic* (Montreal: Eden Press, 1983), 15.

13. Ellen Moers, *Literary Women* (Oxford: Oxford University Press, 1977), 151.

14. Stephenie Meyer, *Twilight* (Oxford: Oxford University Press, 1977), 160.

15. Auerbach, *Woman and the Demon*, 1982.

16. Anne Koenen, *Visions of Doom: Plots of Power* (Frankfurt am Main: Vervuert, 1999), 233.

17. Auerbach, *Our Vampires, Ourselves.*

Bibliography

Auerbach, Nina. *Woman and the Demon: The Life of a Victorian Myth.* Cambridge, Mass.: Harvard University Press, 1982.

Auerbach, Nina. *Our Vampires, Ourselves.* Chicago: University of Chicago Press, 1995.

Creed, Barbara. *The Monstrous-Feminine: Film, Feminism, Psychoanalysis.* London: Routledge, 1993.

Fleenor, Juliann, ed. *The Female Gothic.* Montreal: Eden Press, 1983.

Koenen, Anne. *Visions of Doom, Plots of Power.* Frankfurt am Main: Vervuert, 1999.

Lurker, Manfred. *Dictionary of Gods and Goddesses, Devils and Demons.* London: Routlegde & Kegan Paul, 1987.

Moers, Ellen. *Literary Women.* Oxford: Oxford University Press, 1977.

Patai, Raphael. *The Hebrew Goddess.* Detroit: Wayne State University Press, 1990.

Twitchell, James B. *The Living Dead: A Study of the Vampire in Romantic Literature.* Durham, NC: Duke University Press, 1997.

Online Sources

http://www.bbc.co.uk/news/entertainment-arts-12665443. Accessed March 10, 2011.

http://www.webcom.com/~gnosis/lillith.html. Accessed June 30, 2003.

http://ccat.sas.upenn.edu/~humm/Topics/Lilith/alphabet.html. Accessed June 30, 2003.

http://www.encyclopedia.com/html/l/lilith.asp. Accessed July 2, 2003.

http://mb-soft.com/believe/tto/lilith.htm. Accessed July 3, 2003.

http://www.skepticfiles.org/moretext/lilith3.htm. Accessed July 4, 2003.

http://www.seekgod.ca/embracnotal.htm. Accessed July 3, 2003.

http://www.lilithmag.com/resources/lilithsources.shtml. Accessed July 4, 2003.

http://www.lilitu.com/lilith/lil_alt-myth.html. Accessed July 5, 2003.

http://www.ucalgary.ca/~elsegal/Shokel/950206_Lilith.html. Accessed July 5, 2003.

http://www.lilitu.com/lilith/khephframes.html. Accessed June 30, 2003.

http://www.biblegateway.com. Accessed October 24, 2003.

9

Vampiresse: Embodiment of Sensuality and Erotic Horror in Carl Th. Dreyer's *Vampyr* and Mario Bava's *The Mask of Satan*

Angela Tumini

Fata Morgana
A blue-eyed phantom far before
Is laughing, leaping toward the sun;
Like lead I chase it evermore,
I pant and run. . . .
I laugh, it is so brisk and gay;
It is so far before, I weep:
I hope I shall lie down some day,
Lie down and sleep.

–Christina Rossetti

A Demon is Born

HISTORICALLY, VAMPIRE LORE HAS REFLECTED the values and social structures of the culture in which it has existed, and it is because of their resilient, elemental nature that the legend of the vampire continues to be explored. Many of the myths started from explaining forms of insanity, diseases, and reasons for death; moreover, along with the morbidly humorous side, many people were buried alive who were believed to be dead and that would also add to the myth. While there is no unique universal definition of vampire lore, virtually in all contexts across every society there are scores of beautiful female vampires roaming the countryside and dark alleys of cities; indeed, the oldest vampire figures were females. Ancestors of the female vampire are to be found in the image of the succubi, for example, who were thought to be demons who seduced and preyed on sleeping males. These "ladies of the night" allegedly drew energy from men in order to sustain themselves and would continue to drain their energy, through sex, until their death. Moreover, Lilith, Adam's first wife, made infanticide her *raison d'être* while being also personified as a licentious demon:

> while God then formed Lilith, the first woman, just as He had formed Adam, except that He used filth and sediment instead of pure dust. From Adam's union with this demoness, and with another like her named Naamah, Tubal Cain's sister, sprang Asmodeus and innumerable demons that still plague mankind. Many generations later, Lilith and Namath came to Solomon's judgment seat, disguised as harlots of Jerusalem.[1]

The infamous Lilith/female association with infanticide is another element of a narrative that supported the development of patriarchal hegemony as a textual means of control that spared no form of social-cultural components. For example, frequently, this morally ambivalent status of women motivated the nakedness in the depiction of goddesses such as Diana and Aphrodite, or even Medusa whose serpent-haired image calls to mind the exposed female sexual organ. The latter has been interpreted as an indication of female sexual liberation from social constraints while reflecting the castration anxiety that was affirmed by Sigmund Freud:

> The hair upon Medusa's head is frequently represented in works of art in the form of snakes, and these once again are derived from the castration complex. It is a remarkable fact that, however frightening they may be in themselves, they nevertheless serve actually as a mitigation of the horror, for they replace the penis, the absence of which is the cause of the horror. This is a confirmation of the technical rule according to which a multiplication of penis symbols signifies castration.[2]

Christian iconography has focused heavily on the image of the serpent in the Garden of Eden as an expression of evil or the Devil. There is evidence of that even in art; a close look at Michelangelo's *Fall and Expulsion of Adam and Eve*, for example, a fresco in the Sistine Chapel, reveals that the serpent is shown with the upper body of a woman and snake-like lower parts. As remarked by Christopher L. C. E. Whitcombe:

> That the human part of the serpent is female is clear from the exposed left breast and from her long blond hair which streams back from her head. The human features appear to continue down as far as the knees. The impression is that her two legs become snake-like limbs just above or at the knee. The upper part of

her snake-legs are wrapped around the tree, the right one coiling over the left, but below it appears that the two become one with a single tail emerging from around the tree onto the ground. Her right arm grasps the tree trunk for support as she stretches out her left arm to meet Eve's upraised left hand (the significance of the left, or "sinister," hand used in the transaction by both Eve and the serpent should not be overlooked).[3]

A primary connection has also always existed among snakes, the moon, and the blood of menstruation and has played a key role in the development of symbolic culture in early human society. Penelope Shuttle and Peter Redgrove argued that:

It is a common cultural image of menstruation that a woman is bitten by a snake-god who comes from the moon. The moon sloughs herself and renews, just as the snake sheds its skin, and so does the sexually undulant wall of the womb renew its wall after one wave-peak of the menstrual cycle: the woman renews her sexual self after shedding blood as the snake sheds its skin. The wavy waters of the tidal sea are comparable to swimming snakes, and a good vaginal orgasm can feel to one's penis like a sea undulant with such snakes: a sea which is, of course, tidal with the monthly period.[4]

Rather than exploring the story of the Divine Feminine, observing that the moon and menstruation were both cyclical in nature, and leading our ancestors to notice other cyclical patterns in nature, scriptwriters and purveyors of supernatural fiction usually have, in the past, ignored the radical range of possibilities open to women relating to these mythological beliefs. They have instead, in several cases, opted to employ plot devices and character twists that served tightly to contain and control their female characters, reflecting the social forces exercised over women in general.

The question of sexism and gender became entrenched in vampirism because of the misogynist tradition long rooted in the belief that "the devil prevailed first with Eve and continues to find easy marks in women."[5] After all, a female vampire is a woman who neither dies nor bears children; thus, she represents the incarnation of subversion in the way that she is able to escape mortality and the pains of childbirth for which women were originally punished after the Fall. Moreover, a female vampire is as strong as her male counterparts and stronger by far than human men; while her lack of remorse and reproductive inability represent a pattern of autonomous rebellion that transcends any normative model of behavior. As Susanne Kord explained, in what pertains to child-bearing:

The female vampire is the antithesis of motherhood: she does not feed her offspring but feeds from it; she does not give life but un-death. At the same time, she offers an analogy to *fatherhood:* like a man she can produce as many offspring as she wants, for as long as she wants. Her parenthood is absolute, that is: independent of a partner; like the male vampire (but unlike men), she has gained reproductive omnipotence.[6]

To allow, therefore, childless and remorseless women to roam free was too dangerous even for the screen or for the pages of fiction. This rhetoric of dangerous order alteration has justified a specific formation of the female vampire myth that constitutes a model of "rebellion" to social codes. The ripple effect of her insurgence would be far too terrifying because the superhuman strength of the female vampire acts as a mirror image for the potential power of all strong women who are unbound by emotional or familial ties. While the power of the male vampire is dangerous in terms of literal destructive potential, in women the consequences reach beyond murder and property damage to spark fears about the collapse of social order itself. The vampiress's pioneering of a sexuality that implies a penetration of her victim with her phallic fangs not only represents a stereotypical masculine trait of aggressiveness, but the danger of a process of feminization of men as well as bisexuality, which contributed to the terrifying threat that 19th-century culture saw in vampirism. Such a threat would constitute a direct attack on what R. W. Connell calls "normalizing theories of masculinity" or "theories that identified psychological health with a narrow orthodoxy in sexuality and emotion."[7]

Vampyr, Carmilla, and Female Transgression

In the world of cinema, Carl Th. Dreyer openly departed from the reigning view of the male vampire figure and wedded the idea of having females in primary roles in his German expressionist-type film, *Vampyr.* For those who are familiar with the works of this Danish master, that is hardly surprising. Dreyer was always particularly sympathetic to the feminine role in human interactions throughout his entire career; and, while the presence of women was intensely physical in his films, it was not in any way concerned with the conventional male fantasy of a feminine abstraction. Instead, when dealing with the question of gender, Dreyer's concern was focused on the negative connotation that had stained the reputation of the "feminine" throughout the times and on the way in which women were historicized and made to be the product of a social and religious construct. These considerations relate to the question of the *Eternal-Womanly* that Geoffrey Ashe, for example, discusses at length: that is the question of how in the world, before the rise of any verified gods, human beings worshipped goddesses. Ashe points out that the early Stone Age gave us no proven images of male deity, whereas it gave us figurines with gross breasts and bellies as exaggerated tokens of motherhood. He then talks about the fact that in passing from pre-history to the oldest recoverable rituals and myths, she takes on many faces: sometimes she is represented as a maiden, sometimes as a mistress, and, at times, as a world-matriarch of immeasurable age. What Ashe concludes is that this is the proof, without dispute, of the importance of an actual goddess-centered religion.[8]

What binds many of Dreyer's works together is precisely how he tackles the discourse of the feminine in relation to the fact that we have moved our consciousness from ancient goddess-centered societies that celebrated feminine sexuality to ones that stigmatize it within a culture that is steeped in hierarchy. While *Vampyr* owes its originality to its being a unique stylistic *tour de force*, it also thrives on illusion, on an intricate intertwining of lights and shadows while suggesting that vampirism is a spiritual disease. Moreover, this film evokes, as no movie ever has, the terror common to all humans: that is the terror of being buried alive. Tom Milne also informs us about the effect of this movie on the public in that "the characters all somehow acquire . . . the same dislocated presence as though they had stepped out of a nightmare."[9] Thus, everything tangible in terms of gory and physical violence is removed in favor of the psychological and nightmarish elements that place the protagonists in a constant state of vacant amazement and sleepwalking-like reverie. The viewers, in consequence, perceive an unsettling feeling of uncertainty and dismay, which makes their experience somewhat disquieting. Yet, while Dreyer's *Vampyr* is exceptional in its dreamy and experimental atmosphere, it is the absence of male vampires that determines its reversal of genre and the roles of Marguerite Chopin, the vampiress, and the semi-transformed Léone, her victim, that mark its distinctiveness. David Rudkin insists on the groundbreaking role of this film within its genre, by pointing out that more than 20 vampire films, mostly Scandinavian, had already been made by 1931 and that, in this new genre, the vampires were predominantly male.[10]

Vampyr's females, mostly Léone and her sister Giselle, were vaguely modeled on the female protagonists of Joseph Sheridan Le Fanu's *Carmilla* (1872), a novel that was amazing in its content considering the time when it was written. This story, which is replete with distinct Sapphic overtones, influenced subsequent generations of beautiful, decadent female vampires, and, within the Gothic genre, it is valued as one of the most renowned female vampire narratives from the Romantic era. Aside from being the first vampire tale whose protagonists are women, *Carmilla* unveils the power of female sexuality by taking the role of the feminine to a new level: a lesbian relationship is the unconcealed subtext of the story and owes no apologies to the traditional heterosexual normative of narrative that would have been more conventional for 19th-century culture. With a strikingly modern approach to narrative, Le Fanu chronicles the development of a vampiric relationship through sensual moments of intimacy between two young women; thus, in *Carmilla,* the male protagonists who brutalize their female victims are totally absent. While empowering females who were far too marginalized and victimized to be seen as heroic at the time, the story usurped male authority by excluding male participation in the bonding of women. It would seem, therefore, that Bram Stoker's classic 1897 novel, *Dracula,* was a response to Le Fanu's lesbian tale of *Carmilla,* which defied the traditional structures of kinship: *Dracula* was intended, therefore, as a necessary step to reaffirm the natural hegemony of patriarchy.

Like *Carmilla,* Dreyer's *Vampyr* implies a seduction of females away from male-structured order, albeit within the usual discourse revolving around a struggle between good and evil, tradition and modernity, and lust and chastity. *Vampyr* first introduces viewers to David Gray, the male protagonist who, having checked into an eerie inn for the night, encounters an old man whose daughter is suffering from an unusual disease. After he experiences a series of bizarre discoveries and hallucinatory dreams, including one of his own death, he eventually learns that a female vampire, Marguerite Chopin, is the demonic presence who is at the heart of the spookiness of the setting where a fair maiden, Léone, crosses paths with her fanged menace. As Rudkin suggests, "Dreyer's onscreen world throbs to echoes of the Latin epitaph sometime seen on old gravestones: Media in vita morte sumus/in the midst of life we are in death. . . . in Vampyr's world, there is neither life nor death. There is only the cold, unremitted estate of the Undead."[11]

Within this unsettling imagery of transient, spectral, human figures whose identities are shifting and uncertain, Dreyer, in a manner that is common to some of his other works, draws attention to what Mark Nash sees as:

> the process of the socialization of desire, its containment by and within the cultural order [that] clearly implies a fixing of what is male and/or female. Transgressions of this rigorously enforced cultural distinction between sex-roles are punished in several ways (e.g. *Joan of Arc,* the witches in *Day of Wrath,* and *Vampyr,* who all exceed the limitations imposed on female desire by the male order).[12]

In *Vampyr* we come face-to-face with a triangular interaction of females, which makes this film unique for its time. The blood-sucking and the "bloodsucked" creatures of the night are not merely there to transform and to be transformed; they are charged with an erotic ambiguity, which imposes a reconfiguration of gender practice. In the words of Alison Peirse:

Léone, one of the Châtelain's two daughters, is drawn outside and into the clutches of Chopin. An exterior long shot frames the scene: beneath a large tree, Léone lies on her back on a stone slab. Black-robed Chopin bends over her neck, but the distant framing denies the spectator the opportunity to see either a bite or blood. However, when Léone is taken to her room, she moans as the nurse sponges her neck, insinuating that Chopin has penetrated her.[13]

Dreyer seems to say that, because of the Symbolic Order of things, lesbian desire must be disguised as vampirism, and that, to make it more legitimate, elements of compulsion, hypnosis, and the supernatural must be present. A recognition of that order means to accept the concept of "hegemony" discussed by R. W. Connell in relation to Antonio Gramsci's cultural argument by which a group claims and sustains a leading position in social life: "Hegemonic masculinity can be defined as the configuration of gender practice which embodies the currently accepted answer to the problem of the legitimacy of patriarchy, which guarantees (or is taken to guarantee) the dominant position of men and the subordination of women."[14]

Because femininity is circumscribed within a circle of limits designed by Gramsci's aforementioned type of hegemonic structure, women are much more likely to fear any expression of sexuality that will define them negatively, whereas men are generally defined positively in their sexual expression and experiences.

In *Vampyr*, the conditions for the defense of patriarchy are shaken further when an incest sensibility is seen naturally to surface through the narrative of the film. Although Giselle's concern for her sister Léone leans toward the verge of fright, she is nevertheless attracted to her side and clearly unable to break free from her captivating charm. Léone's feral bloodlust expression, as her smile suddenly turns from innocent to evil and finally to lascivious toward Giselle, counts as the pivotal moment of the film, which established a counter-tradition of seductive female vampires. Dreyer managed to compound the monstrous element of the female protagonists, Léone especially, with an element of disarming sexual ambiguity, something that was not so apparent in male vampires until Anne Rice's novel *Interview with the Vampire* (1976) influenced a generation of beautiful, decadent male vampires all the way to the dropouts of *The Lost Boys*, directed by Joel Schumacher in 1987.

Contrary to what Stoker's *Dracula* was meant to symbolize, in *Vampyr*, patriarchal normative is not there to repossess the female body for the purposes of male pleasure and exchange. What is more, similarly to Le Fanu's *Carmilla*, the reckless unleashing of female desire is unresolved and uncorrected, but one woman must be a vampire, draining the life of the other woman, yet holding her in a bond stronger than the grave. The closeness of the females also functions as an indicator of an unorthodox attempt to fill the void caused by the absence of a structuring motherly figure. The element of blood-spilling is meant to cause anxiety because the cultural meaning and construction of the "maternal" as a concept in the film is completely upturned, while the positive dichotomies of Mother/Nurturer and Mother/Nature in the benevolent meaning of the concept become completely obscured. As argued by Peirse, "[i]n *Vampyr*, blood (whether shown or insinuated) is explicitly connected to the maternal entity: she punctures the flesh and transgresses the sanctity of the body. As such, the coachman's dripping blood can be read as a triumph for Chopin: corporeal boundaries are transgressed, blood drips and death hangs in the air."[15]

Dreyer's technique of delayed and reverse-action shadows reminds us that this is a setting where the physical laws of the universe no longer apply. It is a world peopled by beings who are at once present and yet somehow shadowy, elusive and unreachable. As viewers we feel at a loss as we fail to grasp the continuously shifting meaning of the images produced by the narrative; all that we see is encrusted in reverie and frozen in a stylized atmosphere that wavers between nightmares and psychic distortions. As Michael Grant best puts it:

> Aporia and contradiction are fundamental to it, and Dreyer accords them a particularly vivid and focused realisation. The action of the film is situated ambiguously, in a world which is that neither of life nor of death. What happens in the film occurs elsewhere, in a place self-consciously created out of cinematic effects, and, as a result, we cannot really be sure of what it is we are seeing.[16]

By sifting through the ebb and flow of the vampire genre, Dreyer raises thought-provoking questions about 18th- and 19th-century gender norms in ways that continue to resonate today. Léone and Giselle, as characters, were registered outside of the primary frame of traditionally accepted vampire stories at the time when *Vampyr* came to life; while Marguerite Chopin, the vampire who is given a surname, was quite striking. Dreyer's attitude was a provocative one in that he seems to accentuate Chopin's disruptive centrality in a world steeped in iron-clad patriarchal norms in which death may be said to have doubled the impulse to life; a world where a strong temporal order is blurred by an oneiric dimension in which spiritual catharsis is replaced by an unpinned Gothic sense of fear.

Bava, the Witch, and the *Femme Fatale*

For his vampiric setting, Italian director Mario Bava discovered Barbara Steele, an intriguing woman whom he introduced to an emerging generation of horror fans with *The Mask of Satan*, also released *as Black Sunday*. Thanks to Bava, Steele subsequently became an iconic image and synonymous of horror movies. At the same time as Bava's work in Italy, French director Roger Vadim made yet another screen adaptation of Le Fanu's *Carmilla,* under the title of *Et Mourir de Plaisir* (released in English as *Blood & Roses*), but nonetheless, female vampires remained few in numbers through the rest of the 1960s and primarily appeared in brief supporting roles either as the victims of the male protagonists or as anonymous members of a group of vampires. The plot of *The Mask of Satan* revolves around the tragic and malevolent figure of Princess Asa who, in the 17th century, had been accused of both witchcraft and incest and had been mercilessly executed by placing a spiked mask on her face. Unintentionally brought back to life by a drop of blood by Dr. Kruvajan 200 years later, she manages to resurrect her brother/lover Javutich and to terrorize the ancient Vadja castle where her own descendants, including her look-alike Princess Katia, continue to live. While Asa is variously stigmatized as a witch, a vampire, and a demon, her real crime is clearly her sexual activeness and her "monstrous" love for her brother Javutich. As famously theorized by Freud "the tendency on the part of civilization is to restrict sexual life [and] . . . its first, totemic, phase already brings with it the prohibition against an incestuous choice of object"[17]; thus, such crime is clearly unforgivable.

Because all incestuous relationships are potentially dangerous, The *Mask of Satan* shows how a curse can destroy and tear apart a family and, indeed, by the end of the movie, there is not much of the family left standing. But other questions are raised: are the bad women sexual and the good women pure? And has this issue been conveying the insults, denigration, or attack connected to feminine sexuality? This way, Bava points to the symbolic devaluing of women in relation to the Divine, which stands as one of the founding metaphors of Western civilization. The answers to these questions amount to the concept of the virgin/whore split, whose cultural construction is a history as old as the history of Eve. The story of the Garden of Eden is one example of how the myths of the ancient goddesses were appropriated and altered to reinforce the subordination of women to the "virtues" of patriarchy. As Laws and Schwartz explain:

The Madonna-whore dichotomy was perpetuated by Judeo-Christian cultural tradition through the two strongest women it presents: Eve and Mary. Sexuality as exemplified by Eve is a constant temptation to man, which must be distanced and distained. Carnality has no part in men's "better" nature, which yearns for union with God. In fact, according to tradition, it was Eve's intervention that ruptured the harmonious relationship between man and God. [The Virgin Mary, on the other hand] is holy precisely because she is sexless.[18]

The whore/witch figure, among other things, has always served as a symbolic threat for male, celibate, and religious authorities because one of the most empowering things about a witch is the relative freedom that she enjoys regarding her sexuality and the complete ease that she enjoys with her own body. The dark, lurking menace of the witch became caught up in the male imagination that pictured her dancing nude around bonfires, participating in polyamorous relationships, while also consuming aphrodisiac herbs and breaking gender constraints. To counter that fear, Mary, the woman who saves man for his eternal spiritual destiny, prevailed in the culture and came to represent a nostalgic longing for the traditional woman. Because Bava's film narrative thrives on this archetypal split of the virgin/whore, its reliance is established on much more than just the brutal violence and spooky, fog-enshrouded ambiance, which is so typical of the vampire genre. Perhaps it is precisely because of that that this work has been regarded as the Italian horror film for people who do not really care for horror films. Although Bava does cater to modern bloodthirsty audiences, his concern lies more in the representation of the "feminine evil," while strictly adhering to his own need for artistic expression. As Troy Howarth aptly pointed out:

> The two women represent opposite sides of the same coin: Asa is corrupt, malevolent and sensual: Katia is pure, kind and virginal. Katia represents the comfort of security, while Asa embodies the thrill of danger. . . . this likewise marks the first appearance of the *doppelgänger* in Bava's work. The *doppelgänger* is a double (physical or symbolic) who embodies the worst aspects of an individual's personality. In *Black Sunday*, this relationship is depicted in traditional mythic/fairy tale terms: Asa is the whore, and Katia is the Madonna. Despite their physical resemblance, they represent opposing aspects of morality.[19]

Though still rooted in classic monster tradition, the *Mask of Satan* is also the product of an inheritance left behind by the images of "terrible beauties" in which so many *fin-de-siècle* aesthetes, in their desire to quench an eternal thirst for an ambiguous but human desire, recognized and celebrated their ideal. The 19th-century culture was quite concerned with lunar influenced, fanged-vampire exploits and female sexuality and menstruation, and by the end of the century, some more subversive aspects, such as necrophilia, avenging sexuality, and religious sadism, became an obsessive idea within various artistic circles. According to Phillippe Jullian:

> There was a powerful current of necrophilia running through the *fin de siècle* in the best Romantic tradition. There are countless dead women in the Symbolists' works, and in his tragic story of Princess Phénissa (1893) Rémy de Gourmont goes as far as vampirism: "abandon the barely deflowered female lamb to the ingenuous embrace of a young wolf, and let him die devouring her. But do not expect her, enriched by your life, to lie down on your tomb and open up the rich gates of her sex to the funeral joker."[20]

Jullian also stresses the importance of "psychopathia sexualis" as a form of *fin-de-siècle* fetishism, and the lure of ambiguous ideals of female beauties, from those of "Lesbos . . . [to] those from Sodom,"[21] imposed on a Decadent Europe by artists such as Dante Gabriel Rossetti and Gustave Moreau and by the erotic images of the *femme damnées* of poets like Charles Baudelaire, Algernon Charles Swinburne, and Jean Lorrain, who catered to a public, according to Jullian, that was described by Laurent Tailhade as:

> Fellatrices, catamites, pimps, ponces, madams, club-owners, all of those who traffic in lust are pictured here in all their hideous ugliness. Pale from the kisses of Lesbos, girls of sixteen beg for superhuman embraces, and, to make them fertile, crave the clutches of a monster. Crazed with perverted lust, the damned souls of love hold out their blotted faces to young males stronger than oaks.[22]

Like any good aesthete, Bava had an obsession with unnatural sexual relationships and his artistic tendency craved for the freedom to push cinematic boundaries and to astonish his public. His sensitiveness to visual art—because Bava was a trained painter himself—and his creative nature led him to a strong belief in the adoption of visual composition in film-making and that is what gives his work its distinctive character. In the film, it is in fact an *objet d'art* that acts as a clue to the unresolved mystery. Asa's portrait, in all its ideal of mysterious and melancholic beauty, is used as the secret passage in the castle; this particular feature enriches the scenes with a shade of sexual symbolism that stands on the basis of its own style. Rather than conforming to the usual practice of vampirism, Bava has his female protagonist, Asa, enslaving her victim Dr. Kruvajan in an unconventional way, by drawing the life and soul from him with a long and terrifying kiss that follows the memorable sequence of her resuscitation. In an explosion of stylistic delight, we see her rotting corpse growing new skin and new eyes, instead of merely rising out of her crypt. Like the Greek sphinx, she is ready to claw, tantalize, and dominate the mortal who comes before her with the reassurance of a soft embrace. In so doing, the film never loses sight of its artistic undertone, bringing to mind, in its unsettling effect, the 1896 painting *Caresses* by Belgian artist Fernand Khnopff. Much of this painting's visual effect relies, in fact, on the woman presented as an enigmatic and dangerous animal, the common guise for a *fin-de-siècle femme fatale*. Charged with mythological weight, Asa exercises her hypnotizing power on Dr. Kruvajan: "Bava's camera seems literally haunted by Steele's ethereal beauty, capturing her otherworldly persona from every considerable angle."[23] As Asa obtains mastery over the doctor by weakening him and disarming him, the public is psychologically drawn into an otherworldly *mise en scène* in which the victim experiences moments of erotic delight followed by a disconcerting mental fatigue. In a fusion of style and substance, Bava exemplifies the erotic power that displaces the doctor's ability to reason alluding to the question of the real danger being inexorably linked to that eternal anxiety about the feminine, while Steele, by appropriately incarnating that anxiety, helped make the vampire genre into what it is today.

Conclusion

While the majority of vampire films depend on gory special effects and thrive on the usage of gallons of stage blood, in *Vampyr* and *The Mask of Satan* the focus is placed on the landscape and on the characters. It is as if Dreyer and Bava were particularly aware that the real terror springs from an unsettling anxiety, which is deep-seated in the individuals' subconscious, not just in their eyes. In both films, the male heroes seem stuck in a spiritual limbo between heaven and hell, where deliverance comes through the eventual banishment of spiritual, rather than physical evil and, in all that, the *vampiresse* represents more a symbol of liberation from the spiritual crisis of the Victorian Age than a blood-thirsty monster. During that time, spiritual distress came about as a direct reaction to the conservative and corrupted religious standards that were promulgated in society. While religion openly condemned most forms of pleasure, it did not oppose or criticize all the material gluttony and decadence resulting from the industrial revolution. Thus, alternative religions, and even the occult, came to be a form of escape from a cynical society that had lost its concern for spiritual integrity. Victorian women, what is more, fitted into a social mold that was crafted appropriately for their passive, emotionally feeble and purely reproductive role within the societal structure, a role that was entirely relegated to the domestic sphere and that called for women to surrender their sexually dominated nature to a more dutiful attitude. The vampire figure represented a symbol of primary importance for women in that it intersected sexual love with romantic love and could be ambiguously interpreted as animal in some contexts, and spiritual in others. In other words, the *vampiresse* could be used as a metaphor for an emerging new woman who was willing to undertake the sexual and intellectual active roles that she had been denied in the restricted "compound" of the patriarchal world. Interestingly, some scholars have even argued against the widely accepted interpretation of Stoker's *Dracula*, opting for a view that is more open toward a reading of its narrative as a social theory in relation to an awakening dawn of the emancipation of women. Valdine Clemens, for example, argues that the roles of Mina and Lucy, in the novel, call for a revised reading of its text, in that they are representative of a transitional transforming stage for women who were to become increasingly more predatory:

The plot of *Dracula* appears to endorse the movement towards female emancipation that was undermining the bastions of traditional male privilege, for Mina is exposed to the danger of becoming a vampire mainly because she has been denied active participation in the men's "moving world." . . . Lucy is a beautiful and charming *femme fatale*, capable of uttering the "heresy" that she would not mind marrying all three men who proposed to her one day. . . . what needs more consideration is Stoker's emphasis on the hard, impersonal, almost reptilian quality of her desire, which gives the impression of being more predatory than amorous.[24]

Drawing from these notions, Dreyer and Bava recognized the intricate web that strings together female repression with transgressive Sapphic tendencies and revolutionary sexual behavior and thought. These tendencies struggled within an extremely polarized world, supported by a frame of misogynistic myths and biblical misconstructions that had been shaped solely by male discretion. Thus, to analyze and understand those myths is to gain a better understanding of Western society itself, and that is what Dreyer and Bava tried to achieve in their films. Traditionally, the vampire genre relies mainly on the effects of the shadowy surroundings of the victims' bedroom where, deep in the night, and in the light of the full moon, the victim's blood is stolen with a bite on the neck or on the throat, or even on the breast. We could add to that, how most films of that kind play vastly on the Freudian notion of the oral stage of psycho-sexual development, exaggerating and mutating the dualistic idea of comfort and pleasure derived from nourishment through sucking.

While Dreyer and Bava re-created that same old-fashioned Gothic atmosphere, so common to the genre, of morbid dread and repressed sexuality perceived through fog and swirling mists, there is much more in their films than at first sight appears. One major concern for them both is to reveal the illusionary nature of what often seems apparent, all within a surprising degree of sophistication, whether founded on expressionistic or artistic techniques. While being aware that a vampire's biography begins with death, they accentuate the notion that, in passing through all the successive stages of degradation, which separate exuberant life from death, what prevails is a "bloody" lustful anticipation, which is nothing more than the lust of awaiting sexual consummation. However, these two films do not attempt to resolve or alleviate the conflict between males' personal lustful desire and its resulting subconscious anxiety, but rather to unmask the origin of that desire itself and to confront it with its ambivalent nature that generated the fear of the coils of Medusa while succumbing to her charm. What transpires in these films is the realization that there is an ancient archetype hidden within each one of us that seeks satisfaction in the most primitive way: by finding its path through our psyche, it becomes relentless in spite of evolved morality. The uncouth erotic sensuality of the vampiress and her unending power of seduction, so repulsive but so lustful, so loving and yet so dangerous, is used in these works to better represent the overt arousal created by those contrasting human emotions, which are steeped in patriarchal mores. These two films owe their originality to the most powerful exploration of this subject: the dread of empowered female sexuality when unleashed and the wish to control her unbridled senses, versus the yearning for the spells of oblivion, the transitional stages from consciousness to unconsciousness, or simply the hidden desire for a "vampiric" orgasmic dimension to which no one is immune.

Notes

1. Robert Graves and Raphael Patai, *Hebrew Myths: The Book of Genesis* (New York: Doubleday, 1964), 65–69.

2. Elisabeth Young-Bruehl, *Freud on Women: A Reader* (New York: W. W. Norton, 1990), 272.

3. L. C. E. Whitcombe, *Eve and the Identity of Women*, http://witcombe.sbc.edu/eve-women/5eveserpent.html, accessed January 25, 2012.

4. Penelope Shuttle and Peter Redgrove, *The Wise Wound: Menstruation and Everywoman* (Harmondsworth: Penguin, 1980), 263–264.

5. Rosemary Reuther Radford, *Women and Redemption: A Theological History* (Minneapolis: Fortress Press, 1998), 128.

6. Susanne Kord, *Murderesses in German Writing, 1720–1860* (Cambridge: Cambridge University Press, 2009), 52.

7. R. W. Connell, *Masculinities* (Berkeley and Los Angeles: University of California Press, 2005), 15.

8. Geoffrey Ashe, *The Virgin Mary's Cult and Re-emergence of the Goddess* (New York: Arkana, 1976), 152.

9. Tom Milne, *The Cinema of Carl Dreyer* (New York: A. S. Barnes & Co. London: A. Zwemmer Limited, 1971), 114.

10. David Rudkin, *Vampyr* (London: British Film Institute, 2005), 21.

11. Rudkin, *Vampyr*, 18.

12. Mark Nash, *Dreyer* (London: British Film Institute, 1977), 57.

13. Alison Peirse, "The Impossibility of Vision: Vampirism, Formlessness and Horror in Vampyr," *Studies in European Cinema* 5 (2008): 164, http://northumbria.academia.edu/Alison Peirse/Papers/226241/The_Impossibility_of_Vision_Vampirism_Formlessness_and Horror_ In_Vampyr, accessed December 13, 2012.

14. Connell, *Masculinities*, 77.

15. Peirse, "The Impossibility of Vision," 165.

16. Michael Grant, "The Real and the Abomination of Hell," *Kinoeye*, February 3, 2003, http://www.kinoeye.org/03/02/grant02.php, accessed December 13, 2012.

17. Sigmund Freud, *Civilization and Its Discontents*, trans. James Strachey (New York: Norton, 1961), 51.

18. Judith Long Laws and Pepper Schwartz, *Sexual Scripts: The Social Construction of Female Sexuality* (Illinois: The Dryden Press, 1977), 13–14.

19. Troy Howarth, *The Haunted World of Mario Bava* (Surrey: FAB Press, 2002), 28.

20. Phillippe Jullian, *Dreamers of Decadence,* trans. Robert Baldick (New York: Praeger, 1971), 111.

21. Jullian, *Dreamers of Decadence*, 106.

22. Jullian, *Dreamers of Decadence*, 103.

23. Howarth, *The Haunted World of Mario Bava*, 28.

24. Valdine Clemens, *The Return of the Repressed: Gothic Horror from the Castle of Otranto to Alien* (New York: State University of New York Press, 1999), 172–173.

10

The Vampire in Native American and Mesoamerican Lore

James E. Doan

THOUGH THE VAMPIRE AS CONSTITUTED in European and North American traditions (undead creatures rising from their graves to suck on the blood of the living, who in turn create more vampires) does not exist *per se* in pre-Conquest Native American or Mesoamerican belief systems, there are comparable sorcerers and witches with vampiric attributes, possibly influenced by Euro-American folklore. Among the Cherokees, for example, consumption (tuberculosis) was said to have originated with a demonic ogre who ate human lungs and liver and resided in a cave in Tusquittee Mountain, North Carolina.[1] The demon would gain access to individuals by appearing as a family member and then put them to sleep, after which he pierced their side with an iron finger. He would remove the lungs and liver without leaving a scar. Although the individuals would waken and go about their business, they would soon sicken and die. The Cherokees eventually tracked him to his lair and killed him by shooting his iron finger, according to the legend. Since his descendants had learned the technique of removing the lungs and liver, consumption continued for a while, but with less malevolence or strength than existed with the original demon. Similar beliefs regarding tuberculosis and vampirism are found among late 18th- and 19th-century Euro-Americans, particularly in New England, which suggests a connection possibly via diffusion, though it is difficult to ascertain in which direction it operated.[2]

Among the Abenaki of New England, a folktale existed of an old male witch similar to the undead European vampire. The witch died and was buried in a tree located in a grove, which served as a burial place. Later that winter an Indian man and his wife chose to camp in that same grove and built a camp fire. After dinner, the wife looked up into the tree and saw "dark things" hanging. Hus husband said they were ancient dead. However, the wife felt uneasy and stayed awake, while the husband slept. Later the fire went out and the wife heard a gnawing sound "like an animal chewing on a bone."[3] The next morning she found her husband dead: his left side was gnawed away, with his heart missing. She came to a lodge and told them what had happened, but they suspected her of killing her husband. They followed her back to the tree, where they found the husband's body and the dead witch hanging from the tree. They took the witch down and took it from its burial shroud, noticing its mouth and face covered with blood.

In rural Tlaxcala, Mexico, the Nahua people have a legend of vampire witches known as *tlahuelpuchi*, shape-shifting humans who take on animal forms and suck the blood of infants at night, causing their deaths.[4] Most of them are female and are generally more powerful than their male counterparts. They have their own society, with individual territory. They make a pact with the local shamans and other supernatural creatures: the shamans won't turn in a suspected *tlahuelpuchi*. Evidence that a victim has been killed by one of these creatures comes from the bruises on the upper part of their body. *Tlahuelpuchi* detach their body from their legs and then go hunting, usually in the form of a turkey or vulture. They have to perform a ritual before entering the house of a victim, flying over the house in the shape of a cross from north to south and then east to west. They must feed on blood at least once a month or they die. The only way to catch one is in the act of feeding. Their families protect them out of shame and if a family member is responsible for the death of one, the curse will be passed on to him or her. They curse cannot be lifted and, if a *tlahuelpuchi* is identified, it must be killed immediately. Garlic, onions, and metal repel them.[5]

Figures existing in pre-Conquest Aztec and Mayan myths bear a resemblance to the Euro-American vampire: for example, Mictlantecuhtli, lord of the underworld, who commands a legion of the immortal dead and is depicted as a gaunt, skeletal figure covered in blood. He had a cult involved with ritual cannibalism (of flesh at least) and is associated with spiders, owls, and bats, which are creatures of the underworld in Mesoamerican myth. His queen, Mictlancihuatl, is depicted similarly and her cult apparently persists in that of *Santa Muerte*, "Holy Death," a popular figure in modern Mexican folklore. According to one Aztec myth, the brother gods, Tezcatlipoca and Quetzalcoatl, make the sky and the earth from the torn body of the ogress Tlaltecuhtli, who would only let crops flourish if she were fed with human blood. Similar to the division of Tiamat in the Babylonian creation myth, *Enuma Elish*, half of her torso is turned into the sky and the other half into the earth. At night, it was said she could be heard howling for the hearts of men to eat, and her hunger had to be satisfied if she were to continue providing nature's bounty, thus explaining the origins of human sacrifice.[6] According to another myth, Quetzalcoatl has to retrieve some bone in possession of Mictlantecuhtli. Then, his fellow gods create the Fifth Race (the current human race) with this grisly artifact, combining it with the blood of the gods to give it life.[7] In the Mayan creation story, *Popul Vuh*, the hero twins, Hunahpu and Xbalanque, endure several trials in the underworld (Xibalba). In one episode, the bat god, Camazotz, associated with death, night, and sacrifice, snatches off Hunahpu's head and carries it to the ballcourt to be used by the gods in their play, though his brother later restores it and he is made whole.[8]

In 1905, the ethnographer Henry Reichert Voth published a myth collected from the Hopi, who speak a Uto-Aztecan language, dealing with the corn goddess, a central figure in much Native American mythology. What makes this tale distinctive is the actualization of her role as a life- and blood-devouring being, nevertheless essential to the well-being of the tribe. The tale is set in Oraibi, the oldest Hopi village that dates from ca. 1150 CE and located in the Third Mesa (northeastern Arizona). A maiden lives near the Honáni kiva (a subterranean structure used in Puebloan ritual, which also frequently represents the entrance from the Underworld through which the Hopi ancestors emerged). She meets a young man and asks if she may accompany him to watch his father's fields, to which he agrees. She brings along some piki rolls made of *blue corn* (notice emphasis on corn throughout), which she offers and he eats, thus breaking a food taboo. She then offers to play hide and seek with him, but she warns him that the one who is found four times will be killed.

She first hides under the growing *corn* and then under some *corn*stalks. The boy can't find her. When he hides under a saltbush, the girl finds him. She next hides inside a *corn* tassel, and again he can't find her. The boy is then aided by the Sun, who throws down a rainbow allowing the boy to hide behind his back. The girl discovers his whereabouts after she squeezes some drops of milk from her breast and sees the sun reflected in them.[9] She next hides in a watermelon, after first crossing through the *corn*field.

The young man is becoming increasingly distraught when he hears a voice, that of Spider Woman (one of the original creators in Hopi mythology), who lets him into her house and covers the opening with a web. The girl searches for him through the *corn*field to no avail, when she pulls out a quartz crystal mirror from her bosom and sees the opening of the Spider's hole reflected in it. Once again, the youth is discovered. The fourth time the girl crosses the *corn*field and watermelon patch, goes down into a ditch filled with water and turns into a tadpole. Even though the boy drinks water from the ditch, he doesn't realize he is looking at the maiden until she finally reveals herself.

The boy has one last chance: Spider Woman tells him to go east to his uncle, the Áhū, a type of worm living in rotten wood. The Áhū puts him in the loose knot of a corner pole made from the piñon tree, but the girl discovers him after she puts the tips of her right-hand fingers into her mouth, wets them slightly, presses the point of her forefinger into her right ear and hears the youth in his hiding place. Then the girl tells him to return to the shelter where she found him. She digs a hole near one of the corner posts, and then tells him to take off his shirt and beads, whereupon she grabs him by the hair, jerks out a knife from behind her belt, bends him over the hole and cuts his throat, letting his blood run into the hole. She closes up the hole, digs another one to the north of it, drags his body there and buries it.

She then takes the shirt and beads and goes home. She meets the boy's parents who ask where he has gone. She tells them that he drove her away from the fields and she doesn't know where he is. They had killed a sheep a while before but, being sad, they don't eat much of it, so the flies begin devouring the meat. Once, when the woman was driving the flies off with a broom, one of them asked her why she drives him away, but offers to find her child after sucking some of the meat. The fly, perhaps representing a shaman or sorcerer,[10] goes to the cornfield where it sees many tracks, finds where the young man had been killed, sucks some of the blood, then goes a bit further north and discovers the grave. The fly then sucks the blood from the first opening and injects it into the boy's body. Soon the boy's heart begins to beat and after a while he rises up. He says he is thirsty and the fly tells him to drink water from the ditch and they will return to his home. His parents are, of course, happy to see him. The fly tells them that the boy must go to the girl's house, where he will find his shirt and beads. He is to ask for them and when she gives them to him he is to shake both of them at her. Also, if the girl offers him píki rolls, he is to reject them, which he does (this time). The girl then brings him into a room where he sees "a great many things . . . that she had taken from the youths she had killed." He shakes his shirt and beads at her, and then leaves her house. The fly tells his parents they should go to the girl's house to meet him. While waiting for him they hear a noise in the house, some clapping and shaking.

When the boy shook his shirt and beads at her, the girl apparently changed into *Tihkuy Wuhti* (literally "child-protruding woman"). She went into an inner room and came out in a white robe, with her hair tied up like that of a married woman, but with her face and clothes all bloody. When she put on this costume, the noise and rattle continued in the room where the clothes of the slain youths were located. Consisting mainly of buckskins and rabbit skins, the clothes assumed the shape of deer, antelope, and rabbits. They rushed out of the room and left the house. Angry, the girl tried to stop them;

she grabbed the last one and, wiping her hand over her genitalia, she rubbed this hand over the antelope's face, twisted his nose and rubbed his horns, and then let him run. She turned to the people assembled outside and told them that after this they would have great difficulty in hunting those animals: if they had let them alone, they would have stayed close by and then there would be no difficulty. She then left the house and disappeared with the game.

After that she lived on the Little Colorado River, where the deer and antelope abounded for a while. Because she had rubbed her odor over them, they can smell humans from a distance, making it difficult to approach them. According to the tale, she still lives there and Hopis claim to have seen her wrapped up in the white robe covered with blood. She controls the game, and hunters make prayer offerings to her of turquoise and nakwákwosis (prayer feathers) dyed with red ochre (symbolizing blood perhaps). These offerings are always deposited at night.[11] Also called *Tiikuywuuti* in Hopi tradition, she apparently received this name because she died giving birth when the child did not emerge. She makes her home almost anywhere and is considered the "mother of all game animals."[12] In another Hopi myth, she is described as a demonic figure, whose "eyes were two hollow pits and her teeth were bared,"[13] similar to a vampire.

The myth provides several quintessential dualisms (e.g., life vs. death, agriculture vs. hunting) mediated through the contest between the youth and the maiden. Notice the number of repetitions in the myth, which, as Claude Lévi-Strauss points out in "The Structural Study of Myth," "make the structure of the myth apparent."[14] Also notice that the boy is supported by the Sun and Spider Woman, considered the "Grandmother of the sun . . . and the great Medicine Power who sang the people into this fourth world we live in now."[15] The maiden is associated with maize or corn, of vital importance to Hopi subsistence and religion. "For traditional Hopis, corn is the central bond. Its essence . . . pervades their existence. . . . Corn is the Mother in the truest sense that people take in the corn and the corn becomes their flesh, as mother's milk becomes the flesh of the child."[16]

The concept of the mother goddess probably came to America with the first Siberian hunters during the Paleolithic era (before 10,000 BCE). From her original role as mistress of the animals (which still survives in the Hopi myth), she gradually became more closely identified with agriculture, particularly in areas such as Mexico, where maize cultivation began perhaps as early as 8,700 years ago.[17] "Just as the mistress of the animals was represented as identical with an animal, so the goddess or spirit of the corn was represented as identical with the ear of maize"[18] (also reflected in the Hopi myth in the number of corn associations we see). Apparently, among the earliest representations of the goddess in North America are miniature female figurines from Tlatilco, portraying the maize ear and the maiden, with long, yellowish corn hair. These are viewed as forerunners of the later Mexican corn goddesses, such as the Aztec Chicomecoatl and Xilonen.[19]

In the Hopi myth we see a strong connection between violent death and sexuality, with blood taking on multiple functions. First, the girl cuts the boy's throat, draining some of the blood into a hole (remember that even in the European vampire tradition, as in Polidori's *The Vampyre,* a knife may be used rather than the vampire's teeth). This represents, at least in part, the fertilization of the earth through the boy's blood. Later, the fly sucks the blood from this hole and inserts it into the boy, bringing him back to life. Finally, the girl transforms into the bloody Tihkuy Wuhti, and she uses her scent (and the blood) to drive off the wild animals. Though she continues to consort with them, they learn to avoid humans. An early 18th-century Iroquoian myth also records a vampiric goddess, the grandmother of Tharonhiaougon ("Upholder of the Sky of Heavens"), of whom it was said:

> She subsisted only on the flesh of serpents and vipers; she presided at death; she likewise sucked the blood of men, causing them to die of illness and weakness. She is the Queen of the Shades to whom they must pay the tribute of everything that has been buried with their bodies; and she forces them to divert her by dancing before her.[20]

Though possibly reflecting Catholic missionary influence, also seen with the borrowing of the Genesis creation story into Iroquois tradition during the 17th century, the evil grandmother is already found in a Huron creation account collected in 1623.[21] Of course, the notion of blood sacrifice to propitiate deities is known from ancient Mediterranean societies since at least the Bronze Age (hence the prohibitions in Genesis and Leviticus on consuming blood with the flesh from which it is derived, in addition to the well-known reference from the novel *Dracula*). In India, the blood cult of the goddess Kālī ("Black") is known from the 6th century BCE onward,[22] frequently shown complete with scythe, trident, bloody mouth, and severed heads.

Not surprisingly, given their proximity, several Native American religions show signs of Aztec or other Mesoamerican influence.[23] For example, some of the spirit beings (Hopi *katsinim*) found in the southwest—for example, the Tewa horned water serpent, Awanyu, and the Hopi figures, Paalölöqangw and Pahana—show a strong resemblance to the Meosamerican plumed serpent, Gukumatz or Kukulcan (in Mayan tradition) or Quetzalcoatl (Toltec and Aztec).[24] Like the Hopi myth, the cults of several Aztec corn and fertility deities included human sacrifice. Chicomecoatl ("Seven Snakes"), goddess of life and fertility, specifically the harvested corn crop, had a young girl sacrificed to her in August or September:[25] Her priests decapitated a girl, collected her blood and poured it over an effigy of the goddess. Her skin was then flayed and worn by one of the priests. Another aspect of the goddess was Xilonen ("The Hairy One"), referring to the hairs on the unshucked maize.

A similar goddess, Cihuacoatl ("Snake Woman"), connected with childbirth, is frequently shown as a skull-faced old woman carrying the spears and shield of a warrior, possibly referring to the pains of childbirth. Spirits of women who died in childbirth were honored as warriors; known as Cihuatateo, they were thought to haunt crossroads at night to steal children and often resemble Cihaucoatl. These entities are probably a prototype for La Llorona ("The Weeping Woman") in modern Mexican folklore and are sometimes viewed as vampires themselves. They also resemble quite closely the Malayan female vampires called *pontianak* or *langsuir*, ghosts of women who have died in childbirth.[26]

Several Aztec gods were associated with corn, including Cinteotl, Xochipilli, and finally Xipe Totec, a god associated with the sprouting of the maize seed in the springtime, to whom some victims were sacrificed by being flayed alive, which symbolized the maize seeds shedding their skin when new growth bursts forth.[27] Other victims were tied to frames and shot with arrows, their blood being allowed to drip onto a round stone symbolizing the earth. This bears a strong resemblance to a Native American ritual, the Captive Maiden or Morning Star Sacrifice, practiced among the Skiri or Skidi ("Wolf") Pawnees of Nebraska as late as 1838.[28]

This sacrifice was directly related to the maintenance of fertility of the soil and the success of the crops. Typically, a warrior would dream of the Morning Star, usually in the autumn, which meant it was time to begin preparations for the sacrifice. The visionary would consult with the Morning Star priest, who helped him prepare for his journey. The warrior, with help from others, would capture a young person from an enemy tribe, usually a girl, though there is an example of a 10-year-old Mexican boy being captured but ransomed before being killed.[29] According to accounts of the sacrifice, it was held in early spring, before the planting of corn. All the male members of the tribe accompanied the victim to the scaffold, to which she was tied when the Morning Star was due to rise. At the moment it appeared above the horizon, one priest would shoot her with an arrow, after which another priest would make "a small cut over her heart. Taking some of the blood, he painted streaks on his face. . . ."[30] Then, the girl's blood was allowed to drip onto buffalo tongue and heart meat held below her, though not on the ground itself. The next day her body was taken about one-fourth of a mile to the east, where it was placed on the ground face down. The priests sang, "The whole earth, she shall turn into. The whole earth shall receive her blood,"[31] after which they spoke of all the animals and plants that would participate in this process. The whole tribe would participate in the general rejoicing, with a feast of the consecrated bison meat, followed by "ceremonial sexual license to promote fertility."[32] Some of the women would dress in their husband's war clothes, dance around and make fun of the men. Among other activities, "They carried the Mother Corn. . . ."[33]

Apparently, the sacrifice was related to Pawnee belief that the first human being, a girl, was born from the mating of the male Morning Star and the female Evening Star who appeared on earth as an ear of corn wrapped in the skin of a buffalo calf.[34] According to James Murie, a late 19th-century mixed-blood Pawnee interpreter of this tradition, the arrow with which the girl is shot represents an arrow that allowed Morning Star to overcome Evening Star, by touching and killing a certain corn plant growing in her vulva, which prevented him from having intercourse with her.[35] In his study of the sacrifice, in comparison with Aztec belief, Robert Hall suggests this is a frost arrow that could wilt corn. This would also explain the timing of the sacrifice during the appearance of the Morning Star in early spring when frost was still a threat to new plants.

Though not directly related to vampirism, the Morning Star Sacrifice represents another example of a view in Native American tradition that "the blood is the life." Though one can find clear examples of Aztec sources for the Pawnee ritual, one cannot discount the influence of the European vampire tradition, particularly because the corn goddess figure in the Hopi myth seems to be rather unique in Native American tradition. Oraibi was the site of the first Spanish mission in modern-day Arizona, the San Francisco Mission, which flourished from 1629 to 1680, when it was destroyed as part of the Pueblo Revolt. After this revolt the Hopis avoided contact with the Spanish, and regular contact with whites did not begin for another 200 years. Christian missionaries could have introduced the concept of the vampire during the early contact period, at which point it might have contributed to Hopi mythology. Based even on these few examples from North America, I believe one could successfully disagree with folklorist Alan Dundes's assertion that: "The vampire is *not* universal by any means. Native Americans do not have vampires."[36]

A final note regarding Native American and Mesoamerican vampires concerns the contemporary Latin American creature known as the *chupacabra* (literally "goat-sucker"). As early as 1974 in Nebraska and South Dakota and a year later in Puerto Rico, there were reports of an unknown beast that attacked livestock and domestic animals, leaving no trace of blood. "Academics and police examined the carcasses and blamed everything from humans to snakes to vampire bats."[37] A recent study has suggested that later reports (from Puerto Rico in 1995) were influenced by depictions of aliens in horror films and that most of the attacks may be traced to coyotes, wolves, or wild dogs.[38] Nevertheless, this has not prevented the *chupacabra* from becoming an icon in popular culture with films, television programs, and books in English and Spanish featuring it. Like that of other vampires, the legend of the *chupacabra* is becoming immortal.

Notes

1. James Terell, "The Demon of Consumption," *Journal of American Folklore* 5 (1892): 125–126, cited in David Keyworth, *Troublesome Corpses: Vampires & Revenants from Antiquity to the Present* (Southend-on-Sea, Essex, UK: Desert Island Books, 2007), 265.

2. See Michael Bell, *Food for the Dead: On the Trail of New England's Vampires* (New York: Carroll & Graf Publishers, 2002).

3. Rosemary Ellen Guiley, "Vampire Sorcerers and Witches," http://www.visionary living.com/2008/09/17/vampire-sorcerers-and-wtiches/, accessed November 13, 2011.

4. Guiley, "Vampire Sorcerers and Witches."

5. See Hugo G. Nutini and John M. Roberts, *Bloodsucking Witchcraft: An Epistemological Study of Anthropomorphic Supernaturalism in Rural Tlaxcala* (Tucson: University of Arizona Press, 1993) for a further discussion.

6. Cited in C. Scott Littleton, ed., *Mythology: The Illustrated Anthology of World Myth and Storytelling* (San Diego: Thunder Bay Press, 2002), 549, 575.

7. Littleton, *Mythology*, 549.

8. Mary Miller and Karl Taube, *An Illustrated Dictionary of the Ancient Mexicans and the Maya* (London: Thames and Hudson, 2003), 44. My thanks to Trevor Borg for this reference.

9. In Mayan myth one may view the otherworld by means of reflective devices such as mirrors or mercury: see Diane Z. Chase and Arlen F. Chase, "The Architectural Context of Caches, Burials, and Other Ritual Activities for the Classic Period Maya (as Reflected at Caracol, Belize)," in Stephen D. Houston, ed., *Function and Meaning in Classic Maya Architecture* (Dumbarton Oaks, Washington, D.C., 1998), 299–332, cited in Diane Z. Chase and Arlen F. Chase, "Ghosts Amid The Ruins: Analyzing Relationships between the Living and the Dead among the Ancient Maya at Caracol, Belize," in J. Fitzsimmons and I. Shimada, eds., *Living with the Dead: Mortuary Ritual in Mesoamerica* (Tucson: University of Arizona Press, 2011), 91. Perhaps the Hopi myth discussed here reflects similar beliefs.

10. The fly sometimes represents a shaman or sorcerer in Hopi tales: see Ekkehart Malotki, coll., trans. and ed., *Hopi Tales of Destruction* (Lincoln: University of Nebraska Press, 2002), 75–77.

11. From Henry Reichert Voth, *The Traditions of the Hopi* (Chicago: Publications of the Field Columbian Museum 8 (1905), 16–21, reprinted in Karl Kroeber, ed., *Native*

American Storytelling: A Reader of Myths and Legends (Malden, MA: Blackwell Publishing, 2004), 97–101.

12. Malotki, *Hopi Tales of Destruction*, 219.

13. Malotki, *Hopi Tales of Destruction*, 95.

14. In Thomas A. Sebeok, ed., *Myth: A Symposium* (Bloomington and London: Indiana University Press, 1955), 105.

15. Paula Gunn, *The Sacred Hoop: Recovering the Feminine in American Indian Traditions* (Boston: Beacon Press, 1986), 19.

16. Dennis Wall and Virgil Masayesva, "People of the Corn: Teachings in Hopi Traditional Agriculture, Spirituality, and Sustainability," *American Indian Quarterly* 28 (2004): 435–453.

17. "Wild grass became maize crop more than 8,700 years ago," National Science Foundation, March 23, 2009, http://www.eurekalert.org/pub_releases/2009-03/nsf-wgb032309.php, accessed on November 16, 2011.

18. Åke Hultkrantz, "The Religion of the Goddess in North America," in Carl Olson, ed., *The Book of the Goddess Past and Present: An Introduction to Her Religion* (New York: Crossroad Publishing Co., 1986), 204.

19. Hultkranz, "The Religion of the Goddess in North America," 204.

20. W. N. Fenton and E. L. Moore, eds. and trans., *Customs of the American Indians Compared with Customs of Primitive Times by Father Joseph Francois Lafitau* (Toronto: Champlain Society, 1974), vol. 1, 168, cited in Demus Elm and Harvey Antone (Floyd G. Lounsbury and Bryan Gick, trans. and ed.), *The Oneida Creation Story* (Lincoln: University of Nebraska Press, 2000), 23.

21. G. M. Wrong, ed., *The Long Journey to the Country of the Hurons by Father Gabriel Sagard* (Toronto: Champlain Society, 1939), 169–170, cited in Elm and Antone, *The Oneida Creation Story*, 23.

22. Cited in Matthew Beresford, *From Demons to Dracula: The Creation of the Modern Vampire Myth* (London: Reaktion Books, 2008), 22.

23. See, for example, Harold Courlander, *The Fourth World of the Hopis: The Epic Story of the Hopi Indians as Preserved in Their Legends and Traditions* (Albuquerque: University of New Mexico Press, 1987); Robert L. Hall, *An Archaeology of the Soul: North American Indian Belief and Ritual* (Urbana: University of Illinois Press, 1987). Because the Hopis, like some other ancient Anasazi (Puebloan peoples), speak a northern Uto-Aztecan language, mythological connections or parallels may pre-date the split between the northern and southern (e.g., Nahuatl) branches of this linguistic group, possibly as early as 5,000–4,500 years ago, by which time some agriculture was already being practiced in the ancestral Sonoran desert region: see Patrick D. Lyons, *Ancestral Hopi Migrations* (Tucson: University of Arizona Press, 2003), 92. Others place the origins of Hopi culture in the Great Basin region, see, for example, Jerrold E. Levy, "Hopi Shamanism: A Reappraisal," in Raymond J. DeMallie and Alfonso Ortiz, eds., *North American Indian Anthropology: Essays on Society and Culture* (Norman: University of Oklahoma Press, 1994), 307–327.

24. Susan E. James," Some Aspects of the Aztec Religion in the Hopi Kachina Cult," *Journal of the Southwest* 42 (2000): 897–926. See also Malotki, *Hopi Tales of*

Destruction, 5–7, for a discussion of human sacrifice in Hopi legends, and possible connections with Mayan and Aztec cults.

25. http://www.matrifocus.com/IMB09/images/chicomecoatl3.jpg, accessed on November 16, 2011.

26. Andrew Hock-Soon Ng, "'Death and the Maiden': The Pontianak as Excess in Malay Popular Culture," in John Edgar Browning and Caroline Joan (Kay) Picart, eds., *Draculas, Vampires, and Other Undead Forms: Essays on Gender, Race, and Culture* (Lanham, MD: The Scarecrow Press, 2009), 167–185.

27. Littleton, *Mythology*, 68–69.

28. Gene Weltfish, *The Lost Universe: Pawnee Life and Culture* (Lincoln: University of Nebraska Press, 1977), 106–118.

29. Hall, *An Archaeology of the Soul*, 88.

30. Weltfish, *The Lost Universe*, 114.

31. Weltfish, *The Lost Universe*, 114.

32. Weltfish, *The Lost Universe*, 114.

33. Weltfish, *The Lost Universe*, 114.

34. Hall, *An Archaeology of the Soul*, 91.

35. Cited in Hall, *An Archaeology of the Soul*, 91.

36. In his article, "The Vampire as Bloodthirsty Revenant," in Alan Dundes, ed., *The Vampire: A Casebook* (Madison: Univ. of Wisconsin Press, 1998), 161.

37. Robert Bartholomew, *Little Green Men, Meowing Nuns, and Head-Hunting Panics: A Study of Mass Psychogenic Illness and Social Delusion* (Jefferson, NC: McFarland and Co., 2001), 17.

38. Benjamin Radford, *Tracking the Chupacabra: The Vampire Beast in Fact, Fiction, and Folklore* (Albuquerque: University of New Mexico Press, 2011).

11

Vampiric Viragoes: Villainizing and Sexualizing Arthurian Women in *Dracula vs. King Arthur* (2005)

Katherine Allocco

A MERICAN POP CULTURE'S CURRENT OBSESSION with vampires has recast the way that we imagine medieval women and their sexuality. Although the appearance of vampires in British literature is a post-medieval cultural phenomenon probably dating to the 19th century, modern comic-book authors have easily crossed chronological borders and relocated the vampire into Arthurian legend. Although, on many levels, this is absurd, there are some historical, literary, and theological analogues, such as the medieval virago who could arguably explain such connections and naturalize such a leap between the literary tradition of the medieval period and modern pop culture. The modern vampire, like the virago, often occupies a heavily sexualized sphere and possesses sexual powers and tendencies that medieval anatomists and theologians would argue should be more appropriately exercised by men and valiant knights, thus making the virago appear monstrous and unnatural. The modern vampire enjoys the frequent spilling of blood, an activity also associated with viragoes and not considered to be a feminine trait by many medieval Europeans.[1] It is not surprising that it is at King Arthur's legendary court that comic-book authors and artists have vampirized female characters, especially Guinevere and Morgan LeFay, the two women traditionally assigned blame for the collapse of Camelot and for the deaths of many valiant knights of the Round Table. In *Dracula vs. King Arthur* (2005), the creators reveal their own anxieties about women's bodies as they explore the theme of punishing and sacrificing sexually confident and aggressive women, as their versions of Arthurian women are transformed into vampires and then punished for their deviant lusts both for blood and for sex, and eventually sacrificed in order to preserve male honor.

Vampires and Medieval Monsters

There were no vampires in medieval Arthurian and Arthurian-related literature.[2] Many scholars agree that the vampire was first introduced into English literature in 1819 by John William Polidori, whose story *The Vampyre* featured the exotic foreigner Lord Ruthven (alias the earl of Marsden) who befriends Aubrey, a hapless young Englishman, and then kills all the people Aubrey loves before he realizes that Ruthven is a vampire.[3] Polidori creates a number of women characters in the story; however, they are victims and have little power at all. In fact, both of the women in Aubrey's life are sacrificed to the vampire. First, Ruthven kills Aubrey's love interest, Ianthe, while in Greece. Then, upon returning to London, Ruthven seduces Aubrey's sister, who is killed on her wedding night. Aubrey discovers her drained of blood. Aubrey, who had promised to protect Ruthven's secrets, struggles with his loyalty to his new male friend, as well as with his sense of honor, and decides to sacrifice the women he loves in order to protect the homosocial bond of friendship he has forged with Ruthven. In this original vampire story, women are denied any form of power and are killed for becoming entangled with the vampire. The women are all victims and do not become monsters themselves. The supernatural power that Ruthven exercises has been gendered and assigned only to men. Although Ruthven is a monster, the romantic tale creates a mysterious and enticing aura around him that permits the reader to forgive him somewhat. Many of these tropes—the male monster and female victim, the struggle to protect male honor, and the sacrifice of women—also appeared in medieval Arthurian and Arthurian-related literature with supernatural themes.

There were several other types of monsters and supernatural creatures in the *Lais* of Marie de France, for example.[4] *Bisclavret* tells the tale of a baron/werewolf who appears as a tragic and romantic figure, rather than a terrifying monster.[5] The unfortunate werewolf possesses no real supernatural powers beyond those of his transformation. Out of a chivalric impulse to protect his lady love, Bisclavret makes tremendous efforts to hide his identity, which he sees more as a defect than a source of power. Soon after the baroness learns of her husband's secret, she betrays him by hiding his clothing, thus rendering him incapable of resuming his humanity.[6] Bisclavret spends years trapped in his werewolf body, although he is able to remain at court because of his demonstrated loyalty to the king, who adopts the gentle beast. Bisclavret and the king create a homosocial masculinist tie, much like Ruthven and Aubrey's, which supersedes the loyalty demanded of his marriage vows and by the code of chivalry, which requires him to protect all ladies, especially a baroness. Bisclavret's character evokes sympathy in the reader, who hesitates to think of him as a monster and irritation with the unfaithful wife who failed to live with the monster and keep his identity secret. The lady suffers by having her nose bitten off by the werewolf and by being physically tortured by the king. Her descendants also bear the mark of her shame as the author tells us that many of the women of her line were born without noses.[7]

France introduces the supernatural in order to heighten the romance and mystery of her tale. She is not interested in villainizing the shapeshifter or in crafting frightening tales. Most importantly, the woman in this tale becomes the victim of the supernatural character. The baroness had to suffer both the physical pain of having her nose bitten off and the torture enacted by the king and the social stigma of knowing that she had passed on a visible defect and sign of humiliation to future generations. The baroness has to make several sacrifices in the story by compromising her body and her honor, but she is still seen as the villain of the *lai* rather than the victim. The wife in this story can easily be read as a victim of the monster she unwittingly married. The baron had kept a secret from her while they were married. She became suspicious because he disappeared for three days each month. She assumed that he had a lover and was unfaithful to her. Reluctantly, he revealed his secret. She is horrified to learn that she had been married to a monster, which France describes in the opening lines as a "ferocious beast which, when possessed by this madness, devours men, causes great damage and dwells in vast forests."[8] The only way that she could save herself was by recruiting a knight to steal his clothes while he was in a werewolf state. The knight she chose was one who had loved her, but whose love she had never returned. Frightened of her monster husband, she sacrificed herself by offering to become the knight's lover if he will only save her from the werewolf. The wife does not want to give herself to this man; she does not want to be disloyal, but she fears for her safety and presumably for her soul.[9]

Yet, readers are not always inclined to sympathize with the baroness. The werewolf remains noble and courtly even when in a bestial form. Because he seems to retain his humanity and his chivalry even while transformed, he must be a truly noble knight deserving of the reader's support and sympathy.[10] Like a modern vampire, Bisclavret exists in between the world of the human and the monster, preserving his manners and grace even when in werewolf form. Given his great nobility, it seems unforgivable for the baroness not to remain by his side. Surely her inability or refusal to recognize his purity and goodness indicates a flaw in her person and in her execution of uxorial duties. Because of this, she becomes the monster, the unfaithful wife, the adulterous conspirator who retaliates against her husband with the same incommunicative dishonesty that had marked his relationship with her. Her punishment then transforms her into a monster, a disfigured freak, who is banished from the king's court to live in exile with her lover and their nose-less daughters. In this tale, the brush with the supernatural injures the female character, villainizing and dehumanizing her, even though she had never possessed any magical powers of her own nor did she harm anyone, though it is implied that her bloodthirsty werewolf husband must have.

There are several Arthurian and Arthurian-related texts that do include stories of magical women who flicker through the forests and disappear as men approach them, such as in *The Wife of Bath's Tale,* or women under enchantment whose behavior prophesizes the acts of great men, such as in Chrétien de Troyes' *Perceval, or The Tale of the Grail.* Chrétien de Troyes's Arthurian romances frequently include enigmatic and unexplained characters and details that lend his tales an aura of phantasmagoric mystery, but the major female characters who possess power and agency seldom wield super-human powers. Even the minor female characters who do seem to be magical rarely exercise control over these strange powers and often operate as agents of the great knights around whom the tale revolves, such as the maiden who never laughs in *The Tale of the Grail.* The jester explains that the maiden will not laugh until she "has seen the man who will be the supreme lord among all knights,"[11] Her enchantment and prophecy serve as a vehicle for male power and for the knight who will assume his place of supremacy among his peers once she has laughed. Her supernatural power is not monstrous, rather it underscores the dependency that women had upon men, thus reinforcing conventional gender roles and promoting heroes. Powerful women, on the other hand, who had freed themselves from their gender roles, often appeared as unnatural women in this literary canon, which made them appear monstrous. Perhaps the best example of the threatening unnatural woman that Arthurian literature and medieval society could offer was the virago.

The Virago

The virago appeared frequently in medieval history, literature, and art. The word takes its root from the Latin *vir,* which means man. Therefore, the virago was specifically construed as a woman who had assumed "male" traits and transgressed popularly accepted gender roles. Women could be considered viragoes for a variety of unfeminine activities, including military activity, wearing male clothing, even celibacy. Unlike the scold or the shrew or the nag, she was reviled not for exhibiting amplified "feminine" roles, such as scolding or nagging, but rather for pretending to be a man. She presumed a power that was not hers and thus upset social norms. This disruption became especially distressing when she began to display male sexual characteristics. The virago was not just unnatural; she was also dangerous and monstrous and often generated society's tremendous anxiety over the unstable and unruly character of women's bodies.

Eve, of course, exemplifies the ultimate virago whose bid for agency and insistence on free will earned such severe punishment that she marked all Christians with original sin.[12] Medieval women struggled against Eve's influence and tried to rise above internal impulses that could be perceived as Evian and thus disruptive to society.[13] Often women were instructed to strive to emulate Eve's foil, the Virgin Mary, whose example of submission and purity provided medieval women with a more desirable counterexample and paradigm of femininity.[14] Mary represented an impossible ideal whose chaste, submissive behavior contrasts sharply with both Guinevere and Morgan LeFay, who are neither sexless nor mothers in a legitimate sense. Because of their adulterous and incestuous sexualities, their Evian behavior distanced them from any association with Marian virtue and thus edged them more toward the camp of the monstrous virago.

Guinevere and Morgan LeFay are not the only transgressive Arthurian women. Arthurian literature is replete with sexually aggressive and dangerous women. Examples can easily be found in Chrétien de Troyes's Lancelot, or The *Knight of the Cart* and *Sir Gawain and the Green Knight*. Throughout their quests, both Gawain and Lancelot find themselves menaced by manipulative women who try to seduce them and compromise their chivalric conduct. In the *Knight of the Cart*, Lancelot must fend off an aggressive host as the lady who lodges him begs him to sleep with her. He submits to her entreaties and lies uncomfortably next to her but will not touch her in spite of all of her clever manipulations. Eventually, she is so humiliated that she leaves.[15] Sir Gawain also must constantly rebuff the flirtatious advances of the Lady of Sir Bercilak's Castle. The author sets her up as the aggressor in the relationship and places her in Gawain's bedchamber again and again. One morning, she slips into his room. "The Hero, embarrassed lay hurriedly back down, pretending to sleep" (lines 1189–1190). She laughs coquettishly and says "you're a careless sleeper to let someone creep up on you like this. You're caught. Unless there's a truce, I'll besiege you in bed" (lines 1208–1211).[16] The dynamic is clear. She wishes to seduce him, but he does not wish to offend his host, whose company and support he values more than hers. Gawain resists her advances and is then rewarded by her husband.[17] Both knights successfully defend their honor from these unnatural and shameless women who only embarrass themselves before the characters and the reader.

The contrast between these sexual viragoes and the Virgin Mary is set up beautifully in *Sir Gawain and the Green Knight*. Gawain has an image of Mary painted inside of his shield (lines 647–649).[18] Moreover, he frequently prays to her for assistance (lines 736–739).[19] The Virgin Mary guides the chivalrous knight on his quest and provides him with strength and spiritual comfort.[20] By the end of the tale, Gawain has proven himself to be noble and good and victorious. Readers are reminded of the proper model of medieval femininity and reassured that the virago cannot supplant the great power of the Virgin Mary. Clearly, women who sought to redefine their limited positions in society and take power for themselves were villainized by their contemporaries and criticized for perverting established institutions and male spheres of power.[21] Most unforgivably, they were perceived as doing so through the vehicle of their own sinful bodies and often in the pursuit of satisfying their own lusts and sexual appetites.

Medieval Sexuality and the Clitoris

Women's sexuality was a popular topic of debate in the medieval period and inspired much discussion about women's bodies and sexual appetites. Medieval European scholars, theologians, natural philosophers, and anatomists inherited their information from Greek and Arabic texts, including such indisputable authorities as Galen and Avicenna, who provided a foundation for further discoveries and observations in the medieval period beginning with Gilbert the Englishman's *Compendium medicinae*, published for King John in the early 13th century.[22] Through their reading and creation of these anatomical works, these scholars were well aware of the clitoris, even if they had a confused notion of what exactly it was or how it functioned.[23] Karma Lochrie argues that in Gilbert's section on the usefulness of foreplay he uses the word *nervus*, a term usually reserved for descriptions of the penis, to refer to the clitoris.[24] Lacking a gynospecific vocabulary, he resorts to the phallic, thus drawing a close connection between men's and women's bodies. This connection between the penetrative penis and the sensitive clitoris exposes his own anxiety and uncertainty about women's anatomy.

Anatomists of both Antiquity and the medieval period understood the clitoris's important role as a site of sexual pleasure but never fully innovated an accurate vocabulary to describe its appearance and purpose.[25] Two primary models seemed to prevail. One viewed the clitoris much as it truly is, as an external female organ that is a site of sexual excitement.[26] The other presented the clitoris as a diseased protuberance that could become uncontrollably enlarged until it resembled a penis, with all its penetrative powers.[27]

This tumescent model proposed an engorged pseudo-phallus that filled with blood and redirected the body's circulatory system with the aim of altering its natural (and inferior) female genitalia. Both models could precipitate fear of a woman's unnaturally aggressive interest in sex and validate the imposition of more normative means of restricting women's sexuality, primarily through marriage, which placed sexual power in the husband's hands and refocused women's sexual energies on procreation and motherhood.

There is a close connection between this second medical model of the clitoris and the virago. Viragos were perceived as women who had altered their physiologies and virilized themselves both in body and mind. The virago arrogantly rejected her natural feminine body and instead underwent a series of unorthodox behavioral changes that affected her very physiology. It was popularly believed that viragoes stopped menstruating because they retained their menstrual fluid.[28] Viragoes' bodies became masculinized because they no longer shed their superfluous fluids in a fashion typical of women, and it was assumed that they now performed these corporal purges in a more masculine manner. As a corollary, the masculine non-menstruating body would presumably soon acquire male sexual desire and possibly even penetrative powers. All of this was highly unnatural and therefore undesirable, thus rendering the virago an object of scorn and disgust. A post-Freudian modern reader could even read this blood-sucking protuberance as a fang which is part of a *vagina dentata*.

This amenorrheic, fanged-vagina virago greedily hordes her menstrual blood and uses it to transform her body into a man's. She bloats on excess blood, not only consuming her own body in an attempt to enter a masculine sphere of power, but she also overturns the assignation of bodily humors that had been entrenched in Western natural philosophy since Hippocrates and Aristotle.[29] In Antiquity and the medieval period, women were not associated with the masculine sanguine humor, which imbued them with hot and wet qualities and with the characteristics of courage and hope.[30] Women, instead, were dominated by the black bile humor and configured as cold and dry, thus making their bodies weaker and less active in conception. The virago changes her medical category and transgresses into a male sphere because of the power she receives from retaining her own blood. This state is a serious gender disorder and appears to prefigure the vampire whose relationship to blood also imbues her with power that she should not possess. A vampire is not entirely different from the amenorrheic virago. Vampires ingest blood and draw their power from feeding off living humans. Given the sexual nature of vampiric feeding, women vampires would naturally feed off male victims taking their blood, the sanguine humor, and therefore gain access to men's bodies in an extremely unorthodox and unregulated way. Just as viragoes obtained the strength of a man, undead vampires acquired the physical strength of the living, which is something that they should not have access to had they remained in their graves rather than being unnaturally re-animated. The female vampire drains men of their blood and virility in order to temporarily prolong her own unnatural existence until it is time to feed again. The vampire becomes a hunter, using seduction and deception to lure men before she bites them, penetrates them, and consumes their masculine power for her own selfish needs and desires—like the medieval virago.

Viragoes and Arthurian Women

Both Guinevere and Morgan LeFay have been cast as viragoes in some medieval literature and in a variety of media in modern popular culture. They have been frequently construed as sexually unconventional and therefore disruptive and destructive women. Guinevere's adulterous relationship with Lancelot leads to Arthur's heartbroken retreat from the public sphere and the fall of Camelot. Morgan LeFay's incestuous liaison with Arthur produces Mordred, the bastard son who is often credited with wielding the mortal blow that destroys "The Once and Future King." Through their rejection of prescribed sexual and gender roles, Guinevere and Morgan imagine themselves to have the same sexual agency as men by choosing their own lovers and transgressing cultural taboos. Medieval women, and particularly medieval queens, were expected to safeguard their chastity and to focus their sexual activity on producing legitimate heirs who they would raise to become wise princes and future kings. Neither Guinevere nor Morgan LeFay produces a legitimate heir, and their sexual choices result in the punishment of barrenness for the queen and a bastard inbred for the sorceress. Their actions lead to the destruction of this paradisiacal kingdom and to a large bloodletting as the knights and Arthur himself are cut down and destroyed. Arthur is the martyr and hero whose spilled blood vaults him into a position of legendary holiness and authority.[31] By contrast, both women are remembered as emasculating viragoes who seem to enjoy the very unfeminine desire to make men bleed and who in modern comics have been transformed into vampires.

Dracula vs. King Arthur

Dracula vs. King Arthur is an independent four-issue mini-series published by Silent Devil. In this comic, Count Vlad makes a deal with Lucifer that allows him to travel back in time to the age of Arthur. The authors are very sympathetic to Dracula, whom, clearly inspired by Bram Stoker, they portray

as a romantic hero who had lost everything he loved in the process of realizing a divine plan and whom they contrast with Arthur, a man that possesses
everything and deserves none of it. Lucifer transforms Dracula into a vampire
and then sends Arthur a vision that initiates the quest for the Grail, thus
facilitating Lucifer's plan to watch Dracula destroy Arthur. Arthur's absence
from Camelot makes the community vulnerable when Dracula arrives and
begins to turn all the major characters into vampires. First, he transforms
Morganna, who had at first resisted him but then succumbed after losing
a magical battle. Readers are not surprised that Morganna, whose lust for
power leads her down all sorts of unholy paths, becomes a vampire. What
is so shocking about the tale is the constant, merciless, and rapid turning of
all the other characters. Guinevere is seduced by Dracula and turned into a
vampire. Guinevere, in turn, seduces and turns Lancelot. Dracula and his
minions then turn Mordred, and Percival's sister, Amide, then Bors, and
then Galahad. The new vampires capture Arthur, whom they tie to a crucifix,
so that Morganna, Lancelot, Mordred, and Dracula can suck and feed from
him. In a full-panel drawing, Morganna hovers hungrily over Arthur's penis
licking her lips and clearly enjoying the feast of this restrained and weakened
man whose essence she now ingests. Her particularly sexual position reminds
readers of her sexual and political perversions and of the close connection of
the female vampire's sexuality and her acquisition of power.

Guinevere's turning is particularly sexual, and she clearly has no desire to
resist Dracula's seduction (issue 2).[32] Dracula tells her that she will no longer
have to be alone and unloved and that her heart and land will be at peace. Once
a vampire, she sheds her Virgin Mary blue dress that covers her wrists and
ankles and slips into a red dominatrix outfit complete with Amazonian breast-
plates and a spider web bodice in which she prances and glides about.[33] Just a
few pages later in the issue, when Guinevere bites Lancelot, she tells him that
he doesn't have to fight for her anymore and that they can be together forever.
She bites him, wraps her hand around his long, hard sword, thus cutting her
own hand, and then licks her own blood before she kisses him. The juxtaposi-
tion of sex, violence, and blood reminds readers of her virago roots and reinforces her role as an adulteress. Even worse, Guinevere clearly shares Dracula
with Morganna, just as she shares herself with Lancelot. She appears to be the
instigator of a complex and sinful web of infidelity and indefensible lust.

Since Thomas Mallory's *Morte D'Arthur*, Guinevere has served as the
scapegoat for the fall of Camelot. In *Dracula vs. King Arthur*, modern writers punish her for her irresistible love for Lancelot, by stripping her of her
humanity and by exposing her adulterous sexuality. In issue 3, when Arthur
confronts the demonic Guinevere who is kneeling at Dracula's feet, she tells
Arthur that she is much happier since Dracula "calmed her, tamed her." She
says that she was so restless before, but that she has now been saved. Dracula

smugly reaffirms her claim and then brags about how he had also tamed Morganna, whom he had "brought to heel." The authors use language that dehumanizes these women who apparently deserve to be thought of as pets or domesticated dogs because they have prioritized their desire for sexual fulfillment and for power over their prescribed uxorial roles. By stepping outside of their "natural" spheres and social roles, they have surrendered the right to be treated as anything but a monster.

Amide, the other woman who is vampirized, is equally objectified. She is hunted, captured, and then taken to Merlin's laboratory. Merlin ties her to a rack and conducts a number of experiments on her in an unsettling form of vivisection. He has no remorse about torturing his former apprentice and seems easily to slip into viewing his former protégée as an inanimate object and exploiting her body. Such a seamless transition implies that Merlin had already had practice in objectifying Amide and in understanding that she was inferior to himself. This relationship is hinted at when he first sends her into danger, by asking her to bring a message to the armies that were battling Dracula's vampire soldiers. Readers wonder if he had intended for her to be turned just for this very purpose. He performs a number of experiments on her in order to educate the knights in the art of vampire killing. Once Arthur returns with the Grail, a distressed Perceval tries to rescue his poor, doomed sister by pouring water from the Grail into her mouth.[34] She explodes in a grisly and graphic full-page dismantling of a woman's body.[35] Merlin barely reacts.

In the 4th issue, Guinevere and Morganna experience grisly deaths similar to Amide's as just punishments for their adherence to Dracula. Guinevere is decapitated by Arthur when they meet on the battlefield. Guinevere, dressed in Amazonian armor and brandishing a sword, backs into Arthur, who addresses her as "my faithful wife" before lifting his sword and drawing it across her neck. Her head flies across the battlefield, and Arthur barely gives it a second thought. Morganna is defeated by Merlin in a battle of "magicks." Merlin manages to turn her own spell against her and reminds her that because she surrendered her soul for vampiric immortality that she is an unnatural woman and that the "earth no longer supports [her] magic." Both women suffer deaths that are unusual for their gender. Guinevere dies as a man does by assuming a warrior's role and striding onto the battlefield. Morganna dies like a soulless demon defeated by a greater sorcerer and immediately banished to Hell. Both of these deaths are presented as understandable and well deserved because neither woman maintained her appropriate gender role. Both women ambitiously pursued a more masculine path toward power by becoming vampires and using their sexuality to try to destroy Arthur. Their bid for power and inappropriate control of their sexuality made them monstrous and dangerous. The only possible atonement would be their sacrificial deaths, preferably in as bloody and disrespectful a manner as possible.

Readers have little sympathy for either woman, not only because of their literary legacy, but primarily also because they enjoyed being vampires. Guinevere embraced the sexual freedom that was now available to her, which is presented as contemptible even though she clearly felt abandoned and un-loved by the king. Morganna revels in her new-found power, the only thing that readers are to believe that she actually values. She happily calls Dracula "master" and willingly participates in his regicidal plots. The proud and ar-rogant Morganna allows herself to be Dracula's servant because she sees it as a more direct avenue to power. Morganna thus admits that she needs a man and that, in spite of her magical abilities and talents, she still doubts her own agency and probably yearns for a more conventional arrangement in which she subordinates herself to a man, except that Dracula is no longer a man. He is a demon who received his own powers through a pact with Satan. Morganna's ill-guided attempt to be both virago and wife fails. So, she is pun-ished. Since she has deviated from the proper uxorial and feminine path of wife and mother, she may not return. In spite of her efforts, no man will have her except for this bloodthirsty vampire whose sponsorship will condemn her soul to hell for eternity. The message is clear and pretty clearly medieval: women who reject their proper gender roles will never be readmitted to con-ventional society and will be made to suffer in their afterlife for their selfish and destructive choices.

It is very telling that the creators do not turn Arthur, who is the only char-acter with possible immortal roots, into a vampire. It is Thomas Mallory's *Morte D'Arthur* that introduces the idea of "The Once and Future King," implying that Arthur will return to save Britain at its darkest hour.[36] This legendary component could have easily lent itself to vampirism. Arthur is not exactly undead, but he does not seem to be entirely dead either. The idea that he will arise from the grave and return centuries in the future (again one thinks of *Camelot 3000*) imbues him with supernatural powers and with an undead status much more vampiric than the other characters. Arthur, how-ever, is constructed as a martyr rather than a demon and as the sacrificial king whose honor remained intact even beyond the grave. His humanity is equally unassailable, and in a Christian worldview, it would impossible to conceive of his martyrdom, particularly at the hand of sinful viragoes, being punished by the curse of vampirism.[37] His masculinity remains equally intact. In the final pages of the 4th issue, Arthur kills Dracula, after he had himself been impaled by Mordred. Rising to his feet, with a wooden lance sticking out of his body, Arthur summons the strength to decapitate Dracula. Then he dies, falling on top of Dracula's bleeding body penetrating Dracula a second time with the lance that has killed him. Dracula's body lies broken beneath the great king in a very sexually domineering pose reminding readers that Arthur's proper monogamous heterosexual body is triumphant over the perverse and demonic Dracula who polluted himself with the undead Guinevere and Morganna.

Dracula vs. King Arthur clearly adheres to the misogynistic literary tradition in which much medieval Arthurian literature was created. The authors' choice to vampirize Guinevere and Morganna and to then kill them both so mercilessly demonstrates the close connection between the virago and the monster. Women who seek to define their own destiny and to pursue happiness on their own terms are not only unnatural, but in this case also supernatural. Once they have stepped outside of nature, as Eve did, they can no longer be protected by the rules of society or chivalry and must be euthanized—preferably in a grisly way. Peggy McCracken has argued that sacrificing women is a necessary initiation ritual for the young knight who wishes to prove himself to his male peers and achieve a fully chivalric identity. She has studied numerous episodes from Grail literature in which both Percival and Gawain are responsible for the rape, abuse, pain, and/or deaths of a number of female characters in Arthurian literature. She notes that once these women have been sacrificed, Percival and Gawain can then be considered proper knights.[38] In *Dracula vs. King Arthur*, the authors sacrifice Guinevere, Morganna, and Percival's sister by not only killing them, but by also condemning their souls to hell after their deaths, thus requiring the ultimate sacrifice from a medieval point of view. Readers feel that this type of sacrifice is appropriate because these women had so dangerously transgressed their own natures, pursued power inappropriately and allied themselves with Satan. Their sacrifice, however, fails to make a knight out of Dracula, who is killed by an undeniably masculine Arthur and remains a monster.

Conclusion

Arthurian women have been villainized for centuries. This latest stage of stripping them of their very humanity and recasting them as vampires and monsters realizes an entrenched misogyny that seeks to punish women who wield power and wish to control their own bodies and sexuality. Sexually aggressive women are particularly distressing for a medieval sensibility, which viewed the virago as upsetting political and social roles and queering any sort of gender norm. Vampires do much of the same. They certainly disrupt social order, and the penetrative vampiric woman strikes fear (and lust) into the hearts of the strongest men. Vampirizing Arthurian viragoes reminds readers that these women are the bad guys, that they are inverted, castrating, selfish monsters who bring down the great kingdom of Camelot. Because of their heinous crimes, these characters must be sacrificed if chivalry, kingship, and knighthood are to succeed. Then and now, there is no room for the woman hero or for the supernatural woman who could save the kingdom and usher in a new age of peace and goodness for mankind. Rather, the medieval virago operates much as the vampire does by flaunting her unnatural power and striking terror into the hearts of righteous men. It is only through their violent and grisly deaths that order can once more be restored and gender norms can be happily resumed, thus establishing a stable and natural society.

Notes

1. Peggy McCracken, "The Amenorrhea of War," *Signs* 28 (2003): 625–643.
2. Recent scholars have produced studies about the folkloric creature, the "revenant," which appeared in some medieval chronicles and could lend themselves to foreshadowing of vampires. The revenant was the reanimated corpse of a dead neighbor or relative who returned from the grave for his or her own evil deeds. Some 12th- and 14th-century English writers mentioned the revenant, including William of Newburgh. See Jacqueline Simpson, "Repentant Soul or Walking Corpse? Debatable Apparitions in Medieval England," *Folklore* 114 (2003): 389–402; Marie Anne Polo de Beaulieu, "Paroles de fantôme: Le cas du revenant d'Alès (1323)," *Ethnologie française*, nouvelle série, T. 33e, No. 4e, VOIX, VISIONS, APPARITIONS (2003): 565–574; Nancy Caciola, "Wraiths, Revenants and Ritual in Medieval Culture," *Past & Present* 152 (1996): 3–45.
3. The full text can be found at Project Gutenberg: http://www.gutenberg.org/ebooks/6087.
4. Marie de France did compose at least two *lais* that were set at King Arthur's court, although *Bisclavret* was not one of those. *Bisclavret* was later expanded by an anonymous Breton author into the lai of *Melion*, which was set at the court of King Arthur. The full text can be found in translation at http://www.liv.ac.uk/soclas/los/Werwolf.pdf.
5. Werewolves seem to have been somewhat popular in medieval literature. See Laurence Hauf-Lancner, "La métamorphose illusoire: des théories chrétiennes de la métamorphose aux images médiévales du loup-garou," *Annales, Histoire, Sciences Sociales*, 40e Année, No. 1 (1985): 217.
6. Marie de France, *The Lais*, trans. Glyn S. Burgess and Keith Busby (New York: Penguin Books, 1999), 69.
7. France, *The Lais*, 71–72.
8. France, *The Lais*, 68.
9. Jerry Root, "Courtly Love and the Representation of Women in the 'Lais' of Marie de France and the 'Coutumes de Beauvaisis' of Philippe de Beaumanoir," *Rocky Mountain Review of Language and Literature* 57 (2003): 15.

10. Caroline Walker Bynum, "Metamorphosis, or Gerald and the Werewolf," *Speculum* 73 (1998): 1001.

11. Chrétien de Troyes, "The Tale of the Grail," in *Arthurian Romances*, trans. William Kibler (New York: Penguin, 1991), 394.

12. Augustine conducted a lengthy analysis of the nature of Eve's soul. He concluded that because her soul had not been created during the original 6 days as Adam's had that it was naturally inferior and thus more inclined toward sin, St. Augustine, *The Literal Meaning of Genesis* ii, trans. John Hammond Taylor (New York: Newman Press, 1982), 99.

13. Elaine Pagels has argued that it was not unusual for the early Christians to interpret the Bible fairly literally and to therefore, perceive all women as potential Eves, Elaine Pagels, *Adam, Eve and the Serpent* (New York: Random House, 1988), 63.

14. Mary was the sexless mother who brought mankind's savior into the world without the taint of sex or sensuality: Peter Brown, *The Body and Society* (New York: Columbia University Press, 1988), 444.

15. Chrétien de Troyes, "The Knight of the Cart," in *Arthurian Romances*, trans. William Kibler (New York: Penguin, 1991), 219–223.

16. Bernard O'Donoghue, trans., *Sir Gawain and the Green Knight* (New York: Penguin Books, 2006), 39.

17. However, Gawain is ultimately punished by Sir Bercilak for failing to reveal a magical garter, which the Lady has given him. Moreover, she has been sent by Morgan LeFay to punish Arthur and his court.

18. *Sir Gawain and the Green Knight*, 22.

19. *Sir Gawain and the Green Knight*, 25.

20. In fact, the author reinforces a Marian model of correct feminine behavior by intimating that Gawain's quest to defeat the Green Knight had probably been instigated by the meddlesome Morgan LeFay whose disregard for honor, propriety, and even manhood forced the great men of Arthur's courts to risk their lives: Clare R. Kinney, "The (Dis)Embodied Hero and the Signs of Manhood in *Sir Gawain and the Green Knight*," in *Medieval Masculinities: Regarding Men in the Middle Ages*, ed. Clare Lees (Minneapolis: University of Minnesota Press, 1994), 55.

21. See Carolyn Dinshaw, Getting Medieval: Sexualities and Communities, Pre- and Postmodern (Durham, NC: Duke University Press, 1999).

22. Galen spoke of women's organs as if they were less perfect versions of men's. Women had testes like men but were unable to produce generative seed from them. Instead, they produced a colder, scantier semen, Galen, *On the Usefulness of the Part of the Body*, trans. Margaret Tallmadge May (Ithaca: Cornell University Press, 1968), 630–631.

23. Karma Lochrie, *Heterosyncrasies: Female Sexuality When Normal Wasn't* (Minneapolis: University of Minnesota Press, 2005), 71.

24. Lochrie, *Heterosyncrasies*, 85.

25. Karma Lochrie has argued that Allison, the narrator of *The Wife of Bath's Tale*, does refer specifically to her clitoris in cloaked terms and that she plays many language games in order to provide herself with an accurate sexual vocabulary, Lochrie, *Heterosyncrasies*, 94–95.

26. Thomas Lacqueur has argued that it was the Austrian anatomist Josef Hyrtl (1810–1894) who finally named the clitoris and derived its name from the Greek verb, which translates as "to titillate," Thomas Lacqueur, *Making Sex: Body and Gender from the Greeks to Freud* (Cambridge: Harvard University Press, 1990), 237.

27. Lacqueur, *Making Sex*, 92.

28. Lochrie, *Making Sex*, 88.

29. Aristotle, *De Partibus Animalium I and De Generatione Animalium I*, trans. D.M. Balme (Oxford: Clarendon Press, 1992), 47.

30. Peggy McCracken has argued that "legendary, fictional and historical narratives from pre-modern Europe imagine the heroic relationship between blood and war in gendered terms," McCracken, "Amenorrhea of War," 626. Bleeding on the battlefield was considered to be much more honorable and masculine than any type of bleeding that women tended to do. Menstruation and childbirth were viewed as colder and weaker activities, reminding the medieval audience again of how unnatural it was for a woman to fight, bear arms like an Amazon, or bleed from a wound inflicted in battle. Given how gendered even the biological act of bleeding could be, it becomes clear that medieval women were limited to a very specific relationship with blood and that any type of physical contact, especially with men, that resulted in bleeding or blood loss was considered unnatural and possibly monstrous. Therefore, Amazons and viragoes transgressed yet another social norm by trying to redefine their relationship with their own blood and with male warriors.

31. Iain Thomson, "Deconstructing the Hero," in *Comics as Philosophy*, ed. Jeff McLaughlin, (Jackson, MS: University of Mississippi Press, 2005), 112–114.

32. Please note that there are no page numbers in any of these issues.

33. The spider web evokes images of other bloodsuckers and may also pay homage to *Camelot 3000* in which Morgan LeFay resurrects herself into an enormous black widow (issue 12, p. 18). The Amazonian reference is also relevant to the legacy of the virago. In medieval literature, Amazons serve as a popular form of fictional viragoes and sexual deviants. Since Antiquity, authors told stories about these warrior women who lived isolated on an island without men and ruled by queens who had no king consort. In addition to such overt political deviation, they also physically mutilated their own bodies as a clear statement that they had rejected traditional feminine roles. By cutting off their right breasts, they improved their archery skills, and also eliminated their maternal powers by reducing their ability to breastfeed. They pursued their virago's agenda so thoroughly that they altered their very bodies, effectively distancing themselves from any future comparison to the Virgin Mary. Queens Penthesilea, Hippolyta, and Menalippe were warrior women whose interactions with men took place either on the battlefield or during their annual sexual encounters with strangers from a neighboring tribe who were essentially used for their semen and little else. These Amazons descended on the Gargareans once a year to impregnate themselves and then they left. With the Amazons we can see another vampiric precursor. The Amazon women suck the men dry of both blood and semen with little attachment to the various men that they either attack or with whom they have sex. They weave a path of destruction and sexual deviance wherever they travel, killing great heroes and stealing their sperm. Their behavior makes great warriors shudder

and seek shelter from these monstrous women. These viragoes completely disrupted society and presented an unwelcome threat to proper models of feminine virtue and demure queenship. Although there were no direct references to Amazons in Arthurian literature, their reference in such popular and canonical works as *The Canterbury Tales*, *The Book of the City of Ladies*, and Boccaccio's *Teseide* demonstrate that their legends circulated widely in the medieval imagination.

34. Peggy McCracken analyzes the myriad relationships that Percival has to blood throughout his quest for the Grail, Peggy McCracken, "The Poetics of Sacrifice: Allegory and Myth in the Grail Quest," *Yale French Studies* 95 (1999): 152–168.

35. Amide has appeared in Arthurian literature under many other names, including Dindraine and Helibel. She also frequently appears without a name in many stories. Nonetheless, she usually functions as a sacrificial figure. In *Le Morte D'Arthur*, it is through her selfless and Christ-like death that she saves a countess by giving her own blood (Book XVII chapter 11). Sir Thomas Malory, *Le Morte D'Arthur*, Volume II (London: Penguin Books, 2004), 348–351. Amide/Dindraine's action opposes that of the vampire who takes blood from the living.

36. On Arthur's tomb is written "*Hic Iacet Arthurus, Rex Quondam Rexque Futurus*": Sir Thomas Malory, *Le Morte D'Arthur*, Volume II (London: Penguin Books, 2004), 519.

37. See W. M. Ormrod, "Monarchy, Martyrdom and Masculinity: England in the Later Middle Ages," in *Holiness and Masculinity in the Middle Ages*, ed. P. H. Cullum and Katherine J. Lewis (Toronto: University of Toronto Press, 2005), 174–191.

38. McCracken, "The Poetics of Sacrifice," 158.

12

"If I Wasn't a Girl, Would You Like Me Anyway?" Le Fanu's *Carmilla* and Alfredson's *Let the Right One In*

Jamieson Ridenhour

THERE HAS NEVER BEEN A SATISFYING FILM adaptation of Joseph Sheridan Le Fanu's classic vampire novella *Carmilla*. The more famous attempts, such as Roger Vadim's *Blood and Roses* (1960) and Hammer Studios' *The Vampire Lovers* (1970), jettison the novella's more subtle themes in favor of an exploitative sexuality bordering on soft porn.[1] The focal point of Le Fanu's tale is Laura, a 19-year-old girl whose reporting of events presents the reader with a tale of female intimacy composed of equals parts allure and aversion. Most films that purport to be based on *Carmilla* substitute a prurient, decidedly male gaze, which is more concerned with physical lesbianism than with the emotional dynamics at the heart of Le Fanu's original.

The film that perhaps comes closest to replicating Le Fanu's effect is Gabrielle Beaumont's 1989 made-for-TV film, "Carmilla," part of the short-lived *Nightmare Classics* series. There are flaws and inexplicable variations—Ione Skye's oddly infantilized protagonist, the shift in setting from Austria to the antebellum South, Roddy McDowell acting good-old-boy Southern as Inspector Amos—but the production at least gets the central idea correct: *Carmilla* is the story of a lonely child who finds a loving relationship with a similarly lonely companion. When that companion's monstrous nature is revealed, the protagonist feels conflicted but ultimately is unable to completely reject the only friend she's ever had. In Beaumont's "Carmilla," this emotional focus nearly works, but it is unfortunately marred by poor acting and inconsistent plot elements, along with a 1-hour running time, which truncates character development.

Still, Beaumont's "Carmilla" is worth searching out—it is hard to find commercially, but has recently showed up in parts on YouTube—for Meg Tilly's ethereal turn as Carmilla and for the tantalizing glimpse of what a real *Carmilla* film might entail: a sense of growing menace arising within a fierce and romantic friendship. But it is only a glimpse. More recently, however, the romantic friendship theme has surfaced in a wholly remarkable retelling, Tomas Alfredson's *Let the Right One In* (2008, original Swedish title *Låt Den Rätte Komma In*), based on John Ajvide Lindqvist's 2004 novel of the same title. The script, adapted by Lindqvist in consultation with Alfredson, strips away peripheral subplots and backstory from the novel in order to underscore the central narrative: that of lonely, 12-year-old Oskar and his growing relationship with Eli, the dark-haired girl who moves in next door.

Even a cursory glance at the two narratives reveals remarkable similarities. Laura, Le Fanu's narrator, is a lonely girl living in isolation with her father in the Austrian wilderness. Her need for friendship has become the defining desire in her life. She uses the word *lonely* to describe her situation multiple times and stresses the social isolation under which she lives. Upon learning that General Spielsdorf, an acquaintance of her father's, will not be bringing his niece to visit, Laura reacts with tears, though she has never met the girl. "I was more disappointed than a young lady living in town, or a bustling neighborhood, can possibly imagine," she tells the reader. "This visit, and the new acquaintance it promised, had furnished my day dream for many weeks."[2]

Laura is therefore ripe for the connection to come. Carmilla enters Laura's life when her carriage overturns near the family's *schloss*, and a woman calling herself Carmilla's mother entreats Laura's father to take care of her daughter until she returns from a lengthy and mysterious errand. The friendship between the two girls is fueled by what seems to be a mutual recollection of a childhood nightmare wherein 6-year-old Laura was visited by a fully-grown Carmilla. But even taking this shared experience into account, their relationship is sudden and intense:

> Now the truth is, I felt rather unaccountably towards the beautiful stranger. I did feel, as she said, 'drawn towards her,' but there was also something of repulsion. In this ambiguous feeling, however, the sense of attraction immensely prevailed. She interested and won me; she was so beautiful and so indescribably engaging.[3]

Carmilla reciprocates, embracing and kissing Laura at the end of their first brief meeting as if they were the closest of companions. Laura reflects that

> [y]oung people like, and even love, on impulse. I was flattered by the evident, though as yet undeserved, fondness she showed me. I liked the confidence with which she at once received me. She was determined that we should be very near friends.[4]

They do, of course, become "very near friends," but Laura's strange sense of attraction/repulsion continues. This contradictory feeling, felt at both the emotional and physical level, is the beating heart of the literary vampire. For Laura, the attraction she begins to feel for Carmilla is mitigated by the intense passion that Carmilla evidences toward her. Laura describes these passionate episodes as "fits," but they are weirder and more forceful than that word encompasses. Carmilla embraces Laura, covers her with kisses, and tells her: "I live in your warm life, and you shall die—die, sweetly die—into mine."[5] Laura's reaction should naturally be to recoil from this odd behavior, but she finds her response more complicated:

> In these mysterious moods I did not like her. I experienced a strange tumultuous excitement that was pleasurable, even and anon, mingled with a vague sense of fear and disgust. I had no distinct thoughts about her while such scenes lasted, but I was conscious of a love growing into adoration, and also of abhorrence. This I know is paradox, but I can make no other attempt to explain the feeling.[6]

Laura's paradox is thrown into stark relief when Carmilla's true nature is revealed. General Spielsdorf visits and tells the full story of his niece Bertha's decline and death. It is obvious to everyone listening that the creature who insinuates itself into the general's household and preys on his niece is Carmilla (even to Laura's willfully thick father), but immediately after hearing the tale Laura expresses her joy at hearing Carmilla approach. Years after the men of the story, bolstered by doctors and government representatives, band together to stake and dispatch Carmilla, Laura continues to listen for her at the door, remembering her fiendish friend with "ambiguous alternations."[7]

Oskar, the 12-year-old protagonist of Alfredson's *Let the Right One In*, is likewise a lonely child living in an isolated situation, and like Laura he develops feelings for a dark visitor, which are rife with "ambiguous alternations." Oskar is also the child of a single parent household; his occasional visits to his estranged father are marred by his father's alcoholism and emotional distance, and his mother is scarcely more involved. Oskar lives in Blackeberg, a suburb of Stockholm, and thus much more heavily populated than the Austrian woodlands where Laura and her father have their *schloss*. Oskar's isolation is social—he is a bullied outcast, the chosen victim for the cruelty of his sadistic classmates. Like Laura, one of his defining characteristics is his loneliness, a longing for connection that he has no hope of finding. In a classic example of pathetic fallacy, Blackeberg's snowy landscape (beautifully captured by cinematographer Hoyte Van Hoytema) becomes the outward expression of Oskar's cold and solitary life.

Into this frozen world comes Eli, who appears like Carmilla in a vehicle accompanied by someone purporting to be her parent. Hakan is actually a procurer, Eli's companion who commits serial murder in order to supply her with blood. The world perceives him to be Eli's father, just as the woman in black velvet presents herself as Carmilla's mother in Le Fanu's novella. Eli moves in next door to Oskar, so that, like Laura and Carmilla, they are in adjoining bedrooms, albeit in different apartments.

Eli is at first reticent to connect with Oskar. Practically her first words to him are "Just so you know, I can't be your friend." Oskar reacts petulantly ("Are you so sure that I want to be your friend?"), but it's only what he expects. At their next meeting, however, Eli's fascination with Oskar's Rubik's Cube elicits a tentative reaching out, which quickly develops into a stronger bond.

There are numerous parallels between *Let the Right One In* and *Carmilla*, both cosmetic and thematic. The pairing of the two main characters is striking. The Gothic doppelgänger trope is common in vampire literature, and both of these narratives make ample use of it. Both feature a fair-haired protagonist haunted by a dark-haired revenant,[8] and both imply that the connection between the two central figures is due in part to an already existing affinity. Laura's desire for love and friendship is mirrored by Carmilla, who says early on "I have never had a friend—shall I find one now?"[9] Likewise, Eli's violence is a reflection of Oskar's latent aggression; at their first meeting Oskar is stabbing a tree with his knife, pretending he is revenging himself on Conny, the chief bully at his school. Eli herself makes this linking explicit in a later conversation, after Oskar protests his difference from her. "I don't kill people," he says. Eli replies "No, but you'd like to." In an attempt to overcome Oskar's aversion to his realization of her true nature, Eli asks him to imagine what her life is like: "Be me for a little while." But she has already made it clear that Oskar *is* her in a fundamental way.

Similarly, in both *Let the Right One In* and *Carmilla*, the relationship between the main characters develops into more than friendship, though once again Eli is reticent at first. During the first few times they meet, Oskar tries to find out more about Eli by questioning her. Over a hundred years earlier, Laura had done the same thing, finding Carmilla evasive in her answers. Carmilla refuses to divulge her family name or any information about her background, responding to Laura's repeated inquiries with "a coldness, it seemed to me, beyond her years, in her smiling melancholy persistent refusal to afford me the least ray of light."[10] Eli's response to Oskar's questioning could be described thus. The third time they meet, after Eli has solved Oskar's Rubik's Cube and the ice between them has broken somewhat, this exchange occurs:

Oskar: What's your name?
Eli: Eli. What's yours?
O: Eli? I'm Oskar. How old are you?
E: 12 . . . more or less. What about you?
O: 12 years, 8 months, and 9 days. What do you mean "more or less?"

E: (no answer)

O: When's your birthday?

E: I don't know.

O: Don't you celebrate your birthday? Your parents . . . they've got to know.

E: (no answer)

Like Carmilla, Eli's answers are either unsatisfactory or nonexistent. Like Laura, Oskar continues to question his new friend at intervals, coming no closer to understanding her even as his affection for her grows.

Both vampires, it should be noted, display evidence of their nature in brief ways (Carmilla's aversion to hymns, Eli's inability to eat regular food without vomiting), but neither Laura nor Oskar recognize these signs. Carmilla and Eli both prey on the local populace, feeding and killing among the working classes while cultivating a romantic attachment with their chosen companions.

The romance is largely verbal in both cases, though Laura and Carmilla also do a fair amount of kissing and embracing. Carmilla's swooning 19th-century entreaties ("You are mine, you *shall* be mine, you and I are one forever"[11]) become simpler and sweeter for the younger Oskar, who merely asks Eli outright if she'd like to go steady. Eli agrees after ascertaining that you don't "do anything special" in order to go steady; Oskar does not at first realize the long-term implications of this agreement ("It'll be you and me," Eli promises), and he responds to her acceptance with simple happiness and wonder.

It is no surprise that there are so many similarities between these two narratives; John Ajvide Lindqvist admits to having drawn inspiration from Le Fanu's novella. In a posting on *We, The Infected*, an online discussion forum dedicated to the novel *Let the Right One In* and its film adaptations, Lindqvist responds to a commenter who points out parallels between *Carmilla* and Lindqvist's work. Lindqvist remembers:

> I actually got the idea of the boy befriending the vampire from *Carmilla*. Before writing *Let the Right One In*, once I had decided that the "monster" was going to be a vampire (that wasn't clear from the beginning), I saw some vampire movies and read some vampire books. Or actually I just read *Carmilla* and *Lost Souls* by Poppy Z. Brite. . . . I knew before reading *Carmilla* that the main character was going to have some sort of relation with the vampire, but with *Carmilla* came the very simple and complex idea that the relation in question would be love. One of the most difficult things in writing the book was to portray that budding love in small, humdrum steps instead of the gothic swooning of *Carmilla*.[12]

So the core of *Let the Right One In* was lifted intact from *Carmilla*, and the analogues detailed are natural extensions of that initial inspiration. But upon closer inspection, the differences between the two stories are as great as the similarities. Christopher Frayling identifies three varieties of literary vampire extant in the late 19th century: the aristocratic vampire (modeled on Lord Byron by John Polidori in *The Vampyre*), the *femme fatale* (such as Geraldine in Coleridge's *Christabel*), and the vampire of folklore.[13] As I point out elsewhere,[14] Le Fanu combined the vampire of superstition with the Byronic vampire aristocrat and the *femme fatale* vamps of John Keats and Samuel Taylor Coleridge to create a powerful new hybrid. Carmilla's titled background is hinted at throughout, before she is finally revealed as the Countess Mircalla Karnstein. Her *femme fatale* credentials are made obvious by simply comparing Le Fanu's text with that of *Christabel*,[15] though *Carmilla* alters the basic idea of the *femme fatale* in several important ways.

Most striking is the way in which *Carmilla* echoes the vampire of folklore. Le Fanu, writing early in the history of vampire fiction,[16] makes much use of the folkloric roots of the vampire, using reports from Dom Calmet's 18th-century *Treatise on Vampires and Revenants* (recently translated into English by Reverend Henry Christmas[17]) as an important source. This is most evident in the plague-like deaths of the peasants who are Carmilla's primary food source and in the off-stage staking of the vampire, the description of which is lifted nearly whole cloth from Calmet's report of the staking of Peter Plogojovitz. Le Fanu even puts his staking scene in an official report, complete with certified medical witnesses, à la Calmet.

Le Fanu naturally relied on the established tropes of a literary figure barely half a century old. Alfredson and Lindqvist, creating *Let the Right One In* 140 years later, have to contend with an exponential proliferation of vampire novels, stories, films, TV programs, comics, cartoons, and breakfast cereals that arose in the intervening years. *Carmilla* was itself a foundational influence on Bram Stoker's *Dracula*, and the 1931 film version of *Dracula* ensured the vampire a permanent place in the Western cultural pantheon. The millennial vampire is more varied in its aspect, and its consumers are much more knowledgeable about its identity.

By the end of the 20th century, one common permutation of the vampire was that of disturbed but ultimately redeemable love interest. This idea of the "good" vampire, trapped and troubled by the requirements of his own nature, is seen most ubiquitously in the *Twilight* franchise, but the concept is at least as old as Anne Rice's 1976 seminal novel *Interview with the Vampire*, in which Louis spends an entire novel struggling with the implications of the blood he must drink. Angel, the vampire with a soul in Joss Whedon's *Buffy the Vampire Slayer* TV series, eschews human blood altogether, as does Edward Cullen nearly a decade later in Stephenie Meyer's *Twilight* series and Mick St. John in the short-lived TV series *Moonlight*. Mitchell, one of the main characters in the British series *Being Human*, is a vampire who not only gives up blood but also leads fellow vampires in a sort of Alcoholics Anonymous group for blood-drinkers. All of these "good" vampires are presented as objects of desire: romantic brooding men whose dark and bloody past is an obstacle to be overcome. This is more than a softening of the Gothic anti-hero, the dark Byronic Rochesters and Heathcliffs who haunt romance and sensation fiction of the 19th- and 20th century, though it is that as well. Mitchell, Angel, Mick St. John, and company are grappling with psychological demons; it is no coincidence that the metaphor of addiction frequently recurs in these millennial vampire tales. All of these creatures stand in stark contrast to vampires like Carmilla, who exults in her nature and offers vampirism to Laura as an eternal romance. "Instead of being cast as horrifying monsters," writes Patrick McCormick, "these Millennial vampires turn out to be decidedly human creatures, troubled adolescent souls struggling mightily to gain some measure of control over passions and hungers threatening to make a mess of their lives and loved ones."[18] This is vampirism as emotional damage, and the best therapy seems to be the love of the equally damaged heroine.

You would be hard-pressed to find two people more emotionally damaged than Oskar and Eli. Oskar's systematic abuse by Conny and his middle-school cronies has left him a whipped dog of a boy, flinching at shadows and hiding in bathroom stalls. His absent father and emotionally distant mother only make him feel as alienated at home as he does at school. Until the arrival of Eli, Oskar has not a single friend.[19] Eli is likewise lonely and seems to carry the weight of her many years of isolation as a resigned sadness: "Just so you know, I can't be your friend." The two children at the center of Alfredson's film need each other on a basic level, and this need is predicated on their individual psychological scarring.

Eli is not as squeamish about killing as Angel or Edward Cullen; she not only kills for food with an animalistic savagery, but she encourages Oskar to use violence to protect himself. Her rescue of Oskar from the bullies in the pool is brutal and excessive, and afterward a gore-streaked Eli smiles at Oskar in contented triumph. Oskar's own violent impulses are pointed out to him by Eli in the conversation quoted previously and to the audience at the film's beginning, when he imagines stabbing his bullies with the knife he keeps hidden under his pillow. He is well-matched in Eli, a dark doppelgänger who draws life from the blood he is too frightened to spill.

But even though Eli kills when necessary (or when her loved one is threatened), she also struggles with the realities of her nature in very real ways. Her odd arrangement with Hakan, who brings blood to her so she does not have to kill directly, is ostensibly designed to keep her true nature hidden, but it also functions as a method of distancing Eli from her victims, a buffer between her and the reality of what she is. When Hakan fails to return with the blood from his first murder in Blackeberg (he is a singularly inept serial killer), Eli is furious with him: "Do I really have to take care of this myself?" This scene with Hakan is the only time we see Eli angry; even at her most violent, as with the bullies at the pool, Eli does not lose her composure. Her rage in this scene is an indicator of her reluctance to engage directly with her hunger. It is significant that the only other true loss of self-possession Eli displays in the film is when Oskar cuts his hand in the basement. Eli's inability to control her bloodlust is frightening to see but more powerful is her frantic dismay at giving in to it in front of Oskar. When she later points out Oskar's inherent violent impulses, Eli asks him to imagine what it would be like to have no choice but to kill. "I do it because I have to," she says, "Be me, for a little while."

But Oskar isn't able to immediately "be" Eli. Despite his violent fantasies and his serial killer scrapbook, when confronted with a real killer, Oskar is thrown into a conflicting set of emotions that Le Fanu's Laura would recognize all too well. He refuses to take money from Eli because it has been stolen from the people she has killed, and he defends his own impulses by emphatically stating that he has never acted on them. The closest Oskar actually comes to committing violence is when he threatens to stab Lacke as the latter is preparing to kill Eli as she sleeps. When Eli awakens and does the killing for him, Oskar throws his knife away in apparent disgust. Afterward, when Eli and Oskar share their only kiss in the film, Eli's blood-smeared mouth is a striking visual metaphor of the violence that grounds their relationship and also of the attraction/repulsion theme around which all vampire tales orbit.

Like Laura, Oskar's attraction to Eli and what she offers him is ultimately stronger than his aversion to her vampire nature. This is demonstrated by parallel scenes in the two tales, in which a powerful visual confirmation of the vampire elicits protective feelings from the human protagonists. In *Carmilla*, Laura has recurring nightmares in which she hears a female voice speaking to her from a distance. She remembers:

> One night, instead of the voice I was accustomed to hear in the dark, I heard one, sweet and tender, and at the same time terrible, which said, 'Your mother warns you to beware of the assassin.' At the same time a light unexpectedly sprang up, and I saw Carmilla, standing, near the foot of my bed, in her white night-dress, bathed, from her chin to her feet, in one great stain of blood.
>
> I wakened with a shriek, possessed with the one idea that Carmilla was being murdered. I remember springing from my bed, and my next recollection is that of standing on the lobby, crying for help.[20]

In *Let the Right One In*, Oskar doesn't believe the superstitions around vampires and forces Eli to come in to his apartment without being invited. Upon entering, she begins to shake and blood springs from her body in a dozen places. Oskar rushes to embrace her, frantically calling out the words of invitation to save her. Both vampires stand revealed, covered in a "great stain of blood," and both protagonists' first impulse to is to protect their bloody friends.

The difference, of course, is the difference between the 19th-century vampire and her millennial progeny. Laura does not understand what she is seeing, either through naivety or willful misapprehension, and assumes that Carmilla is under threat from an outside assassin. For Oskar, Eli's sanguine exposé is not revelation but confirmation, and when he folds her into his protective embrace he knows full well what he holds. Eli's character is no longer a secret.

Eli had other secrets, however, and it is in those secrets that we find the most surprising parallel with *Carmilla*. As we have seen, *Let the Right One In* has a number of correlations with Le Fanu's novella. Most obviously, both stories feature a young vampire who develops a relationship with a lonely child its own physical age. In both cases the attachment is one in a long line of such, and in both cases the protagonist struggles with a strong attraction to the vampire coupled with a moral repulsion to the vampire's nature and behavior. More significantly, both stories effectively blur the traditional gender roles for stories of vampiric sexual predation: *Carmilla* in its clear depiction of a lesbian vampire, and *Let the Right One In* in its presentation (implicit in the film and explicit in the source novel) of two boys in a relationship, even though Oskar assumes for most of the movie that Eli is a girl. This sexual ambiguity is a staple of vampire fiction but is noticeably absent in recent popular versions of the romantic vampire trope, which are avowedly heterosexual in their attentions.[21]

Carmilla's lesbianism is overt, even without the reductive film adaptations mentioned in the opening of this chapter. Nina Auerbach calls Carmilla "one of the few self-accepting homosexuals in vampire or any other literature" and attributes this to gender, pointing out that "no male vampire of her century confronts the desire within his friendship."[22] Auerbach thus finds that Carmilla is a different breed from the standard *femme fatale* vamps of the 1890s, female creatures who preyed only on men. Edward Burne-Jones's painting *The Vampyre* and its companion poem by Rudyard Kipling are representative examples of this trope, culminating in the film career of Theda Bara in the early 20th century. Carmilla is not one of these; she is not merely predator but friend, and apparently uninterested in men as either prey or companion. She differs also from the friendship offered by male vampires before her, set apart from "Ruthven, Varney, and the rest in intensity rather than kind: as a woman, the vampiric friend releases a boundless capacity for intimacy."[23] Like the best monsters, Carmilla stands in a liminal space, one where friends and lovers become predators, where the lines of traditional sexuality are blurred.

Laura tries to force Carmilla's behavior to fit what she understands to be sexual norms:

> Respecting these very extraordinary manifestations I strove in vain to form any satisfactory theory—I could not refer them to affectation or trick. It was unmistakably the momentary breaking out of suppressed instinct and emotion.
>
> [W]as there here a disguise and a romance? I had read in old story books of such things. What if a boyish lover had found his way into the house, and sought to prosecute his suit in masquerade, with the assistance of a clever old adventuress. But there were many things against this hypothesis, highly interesting as it was to my vanity.[24]

Ultimately, however, Laura is forced to admit the reality of Carmilla's nature, though she never directly addresses what conclusions can then be drawn about her own.

Eli's secret is not that she is a vampire, but that she is a boy. In Lindqvist's novel, a fully realized backstory leaves no doubt as to this fact. Eli was turned in the 18th century by a vampire who castrated him and drank the blood from the wound, an event explicitly shown to Oskar through a form of thought-sharing. Eli's gender is mutable throughout the novel, Lindqvist's pronouns shifting from "she" to "he" and "her" to "him" depending on the perception of the current point-of-view character.

The origin narrative is excised from the film, and Eli's secret is revealed to Oskar and the viewer through hints and signs. Each time Oskar tries to directly address the growing romantic feelings between them, Eli tells Oskar that she[25] is not what he thinks. "If I wasn't a girl," Eli asks at one point, "would you like me anyway?" Oskar supposes he would, but the question confuses him. Later, when Oskar asks if Eli will be his girlfriend, the answer is even more direct: "Oskar, I'm not a girl." The audience assumes that Eli is referring to being a vampire, but at this point in the film Oskar has had little indication of that dark part of Eli's life. His response, "Okay. But do you want to go steady or not?" could indicate a willful naivety similar to that of *Carmilla's* Laura. But it is also possible that Oskar understands what Eli is telling him but doesn't care, that his happiness in finding a soul mate trumps anything as trivial as gender.

This may well be the case. Gender is not a topic of conversation between them again, though Eli's castration is graphically demonstrated when Oskar peeks at Eli changing clothes. It is a very brief glimpse, so brief that the audience, having been given no more clues than Oskar, can be forgiven for misunderstanding what they have seen. If Oskar understands, thus having Eli's strange comments about not being a girl fully explained for the first time, it in any case does not alter his relationship or change the way he acts toward her. It is soon after this scene that Oskar nearly stabs Lacke to defend Eli from assault, and, of course, by the end of the film Oskar is willing to give up his life in Blackeberg to be Eli's lifetime companion.

In context of how *Let the Right One In* functions on a thematic level, it makes sense that Eli's gender would ultimately be a non-issue. The film is not about sex, *per se*, not concerned at all with sexual desire. The prepubescent protagonists of *Let the Right One In* are also pre-sexual, at least insofar as we are shown. When Eli huddles naked in Oskar's bed after the death of Hakan, the most physical contact the children engage in is holding hands. This is the final and most crucial difference between *Let the Right One In* and Le Fanu's *Carmilla*. *Carmilla* is certainly about sexual awakening, among other things, and about Laura's burgeoning sexual awareness finding liberation through the actions and encouragement of the sexually free vampire. In *Let the Right One In*, it is violence—not sex—that Oskar is holding nascent within, a violence that finds its expression in Eli's encouragement and demonstration.

Significantly, Eli does not prey on Oskar. Unlike Carmilla, she does not try to turn her human love into a vampire. But Eli's empowerment of Oskar, direct and indirect, does transform him. Oskar absorbs and performs Eli's violence for self-preservation. John Calhoun writes that "horror is all about the breakdown of forces that are supposed to govern and provide reason for our existence," going on to argue that Oskar's "savagery naturally rises to the fore" due to lack of parental supervision or religious guidance.[26] Whether or not this is true, Oskar's survival depends on violence, just as Eli's does. Both enact this violence to protect Oskar—he on the ice when he strikes back at Conny, she in the pool when she butchers Oskar's bullies. The ending of the film, in which the two children take a train to an unknown somewhere, shows Oskar contented, smiling, belonging, and loved for the first time in his unhappy life. It is a happy ending to what is ultimately a love story, but it is underscored by the brutality necessary to achieve it. In Le Fanu's 19th century, the status quo wins, asserting accepted norms and "saving" Laura, who spends the rest of her life hearing Carmilla's footstep at the door. Alfredson's millennial children find love and belonging by inviting them in, along with the blood and intimacy that are their inextricable counterparts.

Notes

1. As Nina Auerbach says of *The Vampire Lovers*, the vampire women are reduced to "interchangeable stuffed breasts," *Our Vampires, Ourselves* (Chicago: University of Chicago Press, 1995), 58.

2. Joseph Sheridan Le Fanu, *Carmilla* [1872], ed. Jamieson Ridenhour (Kansas City: Valancourt, 2009), 6.

3. Le Fanu, *Carmilla*, 19.

4. Le Fanu, *Carmilla*, 20.

5. Le Fanu, *Carmilla*, 22.

6. Le Fanu, *Carmilla*, 22–23.

7. Le Fanu, *Carmilla*, 83.

8. See also the pairing of Mina and Lucy in Stoker's *Dracula* (1897), a novel that makes frequent and self-conscious use of *Carmilla* as source material.

9. Le Fanu, *Carmilla*, 19.

10. Le Fanu, *Carmilla*, 21.

11. Le Fanu, *Carmilla*, 23.

12. John Ajvide Lindqvist, "Re: LMI and Carmilla," *We, the Infected*, http://www.let-the-right-one-in.com/forum/viewtopic.php?f=8&t=4242, accessed December 22, 2011.

13. Christopher Frayling, *Vampyres: Lord Byron to Count Dracula* (New York: Faber and Faber, 1992).

14. In the Introduction to the Valancourt edition of *Carmilla* (2009), *xi*.

15. Arthur Nethercot has already done this in "Coleridge's *Christabel* and Lefanu's *Carmilla*," *Modern Philology* 47 (1949): 32–38.

16. Le Fanu's main literary source material, Coleridge's *Christabel* (1816), is arguably the first vampire tale in English.

17. Dom Augustine Calmet, *Treatise on Vampires and Revenants: The Phantom World*, trans. Henry Christmas (Brighton: Desert Island Books, 1993).

18. Patrick McCormick, "It's in the Blood," *US Catholic* 75 (Dec. 2010): 40–41.

19. This isn't as absolutely true in the novel, where Oskar is friendly with a rebellious neighbor named Tommy. Tommy's character was left out of the film, resulting in Oskar's total quarantine from healthy human relationships.

20. Le Fanu, *Carmilla*, 44.

21. *Twilight* is the most popular example, but *Buffy the Vampire Slayer* and the *Vampire Diaries* also keep their vamp relationships straight, although *Buffy* does feature a sympathetic portrayal of lesbianism in the character of Willow Rosenberg.

22. Auerbach, *Our Vampires, Ourselves* 43.

23. Auerbach, *Our Vampires, Ourselves* 45

24. Le Fanu, *Carmilla*, 23.

25. One of the difficulties of writing about Eli is this mutability of gender. I have chosen to continue with feminine pronouns to avoid confusion and because the film for the most part presents Eli as female.

26. John Calhoun, "Childhood's End: Let the Right One In and Other Deaths of Innocence," *Cineaste* 35 (Winter 2009): 31.

IV

OLD AND NEW WORLD
MANIFESTATIONS OF THE VAMPIRE

13

A Cultural Dynasty of Beautiful Vampires: Japan's Acceptance, Modifications, and Adaptations of Vampires

Masaya Shimokusu

IN LATE AUGUST 2011, THE JAPANESE VERSION of *Dracula, the Musical* appeared on stage in Tokyo.[1] The musical was originally performed in the United States, including Broadway, and was later staged at an old castle in Graz, Austria. The internationally renowned musical composer Frank Wildhorn composed the score, and Don Black and Christopher Hampton wrote its lyrics. For the performances in Western countries, male actors played Dracula in accordance with his gender. On the Tokyo stage with Japanese lyrics, however, the actress Yōka Waō acted the role of Dracula (see figure 1). This casting, suggested by the composer Wildhorn himself, was striking but acceptable for the Japanese audience.[2] Waō had a long career of playing male roles in Takarazuka Revue, an all-woman musical troupe having enjoyed lasting popularity in Japan.[3] Moreover, many Japanese were accustomed to seeing *beautiful* vampires luring humans regardless of their gender. On the stage, Waō's Dracula was cool, merciless and beautiful and, when seducing female characters, the vampire's sexuality was ambiguously represented. The Japanese have nurtured and developed their own images of vampires, especially after World War II. In 21st-century Japanese popular mentality, vampires can or even should be beautiful.

This chapter will demonstrate how the Japanese accepted vampires from Western literary works and how they later made use of the creatures in diverse cultural media and developed their own works with vampire motifs in various artistic fields. Before Japan began to negotiate with Western imperial countries and chose her way to advance as a modern nation state, vampires had not lured the Japanese. Originally, there seemed to be no blood-sucking, immortal creatures in Japanese folk tales or legends. Chiefly after World

Figure 1.   A Beautiful Vampire: Yōka Waō as Dracula in the Japanese production of *Dracula, the Musical* (2011) © SHINOBU IKAZAKI

War II, visualized vampires penetrated into the depth of Japanese popular imagination and, since then, the Japanese have developed images of beautiful vampires. Most of them are male and they often disturb the sexual boundaries of humans.

In order to examine this process, I will focus on a number of literary works or those in other artistic fields representing Japanese vampire culture. The number of Japanese cultural works with vampire motifs is so enormous that it is impossible to examine all of them. Therefore, my selection in this chapter is arbitrary to some extent, but most of the works discussed here, especially after World War II, have been popular among the public, and also, in most of them, you can find beautiful vampires.

Critical assessments of Japanese vampire works are rare to date. However, exceptions include Asahiko Sunaga's brief overview of Japanese vampire literature[4]; Masao Higashi's selections for vampire anthologies such as *Chi to bara no ekusutashī* (*The Ecstasy of Blood and Rose*, 1990) and *Shiki no ketsuzoku* (*The Kith and Kin of Corpse Demon*, 1999). In particular, Mari Kotani's study of Japanese vampire literature contains parallels with this chapter. Kotani is one of the contemporary leading critics of science fiction and popular culture, and her 2005 study, *Tekunogoshikku* (*Techno-Gothic*), investigates Gothic culture in materials from various artistic fields. Although I will simply focus on the appearances of beautiful vampires, Kotani, in *Tekunogoshikku*, considers that vampires in Japanese novels represent "Others" or foreignness for the Japanese and she selects such works.[5] Nevertheless, although we discuss vampires from different perspectives, many of the works Kotani selected, especially those from the 1970s to the 1990s, are discussed in this chapter, too. One of the reasons why our selections of vampire works in these periods coincide may be that Kotani also paid attention to the transgender aspects of modern popular culture; beautiful vampires often lure both males and females regardless of their gender when they were human.

The Coming of the Dark: The Early Influx of Vampires into Japan

Although Japan may be one of the Western-type advanced countries, it is situated in the Far East. It is certain that, in ancient Japan, some tribes recognized the spiritual power in blood and returns from the dead were often incorporated into many folk legends or tales, but immortal blood-sucking creatures did not seem to exist in Japan, even in the fantasy of Japanese people. However, after Western vampires had flowed into Japan with the mass of Western literature, they seemed swiftly to start fascinating Japanese intelligentsia.

In the latter half of the 19th century, Japan rapidly westernized. Previously, for more than 200 years, the Japanese Tokugawa Shogunate had isolated the country from foreign countries. However, Western powers finally forced Japan to open its ports in the middle of the 19th century. Shortly after the imperial nations' fleets arrived on the coasts of Japan, the new Meiji government was established in 1868 and took over from the Tokugawa Shogunate, which led to the end of the rule of *samurai*. The new Japanese government was eager to catch up with Western, advanced countries and struggled to avoid being colonized. It devoured any kind of knowledge on Western countries, including cultural matters. They sent many eminent young scholars to various Western countries and encouraged them to bring Western knowledge and technologies back home with them. Consequently, a great number of Western documents, including literature, flowed into Japan, and many Japanese writers began to read Western literature. Some translated it; others rearranged it and created their own stories, dramas, and poems to fit the new Japan.

In the forward to Kōjin Karatani's *Origins of Modern Japanese Literature*, Fredric Jameson insightfully points out that Japan tried to adopt aspects of the Western Enlightenment as soon as possible and condensed the adoption process into just 100 years.[6] Considering this context, we can see why Japanese intellectuals accepted Shakespeare, Romanticism, Realism, and other trends of Western artistic movements at the same time in the late 19th century. They attempted to digest them and create some artistic achievements in their own language. Furthermore, during this modernization of Japan, the population of the literate public increased explosively. Before the foundation of the Meiji government, the Japanese had two kinds of language: one for writing and the other for speaking. Only the samurai ruling class appropriated its written language. Once Japan became involved in imperial power struggles, it hastily became a modern nation state for protection. The country needed an educated public to work for the nation. The Meiji government started to integrate writing and speaking into one Japanese language; the politician Arinori Mori (1847–1889) even proposed that a simplified English should be adapted as the nation's language. As a result, Japan could boast a highly literate population by the early 20th century.[7] Many such readers fervently called for more materials to read, especially those they could enjoy. New texts that they could easily understand were ideal.

With the simultaneous acceptance of various literary modes and the growing readership, some Japanese drew their attention to one of the universal elements in Western literature: fear and horror. According to H. P. Lovecraft's famous generalization of human emotion: "The oldest and strongest emotion of mankind is fear."[8] As early as the late 19th century, several Japanese writers such as Ruikō Kuroiwa (1862–1920) began to show strong interest in Victorian ghost and supernatural stories and translated them.[9] Other Japanese writers also translated Gothic literature and stories featuring horrific supernatural beings. Moreover, some authors created their own work based on these genres.

Among the stories importing Western fear, some Japanese writers discovered vampires in the early 20th century. One of the most prominent writers in Japanese literary history, Ryūnosuke Akutagawa (1892–1927), translated Théophile Gautier's "*La morte amoureuse*" in 1914 when he was a student at Tokyo Imperial University. He selected "Clarimonde" as a title to the story probably because he translated one of the English translations of Gautier's story. Furthermore, he did not use the word *kyuketsuki*, the authentic Japanese translational term for the word *vampire* in later generations. A few Japanese writers later translated this story of Gautier with the word *kyūketsuki*. In 1932, another famous writer of belles lettres, Haruo Satō (1892–1964), published the translation of John Polidori's *The Vampyre*, although his disciple[10] actually translated it.[11]

It is not clear who became the first person to use the word *kyūketsuki*. Masao Higashi points out that Kumagusu Minakata (1867–1941), a globally famous naturalist and erudite writer, used the word in his articles submitted to an anthropological magazine in 1915.[12] Among literary figures, Rampo Edgawa (pseudonym of Tarō Hirai, 1894–1965) may have used the word first. He published a short essay with the title, "Kyūketsuki," in 1926. The novelist also uses the word *vampire*, phonetically expressed in Japanese, in the essay.[13]

Kōnosuke Hinatsu (1880–1971) was a poet and scholar of English literature. As a poet, he invented his own poetic style, as he puts it, "Gothick-Rōman-tai" (Gothic-Romantic style), in his early career.[14] He wrote abstruse poems with kaleidoscopic imagery of alchemy or Satanism and became one of leading figures of Japanese literary modernism in the early 20th century. Moreover, he played a great role in spreading the images of Western vampires among Japanese readers. He published a general overview on the legends of vampires in Europe in his *Kyūketsuyōmiko* (*A Study on Vampirism*), published in 1931. The book, heavily dependent on Montague Summers's *The Vampire: His Kith and Kin* (1928) and *The Vampire in Europe* (1929) as he himself states in the preface, came out as volume no. 11 of collected works of sexology. Hinatsu also published a short essay titled "Kyūketsukitan" (Vampire Tales), in the same year.

It is noteworthy that few Japanese seemed to know Count Dracula in this period. In the aforementioned essay, Edgawa does not refer to Bram Stoker's *Dracula*, although he was eager to read overseas detective- and fantasy novels in English. In *Kyūketsuyomiko*, Hinatsu briefly mentions Stoker's novel and its dramatizations,[15] but they are treated at the very end of a section dealing with vampires in literature as the newest piece of information at that time.

I started this chapter with the description of a beautiful vampire on the present-day stage in Japan, but when we read the writings of Rampo or of Hinatsu on vampires, we are hardly impressed with their beauty. Most of the vampires appearing in their texts are folkloric ones, such as people buried too early or corpses that did not decay in their coffins. The Japanese were already lured by the uncanniness of vampires in the early 20th century, but they had not recognized them as beautiful or elegant yet.

The Rise of the Dark Beauty: The Development of Beautiful Images of Vampires in Japan after World War II

Since Stoker deliberately describes Dracula as an ephemeral and evaporative creature in the novel, *Dracula*, the readers can hardly pin down the vampire's figure or image by reading the text. However, thanks to filmed versions of *Dracula*, most of us generally have clear images of the Count. The aristocratic figures performed by Bela Lugosi and Christopher Lee must still be dominant images among us, even among the Japanese. As the development of the film industry simultaneously took place in the period of Japan's westernization, Japan could enjoy the fruits of the swiftly emerging media with the Western world. They imported Western movies as soon as they were released. One of the Universal horror movies, Tod Browning's *Dracula*, featuring Bela Lugosi, was first released on February 12, 1931,[16] and it appeared on the screen in Japan on October 8, 1931, according to *Internet Movie Database*.

Nevertheless, Stoker's *Dracula* had not been well known yet among Japanese readers in the 1930s, which allowed a detective story writer, Seishi Yokomizo (1902–1981), to write a vampire story, "Dokuro kengyō" (The Lord of Skulls), in 1939. Designing the story's setting in early-19th-century samurai-ruling Japan, Yokomizo nearly plagiarized the plot and main characters from Stoker's *Dracula*. The supernatural villain, Shiranui Kengyō, sucks blood and turns victims into vampires.[17] The protagonist Akenosuke Kitō becomes a prisoner of the vampire living on an isolated island. The island is full of wolves, like in the woods of Transylvania, and while dozing, Kitō is about to be attacked by the wives of the vampire just like Jonathan Harker at Dracula's castle. Shiranui Kengyō, or the Lord of Skulls, departs for Edo as

Count Dracula heads for London. The story contains characters corresponding to Van Helsing, Mina Harker, Lucy Westenra, and even mad Renfield.

As we see, although Japanese people had rarely known Stoker's *Dracula*, Bela Lugosi's Dracula appeared in Japan in the 1930s. However, World War II prevented the influx of Western culture into Japan in the early 1940s. The Japanese Imperial Government banned various cultural matters related to Western countries to prevent its citizens from sympathizing with their enemies. After the defeat of World War II, the Japanese gradually prepared to reconstruct their country and began fully to accept Western culture again. As Japan grew up from the bombarded and wasted land as a new economic power, the Japanese raised their living standards. In the 1950s, Japanese people eagerly restarted consuming vampire productions coming from the Western world.

In 1958, Hammer production's *The Horror of Dracula*, directed by Terence Fisher, was released. The Dracula performed by Christopher Lee in this movie had a strong impact on the audience, and his figure has become a global cultural icon. The series of *Dracula* movies performed by Lee were successively produced and exported to Japan. Moreover, they often appeared on TV. Lee's Dracula established an authentic image of Dracula in the popular mind-set of Japanese, probably partly confused with Lugosi's Dracula.

In the middle of the 1960s, "Dracula" had nearly become a common appellation for vampires among the Japanese. Dracula was caricaturized, parodied and consumed in Japanese popular culture, just like the Count in *Sesame Street*. In 1965, the cartoonist duo Fujiko Fujio started serially publishing *Kaibutsukun* (*The Prince of Monsters*).[18] The target readers were elementary school children. The Prince of Monsters determines to live alone among humans. His three caretakers, Frankenstein's monster, Wolf Man, and Dracula, come to see him only during the night. This Dracula, drawn by Fujiko, is snobbish and meticulous, and even resembles a mother who constantly chides and annoys her children. In its first story, a boy living in the flat next to the Prince's watches a TV program with the title *Three Monsters*: Frankenstein's monster, Wolf Man, and Dracula.[19] Fujiko Fujio clearly describes them based on the monsters appearing in the Universal horror movies originally released in the 1930s. In due course, the three characters scare the boy and, when he sees Dracula, he cries, "Dracula!" not "Vampire!"[20] This cartoon plainly shows how the Japanese public had adopted the filmed Dracula by the middle of the 1960s.

In the same period, Japanese readers came easily to access Stoker's *Dracula*. In the late 1950s, Teiichi Hirai (1902–1976) first translated *Dracula*, although it was an abridged version. Hirai energetically and continuously translated and introduced many scary Western stories, including Joseph Sheridan le Fanu's

Carmilla (translated and published in 1970) and has been praised as a champion translator of horror fiction among Japanese bookworms. In 1971, Hirai's complete translation of *Dracula* was published. We should notice that, as mentioned, Dracula had already been parodied in various media before this publication. Hirai's translation ensured *Dracula*'s masterpiece status among hard-core horror fiction readers in Japan. Due to the skillful and rhythmical narrative containing a rich vocabulary, many regarded his work as the decisive translation of the classical story of the vampire; however, it includes many mistranslations. It was in the last year of the second millennium (2000) that a pair of Japanese scholars, Akihiko Agatsuma and Ai Tanji, dared to publish a new translation. Hirai's translation, however, is still being reproduced and enjoys a wide readership even now.

Thus, the spread of the images of the visualized aristocratic vampires among the Japanese and the appearance of the authentic translation of Stoker's *Dracula* provided the soil in which Japanese beautiful vampires were nurtured on their own. The *tanka* poet Asahiko Sunaga (1947–) published the aforementioned study on vampires, *Chi no arabesuku* (*Arabesque of Blood*), in 1978. He intended to connect the folkloric origins of Western vampires with the widespread contemporary images; its newly enlarged version was published in 1993. At the beginning of the book, Sunaga reveals his own personal image of vampires, skillfully generalizing the image that many Japanese must have shared when the first edition of the book was published in the late 1970s. Sunaga introduces why vampires attracted him. The reason was that he saw a tall beautiful young man walking along the hall of an old castle with a black mantle lined with vivid red cloth in a foreign movie the title of which Sunaga could not even remember.[21] The origin of Sunaga's image is vague, but the image of the vampire itself is extremely clear.[22]

Sunaga himself wrote short stories featuring beautiful male vampires mainly in the 1970s. The vampires clearly share the image of the vampire described at the beginning of Sunaga's study. Many of them seduce young males, and their stories consequently have a strong flavor of homoeroticism. Furthermore, some of them can be recognized as short sequels to *Dracula* with settings in Transylvania. These short stories have often been chosen for anthologies, including those of Sunaga's own works such as *Tenshi* (*The Angel*, 2010).

There is no doubt that, since the 1970s and 1980s, Anne Rice's *Vampire Chronicle* series has also established modern images of beautiful male vampires. The first novel, *Interview with the Vampire*, was published in 1976. However, we should consider the fact that its Japanese translation came out in 1987, and that Rice's beautiful vampires destined eternally to roam around the world needed the help of the novel's film adaptation, released in 1994 with Tom Cruise and Brad Pitt as vampires, to spread their decadent and elegant images overseas.

In 1971, the same year of the publication of Hirai's complete translation of *Dracula*, Ryō Hanmura (1933–2002) published a milestone among Japanese vampire novels, *Ishi no ketsumyaku* (*Bloodlines of Stones*). This novel cannot be called a "pure" vampire novel because, in addition to vampires and werewolves, it contains a mixture from different genres, such as the legend of Atlantis, worldwide megalithic monuments, a legendary cult of assassins, and the sexual esotericism of ancient religions, and it describes long conflicts between the privileged minority and the exploited majority in human society. The vampires are infected with a kind of sexual disease. They can obtain immortality but need human blood in their transformation process. In this heavily Marxist vampire novel, those who are selected as the privileged infectees are beautiful or extremely rich people. Physical beauty is regarded as one of the indispensable attributes for vampires in this popular Japanese novel.

In the middle of the 1970s, before the appearance of Anne Rice's Lestat, a Japanese female cartoonist created beautiful boy vampires living immortal lives with decadent backdrops. Moto Hagio's *Pō no ichizoku* (*The Family of Poe*) continually appeared in a Japanese girl's comic magazine, *Hana to yume* (*Flower and Dream*), from 1974 to 1976. In Japan, comics for girls, *shojyo manga* or *shojyo comikku*, have formed a genuine genre of popular culture, and this vampire cartoon work has been estimated as one of the masterpieces. Thanks to Hagio's long career and popularity, *Pō no ichizoku* has been reissued in various editions. It describes the miserable destinies of an eternal 14-year-old vampire, Edgar, his family, and mortals who happen to engage with them. For nearly 200 years, the beautiful boy vampire cautiously selects mortals who may be able to share the destiny of the undead. Most of the human characters with whom Edgar deeply engages are boys in their teens; Edgar chooses them as his victims or eternal partners.

While Hagio's masterpiece was serialized within a short time period with many breaks, another Japanese vampire serial story keeps being published as if it never ends. The first novel of the series, *Banpaia Hantā "D"* (*Vampire Hunter "D"*), written by Hideyuki Kikuchi, was published in 1983 as one of a selection of entertainment novels for young adults. In 2010, the 34th novel of the Vampire Hunter D series was published. After destructive wars among humans, vampires suddenly emerge and rule the near-future earth. They are called "aristocrats," and most of them have medievalist tastes for their appearance or residences. In order to resist the oppressive rule of the bloody aristocrats, people hire talented individuals or groups who can compete with and destroy vampires. Among such vampire hunters, the hunter whom people believe is the strongest gives his name as "D." He is a mixed breed between human and vampire who is so beautiful that nobody can imagine any figure surpassing his beauty. Just a glimpse of his appearance infatuates both males and females.

As this general overview of the work's setting and protagonist show, the most beautiful figure in this series is a hybrid of human and vampire. Nevertheless, it is certain that this vampire series has kept powerfully implanting the image of a beautiful vampire in the Japanese popular mindset for several decades. In many stories of D, the antagonists facing the beautiful protagonist often boast of their beauty. Moreover, the reason why D can be the strongest vampire hunter is that he can use the powers and skills of vampires. Among other things, as the name of the protagonist implies, this vampire novel series is inspired by *Dracula*, especially by its filmed version. Kikuchi confesses that he escaped from a cinema house in the middle of the screening of Christopher Lee's *The Horror of Dracula*. He himself identifies this movie as the origin of his attraction to scary movies and stories.[23]

The third novel of this series, *D—Yōsatsukō* (*D: A Wild Hunt*, 1985), was filmed with the title *Vampire Hunter D* and first released in the United States in 1999. Because it was on the screens in the States, the characters speak only in English; they of course spoke Japanese when they were on the screens in Japan. *Vampire Hunter D*, directed by Yoshiaki Kawajiri, is a typical example of the internationalization of Japanese *anime* and of Japanese vampire culture.

In the 1990s, Japan got another vampire novel masterpiece: Mariko Oohara's *Kyūketsuki Efemera* (*Ephemera the Vampire*, 1993). This feminist vampire novel differs from the work mentioned previously because the central figure is female. In this story, the vampires are parasites similar to the "thing" in the movie, *The Thing from another World* (1951). (Actually, Oohara lets the protagonist vampire, Ephemera, recall this movie in the novel.) These parasites increase their life spans by supplanting the bodies of humans. When they hijack males, they generally become pregnant and bear offspring in a rather short term. In this case, the mother and the child need one more body. Thus, they usually stay in female human bodies. Because of this backdrop, all main figures of this novel (i.e., vampires) have the forms of female humans. Among them, Ephemera has *used* a specific body for a long time because it is splendidly beautiful.

In this story, for an unimaginably long time, humans rarely knew about the vampires. In the 22nd century, however, their existence becomes public due to an accident caused by the coming of extraterrestrial beings. In a Far Eastern country (seemingly Japan), humans start hunting vampires, but the vampires exploit the bodies of the all-male extraterrestrial beings and proliferate themselves in a short period; they consequently overcome the danger of the persecution by humans. On the other hand, many human females lose their bodies and lives because of the rapidly increasing vampire population, though pregnant women hijacked by the vampires bear new humans who can live much longer than normal humans. The story ends with the suggestion of the beginning of a new age of humans, new humans, and vampires with the appearance of female humans. The vampires in this fiction are far different from the decadent and lonely image of the male vampire as Asahiko Sunaga described it in the 1970s. The vampires described by Oohara are female, organize a group, become productive, and even obtain a bright future. This vampire novel prophesied the coming of the age of women in the early 1990s. (It even predicted the emergence of the first African American President, which obviously was realized. The character is a man nurtured by a very old vampire profoundly considering the future of the world.)

Diversified Children of the Night: Vampires in Contemporary Popular Culture in Japan

Since World War II, the Japanese have kept creating and enjoying vampires using various cultural media. Along with the representative beautiful vampires discussed previously, many other types of vampires have appeared in Japanese literary or visual works. For instance, a variety of them may be found in the anthologies of vampire stories written by Japanese writers mentioned in the introduction: *Chi to bara no ekusutashī* or *Shiki no ketsuzoku*.

Among Japanese vampire novels without beautiful vampires, Fuyumi Ono's *Shiki* (*Corpse Demon*, 1998) is a remarkably voluminous vampire story. It can be called a Japanese version of Stephen King's *Salem's Lot*. A group of vampires secretly invades a small town situated among the mountains. Normal people turning into vampires confront their own family and friends. The hunters become the hunted, and vice versa. There are neither superheroes nor extremely beautiful nightwalkers in this novel. Humans are like vampires; vampires are like humans. It is worth mentioning here that this novel developed into other media: Ryū Fujisaki drew the cartoon-serial version of Ono's *Shiki* in the graphic magazine *Jump Square* from 2007 to 2011 and this cartoon was also adapted into a television animation in 2010.

Since Japanese readers and audiences have experienced various types of vampires, they can easily accept and enjoy vampire novels or movies coming from foreign countries.[24] In the 1990s, after the release of the movie *Interview with the Vampire*, most of the novels of Anne Rice's *Vampire Chronicles* were translated. In the first decade of the 21st century, the novels of the Daren Shan series were translated book after book and became bestsellers. Recently, young Japanese people have had fun reading the translations of the *Twilight* saga and seeing the movies from the series.

While the dominant image of the vampire in the late 20th century was a very solitary and decadent figure, contemporary young Japanese seem to imagine them as creatures existing in a group. They are numerous and, in some cases, their world is in parallel with our own. We humans communicate, conflict, or even find companionship with them; they are friends, enemies, or even lovers. Examining modern images of vampires in Japanese popular culture, mainly focusing on several vampire cartoons, such as Matsuri Hino's *Vanpaia naito* (*The Knight of Vampire*, 2005–), Yoshitaka Inoue analyzes how two "worlds" of humans and vampires negotiate with each other. Inoue considers that they divide roughly into three patterns: (1) they exist with little or no communication; (2) they conflict with each other; and (3) they co-exist in one society.[25]

Vampires in a subcultural genre, "Light Novels" or *Ranobe*, are worth discussing here.[26] This genre is generally defined as illustrated entertainment novels targeting teenagers.[27] At the turn of the 20th century, the genre explosively developed in the publication industry of Japan. According to the yearly guidebook of the genre, *Kono Raito Noberu ga sugoi! 2012* (*Great "Light Novels" in 2012*), approximately 1400 Light Novels came out under various labels from October 2010 to September 2011. Presently, many publishers dealing with this genre make up duos of writer and illustrator, and the works of such popular pairs have been successively adapted into TV animation programs with the characters designed by the illustrators of the duos. The sales are boosted further by becoming anime. Aki Enomoto points out that most of such animated *Light Novels* develop into other diverse media such as CDs, comics, video games, and the like.[28]

Among the enormous number of publications of *Light Novels*, many include vampire motifs. As we saw previously, Japan has more than a half-century history of acceptance of Western vampires. Moreover, young people in present-day Japan are fond of Gothic characters or images including vampires in popular culture. The targeted readers of *Light Novels* also influence the ages or appearances of main characters in them. In most of the novels, they are high school or junior high school students, and thus many vampires communicating or conflicting with them have the appearance of human teenagers. When the vampires look like boys, they are not necessarily beautiful any more. They can be handsome, cool, or even grotesque. On the other hand, when they look like girls, they are often cute rather than beautiful. For example, in *Itsuka tenma no kurousagi* (*A Black Rabbit Has Seven Lives*, 2008– ; adapted to TV animation in 2011), the protagonist, Taito Kurogane, is a student of Miyasaka High School. A "vampire" (meaning "the most ancient sorcerer" in this novel) bit his neck with two sharp teeth, injected venom and cast the curse of love upon Taito in his childhood. This vampire named Himea Saito comes to his high school as a student—disguised as a lovely human girl.

Conclusion and Epilogue: A Cute Vampire

Before the Western imperial powers opened the then isolated samurai country in the middle of the 19th century, there were no blood-sucking immortal creatures in Japan. With the huge influx of Western cultures, however, the supernatural beings, having charmed Western people for so many years, started entering the mind-set of the Japanese. Though World War II temporarily blocked their influx, in the 1950s and 1960s the film *Dracula* had a strong impact on the imagination of the Japanese public. As a result, the image of an aristocratic dark figure represented vampires for the Japanese in the late 20th century. As Japanese writers created many literary works with vampire motifs, probably in the 1970s, vampires turned into *beautiful* creatures in the popular imagination, and the genealogy of beautiful vampires was established in Japanese popular culture. In most cases, they are males eternally destined to wander around the world. Since throughout the last several decades of the 20th century, the Japanese developed their own vampire culture, contemporary Japanese readers and audiences can accept and enjoy various types of vampires.

At the end of the previous section, I referred to the rise of *cute* girl vampires in *Light Novels*, a genre of contemporary Japanese popular culture. To conclude this chapter, let us examine another cute vampire appearing in Japan in the summer of 2011. I launched this description of the history of Japanese vampire culture by introducing the Japanese version of *Dracula, the Musical*. I saw one of the performances in Hall C of the Tokyo International Forum on August 21, 2011. As mentioned, Count Dracula was beautiful, cruel, and dignified: Yōka Waō, an actress with a long career, performed the vampire role. Since three male dancers played Dracula's three vampire partners, only one other female vampire appeared on the stage. Natsumi Abe, from the pop group Mōningu Musume (Morning Girls), performed the role of Lucy Westenra. Her height is relatively short, and she is cute, rather than beautiful. Lucy/Abe was eliminated in the middle of the performance, but her energetic acting left powerful impressions on the audience. The representation of the beautiful vampire on the stage was of course magnificent but, at the same time, the people in the theatre on that night saw the rise of the cute vampire.

Notes

1. I wish to thank Dr. Simon Humphries, Doshisha University, for reading the manuscript and contributing valuable suggestions and editorial assistance, and Professor Takako Tanaka, Doshisha University, for providing useful pieces of information on Takarazuka Revue. Special thanks to Kyodo Tokyo Inc. for allowing the use of the gorgeous picture of Yōka Waō as Dracula; Mitsuyo Taketsugo, Gene & Fred, gave me a chance to write an essay on vampires developing into this work. I also cannot help showing my gratitude to three ladies living with me: my daughters, Eri and Mari, have been constantly providing the interest-luring information on contemporary Japanese teen popular culture, and my wife, Chikako, patiently allows me to enjoy, with the whole of the family, the stuff that my daughters bring home with them.

2. I contributed an essay to the brochure of the Japanese production of *Dracula, the Musical*. This essay was developed from that work. See Masaya Shimokusu, "Utsukushiki kyūketuki: Dorakyura to kyūketsukibungeitaikoku, Nihon (Beautiful vampires: Dracula and Japan, a country rich with her own vampire culture)," in *Dorakyura, za myūzikaru (Dracula, the Musical)*, ed. Mitsuyo Taketsugu (Tokyo: Fuji Television and Kyōdō Tōkyō, 2011), 44–45, published in conjunction with the musical, *Dracula, the Musical*, performed at the Tokyo International Forum and Umeda Arts Theater.

3. Takarazuka Revue also put on the stage their own original musical featuring a beautiful vampire, *Bara no fūin: Vanpaia rekuiemu (The Seal of Roses: A Vampire Requiem)*, in 2003. The male vampire, performed by Jun Shibuki, roams around the world for nearly 700 years.

4. Asahiko Sunaga, *Chi no arabesuku: Kyūketsuki dokuhon (Arabesque of Blood: A Vampire Reader)*, rev. ed. (Tokyo: Peyotoru Kōbō, 1993), 151–153.

5. Mari Kotani, *Tekunogoshikku (Techno-Gothic)* (Tokyo: Hōmu, 2005), 98–107.

6. Frederic Jameson, Foreword to Kojin Karatani, *Origins of Modern Japanese Literature*, trans. and ed. Brett de Bary (Durham, NC: Duke University Press, 1993), vii–ix.

7. Toshirō Yasuda, *"Kokugo" no kindaishi: Teikokunihon to kokugogakusyatachi (A Modern History of "National Language": Imperial Japan and Scholars of Japanese)* (Tokyo: Chūōkōronshinsha, 2006), 3–33.

8. Howard Phillips Lovecraft, *Supernatural Horror in Literature* (New York: Dover, 1973), 12.

9. Masao Higashi, ed., Commentary to *Goshikku meiyaku syūsei 1: Seiyo denki monogatari (Best Selection of Translations of Gothic Works 1: Western Historical-Fantastic Stories)* (Tokyo: Gakushūkenkyūsha, 2004), 521–525.

10. The famous scary-story translator, Teiichi Hirai, discussed later in this article, was the disciple of Haruo Satō. Hirai is the first Japanese to translate the full text of Stoker's *Dracula*.

11. Maso Higashi, ed., Commentary to *Shiki no ketsuzoku (The Kith and Kin of Corpse Demon)* (Tokyo: Ōtōshobō, 1999), 487–490.

12. Higashi, *Shiki no ketsuzoku*, 488–489.

13. Rampo Edgawa, "Kyūketsuki" (Vampire), in *Edgawa Rampo zenshū (Complete Works of Edgawa Rampo)* (Tokyo: Kōbunsha, 2005), 92.

14. Kōnosuke Hinatsu, *Kokuiseibo* (*Black Virgin Mary*), vol. 1 of *Hinatsu Kōnosuke zenshū* (*Complete Works of Kōnosuke Hinatsu*) (Tokyo: Kawadeshobōshinsha, 1973), 136.

15. Kōnosuke Hinatsu, *Kyūketsuyōmikō* (*A Study on Vampirism*), vol. 11 of *Seikagaku zenshū* (*Collected Works of Sexology*) (Tokyo: Bukyōsha, 1931), 180–181.

16. Skal, David J., *Hariuddo Goshikku*, trans. Katsuo Jinga (Tokyo: Kokushokankōkai, 1997), 235. Originally published as *Hollywood Gothic: The Tangled Web of Dracula from Novel to Stage to Screen* (New York: Norton, 1990).

17. The tombstone of Shiranui Kengyō suggests that this vampire is Shirō Amakusa, a real historical figure, who revolted against the Tokugawa Shogunate, leading Japanese Christians. During the battle in 1638, he died at the age of 17. Japanese folklore has described him as a very beautiful boy.

18. The cartoon duo, Fujiko Fujio, later separated into Fujiko Fujio A and Fujiko Fujio F: eventually the individual authorship was revealed. *Kaibutsukun* was drawn by Fujiko Fujio A, Motoo Abiko. As Makoto Fukuda reported in a *Daily Yomiuri* article, "Monsters Come to Life," on December 23, 2011, this long-forgotten cartoon gained fresh attention because it was adapted to a TV serial drama in 2010, and the TV drama developed into a cinema version in 2012.

19. Fujiko Fujio A, *Kaibutsukun: Yūjohen* (*The Prince of Monsters: Best Selection of Stories of Friendship*) (Tokyo: Shōgakukan, 2010), 16–17.

20. Fujio, *Kaibutsukun: Yūjohen*, 22–23.

21. Sunaga, *Chi no arabesuku*, 2.

22. An erudite scholar of German literature, Suehiro Tanemura (1933–2004), tried to explore the origins of vampires' fascinations, referring to both classical and modern, and Occidental and Oriental cultural works in his influential essay, "Kyūketsuki gensō" (Vampire Fantasy), published in 1968. The essay was compiled with Tanemura's other articles on vampires and published in a book form with the same title in 1982.

23. Hideyuki, Kikuchi, *Banpaia Hantā "D"* (*Vampire Hunter "D"*) (Tokyo: Asahi Sonorama, 1983), 281.

24. Even my translation of Bob Curran's *Bloody Irish*, a collection of vampire short stories based on Irish folk legends, was published on a commercial basis in 2003. (A Dublin publisher, Merlin, originally published it in 2002.) The Japanese publisher considered that the translation of the collection could appeal to Japanese readers. See Bob Curran, *Bloody Irish*, trans. Masaya Shimokusu (Tokyo: Hayakawashobō, 2003).

25. Yoshitaka Inoue, "The Image of Vampires in Modern Japan," *The Annual Bulletin of Praxis and Research Center for Clinical Psychology and Education, Kyoto University* 14 (2010): 36–55, 42–47.

26. Tomomi Yamanaka investigates how the concepts of *Light Novels* have been changing in response to contemporary popular trends. See Tomomi Yamanaka, *Raito Noberu yo doko ni iku: 1980 nendai kara zero nendai made* (*Where "Light Novels" Go: From the 1980s to 2000*) (Tokyo: Seikyūsha, 2010). Hirotaka Ichiyanagi argues that *Light Novels* are a cultural phenomenon complicatedly produced in contemporary Japanese society,: see Hirotaka Ichiyanagi and Yoriko Kume, eds., *Raito Noberu*

kenkyu jyosetsu (*An Introduction to Light Novels*), foreword by Ichiyanagi (Tokyo: Seikyūsha, 2009), 13–15.

27. Tomomi Yamanaka, *Raito Noberu yo doko ni iku: 1980 nendai kara zero nendai made* (*Where "Light Novels" Go: From the 1980s to 2000s*) (Tokyo: Seikyūsha, 2010), 7.

28. Aki Enomoto, *Raito Noberu bungakuron* (*A Literary Study on Light Novels*) (Tokyo: NTT Shuppan, 2008), 185–192.

14

From Russia with Blood: Imagining the Vampire in Contemporary Russian Popular Culture

Thomas Jesús Garza

Beginnings: The Vampire as Russian and the *Other* Russian

FOR MANY FANS AND FOLLOWERS OF THE VAMPIRE in the 21st century, the word itself is synonymous with the name *Dracula* and, as such, begins with Bram Stoker's seminal tale of the blood-drinking count from Transylvania. Though some know that Stoker's account is loosely based on the real-life historical prince of Wallachia, Vlad "Țepeș" Dracula from the 15th century, far fewer know that the word *vampire* is very much a part of the myth and folklore directly from the Slavic lands: the Balkans, Eastern Europe, and Russia. Indeed, the first occurrence of the word in writing is attested in 1047 in a text from the Russian Primary Chronicles in reference to a prince from the Russian town of Novgorod as "*upyr' likhij*," or "wicked vampire."[1] Since then, the use of the word—which changed over time from *upyr'* to *vampir*—to refer not only to the evil, wicked, and blood-thirsty, but actually to the mythical undead, a "being which derives sustenance from a victim, who is weakened by the experience,"[2] has evolved greatly to embrace "vampires" of all types present in Russian culture and society.

In medieval Russian culture, one of the primary suggested "causes" of a human's transformation into a vampire after death is heresy against the Christian church, to which Early Russia subscribed in 988 under Prince Vladimir.[3] This association, that one who acts against the common belief and for the salvation of humankind should become the predatory undead, has led to a post-modern use of the vampire in the cultural production of Russia that carries the meaning of cultural "Other," as used by, among others, Edward Saïd in his seminal work *Orientalism*.[4] Thus, the vampire in the late 20th and 21st century has frequently been employed in Russian popular culture critically to describe elements of contemporary Russian society that are not like the rest of us and usually detrimental to the rest of us. This work examines the use of the vampire image in Russian popular culture, notably in music and film, and how the vampire in these cultural products reflects the nation's fears and anxieties about the vampires among them during the period following the collapse of the Soviet Union and the construction of New Russia.

Gorbachev, *Glasnost'*, and New Vampires

During the Soviet period (1917–1991), the vampire was nearly absent from the official Russian cultural consciousness, save for a couple of notable appearances in official or semi-official venues. Most striking was the 1967 film version of Nikolai Gogol's novella «Вий» ["Viy"], directed by Konstantin Yershov, which officially was the first horror film to be released in the Soviet Union. Replete with witches, werewolves, and ghouls, in addition to vampires, the work was sanctioned as part of the Russian literary canon and as an obvious work of fantasy. Less official, but at least as visible, was a 1971 satirical horror-ballad by the incomparable Soviet bard Vladimir Vysotsky. Invoking his own funeral wake, the song «Мои похороны» ["My Funeral"], like so many of Vysotsky's controversial compositions, is a thinly veiled critique of the "blood-sucking" nature of the Soviet regime, from the critics to the government itself.[5]

Сон мне снится—вот-те на!	I have this dream; here it is!
—гроб среди квартиры.	—a grave in the middle of my flat.
На мои похорона съехались вампиры.	Vampires have gathered for my funeral.
Стали речи говорить,	They all started making speeches,
все про долголетие,	all about long-life,
Кровь сосать решили погодить:	They decided to hold off sucking blood;
вкусное на третье.	it's tasty for dessert.[6]

It is important to note, of course, that like so many of Vysotsky's compositions, the Soviet government never officially sanctioned the performance or recording of these lyrics. But through the efforts of passing along hand-copied lyrics and copies of recordings through the practice of *samizdat*, or "self publishing," Vysotsky's early Soviet vampires succeeded in making it into the Russian consciousness. Vysotsky, regretfully, died in 1980 at the age of 42, just 5 years before his works might have easily been recorded and performed legally in the Soviet Union.

With Mikhail Gorbachev's ascension to power in 1985 after a quick succession of other Soviet leaders following the long period of stagnation under Leonid Brezhnev, a palpable shift in the very fabric of Russian culture and society occurred after he instituted a policy of *glasnost'*, or "speaking out" on issues of political and social concern. Suddenly, topics that earlier would have ensured one's imprisonment or persecution were on the pages of the official Soviet press. Writers and their works, once forbidden, were printed for the first time in their native language. Films, plays, songs—all suddenly enjoyed a new official imprimatur of creative freedom.

Key to the implementation of *glasnost'* for Gorbachev was *samokritka*, or "self-criticism," the practice of searching deeply into oneself, one's surroundings, and society to find what was not right and to try to make it better through public revelation. Inherent in this process was the outright naming of points of weakness in Russian government and society, and the press and products of popular culture were frequently used as the vehicles for such revelations. As *glasnost'* took hold in practice toward the end of the 1980s, subject matter that was virtually unheard or unseen in the Soviet period suddenly became germane for public consumption, especially in popular culture. Among these now permitted subjects, the vampire quickly emerged as both a theme and symbol of New Russia's new constituents.

Rising from the Ashes: Early Post-Soviet Pop-Gothic

Russian popular culture responded relatively quickly to the social upheaval that followed the collapse of the Soviet Union in 1991. Popular music became the immediate venue for much socio-political content in the 1990s, as it had a strong base of musicians and fans dating back to the days of the Soviet underground scene. Previously forbidden groups, such as Kino, Akvarium, Alisa, and others, now performed openly and released records to an eager audience, hungry for themes and lyrics that went beyond the narrow scope of official previously sanctioned tunes about love and happiness. The music of Russia's newly emerging music scene ranged from heavy metal to light rock, from post-punk to gothic. It was in this heady, exciting musical crucible that Russian rock once again returned to the venerable subject of the vampire in its performance. Importantly, however, the *upyr'*, who had lain relatively quiet through more than 70 years of Soviet rule, returned from the dead in a quite different guise; once again the vampire would be used in Russian culture to signify new "Others" in post-Soviet society and once again be employed to vilify the unwelcome visitor among the population.

One of the first performers to invoke the vampire as part of her musical repertoire was the singer Linda (née Linda Gejman). A native of Soviet

Kazakhstan, Linda quickly built her career on writing and performing electronic music, often with an ethnic flair, and spearheading in Russia the genre known as "trip hop." Her first album, «Песни тибетских лам» [*Songs of Tibetan Lamas*], appeared in 1994 and included the vampire-inspired song, «Девочки с острыми зубками» ["Little Girls with Sharp Little Teeth"]. The lyrics of this song are explicitly vampiric, and "traditional" in their references to fangs and blood:

Они уходят ночью,	They come out at night,
Не остановить!	Don't stop!
Они кусают плечи,	They bite shoulders,
Это не забыть!	Don't forget this!
Смотри! Они с острым клыком	Careful! They have a sharp fang
Тебя зовут красивым ногтем!	They call you with a pretty fingernail!
Они оставят после	Later they'll leave
На тебя следы,	Tracks on you,
Как отставляют кошки	Like cats leave behind
От такой игры!	From such a game![7]

Perhaps intentionally, the song's vampiric impact (i.e., horror) is greatly softened by the use of diminutives throughout: little girl, little teeth, etc. As one of the first products of Russian popular culture to foreground the theme of the vampire, Linda's song benefited from the lighter touch and became a video hit for the performer.

The following year, in 1996, Linda released her second album, the commercially successful «Ворона» [*The Crow*] with an eponymous single and music video. This song was replete with gothic images of death, blackness, and faceless, zombie-like creatures, though it lacked explicit vampire imagery. However, Linda's role in promoting the nascent gothic genre to the fore of Russian popular culture cannot be overstated.

While Linda imbued her vampire songs with irony and even humor, another Russian band chose to re-create the high gothic drama of the 19th-century vampire tales reminiscent of Pushkin's Romantic gothic verses, such as "The Bridegroom" or Zhukovsky's "Liudmila." The band Piknik managed to remain viable during the Soviet period by creating albums of the fantastic and supernatural, but not fully embracing the gothic or vampiric. Only after the fall of the Soviet Union did the band release an entire album themed exclusively on the creature of the night. In 1995, the album «Вампирские песни» [*Vampire Songs*] came out, featuring 9 songs, all of them contributing to a brilliant portrait of the classic Russian vampire tale. Notable in the collection is «Лишь влюблённому вампиру» ["Only for the Vampire in Love"], which is ballad-like in its telling of the relationship between a male vampire and his gentle, female victim:

Он идёт походкой лунной	He walks likes the moon to a
В дальний сад, где ночь без дна,	Distant garden, where the night is deep,
Где за оградою чугунной	Where behind the iron gate
Бродит девушка одна,	A girl strolls alone,
Бродит девушка одна.	A girl strolls alone.[8]

This album played a major role in creating the post-Soviet gothic sound and culture that enjoyed popularity in Russia in the mid-1990s. While Piknik's contribution might seem to be on the surface somewhat derivative of the much earlier Russian Romantic gothic movement, the melodies and lyrics nonetheless add to the portrait and character of the new Russian vampire that was forming in the 1990s.

Just a year following the success of Piknik's *Vampire Songs*, another female artist added her voice to the growing presence of gothic and vampiric themes in Russian popular music. Lika Starr (née Lika Pavlova), known simply as Lika, added a euro-disco dance beat to the vampire theme. In 1996, her song *"Odinnokaja luna"* ["Lone Moon'] became an instant hit. Though the lyrics contain not a single literal reference to vampires, vampirism, or blood, they do—from the title on—invoke a strong sense of the vampiric and the gothic:

Скоро наступит утро,	Soon it will be morning,
Скоро придёт рассвет.	Soon dawn will arrive.
Дай мне одной минутой	Give me just one more minute
Вновь позабыть весь свет.	To forget the whole world again.
Перед моей дорогой,	Before I hit the road,
Дай мне любви глоток.	Give me a sip of love.
Знаю, что этой ночью	I know that tonight
Ты, как, я, одинок.	You're alone like me.[9]

The invocation of the night and the moon from the title, and the subsequent description of a passionate and dependent relationship, the need to leave before dawn, and the reference to a "sip of love" all draw a quite convincing portrait of a vampiric encounter. But as if the lyric evidence were not enough, the video clip that accompanied this song's release in 1996 and aired on Russia's pre-MTV music video program, «Музыкальное обозрение» ["Musical Review"]. makes the vampire connection vividly.

The video for "Lone Moon" portrays a group of Russian gangsters kidnapping a young woman (played by Starr) and showing the ills of the New Russian underworld: prostitution, drugs, gun smuggling, and human trafficking. The video is dark and foreboding, not merely in its subject matter, but in its visual presentation. As the woman's boyfriend desperately tries to locate her and becomes entangled with other gangsters himself, we anticipate an unfortunate ending for the kidnap victim—an ending that might have seemed entirely appropriate in the seemingly lawless days in Russia's capital city in the 1990s. But in an unexpected twist, just as the video reaches its final seconds, both the young woman and her boyfriend turn into vampires and quickly dispatch the criminal element around them. Suddenly, the "victims" become the predators in Moscow's topsy-turvy gangland environment, and the Other, in this instance, is Russian young people. The vampire image unexpectedly is re-imagined as a positive attribute, empowering the youth to rise up and fight the tide of corruption and crime that is the new plague on New Russia. Of course, the entire presentation of the vampire in the clip is not entirely tongue-in-cheek. While the postscript on the screen at the end of the video states:

> Все события и персонажи этой истории вымышлены,
> любые аналогии исключены
> All events and characters of this story are fictional,
> any similarities are unintentional[10]

The message to viewers is clear: we all know that there are monsters are in our society, and now we know who they are—and we are *not* the monsters—at least not yet!

Female artists did not have a monopoly on exploiting the vampire theme in popular music in the 1990s. In 1997, one of Russia's seminal all-male rock-n-roll bands, Nautilus Pompilius, released the album «Яблокитай» [*Yablokitaj*, or *AppleChina*], which contained the single «Нежный вампир» ["Gentle Vampire"]. With lead singer Vyacheslav Butusov's baritone fronting the lyrics, "Gentle Vampire" became one of the first overt and chilling re-imaginings of the Slavic vampire in post-Soviet Russia. The words to the song, in contrast to earlier efforts, invoke the vampire and its place in the Russian cultural consciousness explicitly—from the title to its refrain:

Холоден ветер в открытом окне.	A cold wind in an open window.
Длинные тени лежат на столе.	Long shadows lie upon the table.
Я таинственный гость	I am the secret guest
в серебристом плаще,	in a silvery coat,
И ты знаешь зачем я явился к тебе.	And you know why I've come to you.
Дать тебе силу,	To give you strength,
Дать тебе власть.	To give you power.
Целовать тебя в шею,	To kiss you on the neck,
Целовать тебя всласть,	Kiss you to my heart's content,
Нежный вампир.	A gentle vampire.[11]

But this song does not merely convey a neo-Romantic portrait of a New Russian vampire; the lyrics go on to chide the potential victim in a striking critique of Russia's new youth and of the country itself:

Подруги твои нюхают клей.	Your girlfriends sniff glue.
С каждым днём они становятся	Every day they become
Немного глупее.	A little more stupid.
В этой стране вязкой как грязь,	In this country sticky like mud,
Ты можешь стать толстой	You can become fat
Ты можешь пропасть.	You can disappear.

Much more a reprise of the Lika song "Lone Moon," "Gentle Vampire" reminds the listener that the presence of vampires is hardly the worst thing in the country at the moment. Indeed, the lines of the song about the vampire himself are much more empowering and consoling, while the words about the status quo in the country are entirely unfavorable and negative, implying once again that vampires are not the real monsters in New Russia.

As if to emphasize the critical timbre of the lyrics, "Gentle Vampire" was selected by the director, Aleksej Balabanov, to be featured in his film «Брат» [*The Brother*] later that same year. The film, like the song, presents contemporary Moscow and St. Petersburg as overwhelmingly crime-ridden, destitute, and soulless. Only the film's hero, Danila Bagrov, a de-mobbed veteran of the Russian army during the first Chechen war, seems able to maintain a sense of moral equilibrium in the post-Soviet social chaos, but as a result constantly falls victim to the denizens of the changed cityscape. Not coincidentally do we learn that he is a great fan of the group Nautilus Pompilius, and his search for their music becomes a leitmotif in the plot. Further, the song "Gentle Vampire" is playing when Danila must become a "benevolent monster"—a killer himself—in order to save his beloved brother from a gang of Russian mobsters. Once again, the trope of the Slavic vampire, as a soulless predator, is re-imagined as the lesser of many evils that abound in post-Soviet Russia.

New Century: New Vampires

With the election of Vladimir Putin in the spring of 2000, vampire imagery, along with other negative portraits of the new president, increased significantly in Russian cultural production.[12] With campaign rhetoric that included calls for the complete annihilation of the Chechens in order to put an end to the Chechen War that Boris Yeltsin had begun in 1994, Putin's rise to the presidency created the perfect atmosphere for anti-war, anti-establishment, and especially anti-autocracy artists and citizens to use the vivid and culturally available trope of the vampire to illustrate the barbarism of predatory behavior in Russia in the new millennium. Russian film, theater, and music all included performances that were highly critical of the administration and the direction the country was moving. One of the most striking examples of an overt call for young Russians to "slay the vampires among us" came in the form of an unlikely diminutive Russian rapper named Detsl.

Born Kirill Aleksandrovich Tolmatsky, the young rapper called "Detsl" (meaning "a small amount" or "half-pint" for his small stature) stunned Russian MTV audiences in 2000 with the song and accompanying video called «Кровь, моя кровь» ["Blood, My Blood"]. With a hip-hop performance that many fans of the new genre uniformly derided for its naïveté and immaturity, the song's lyrics and video nonetheless created a sensation for their uncompromising criticism of contemporary Russian urban culture and figures of authority. The song tells the story of a Russian youth who inadvertently finds himself the target of various vampire figures in the city, ranging from drug addicts and gang members to mafia bosses and his own teacher. Having been saved from a nearly deadly vampire attack in the video by a shaman-like figure, he is transformed into a Buffy-style vampire slayer, complete with wooden stakes and mallet. Once empowered, he quickly dispatches a series of vampires, including his own teacher, and—at least for the time being—emerges victorious at the end of the song. The song lyrics describe each slaying following his own attack:

Я приступил к делу, хотя ещё болело тело.	I got to it, even though my body still hurt.
Страшная месть мною владела.	Horrific vengeance ruled me.
Во мне кипело как в тот тёмный вечер,	It boiled in me, like on that dark evening,
Когда меня четыре быка хотели покалечить.	When four thugs wanted to cripple me.
Один любил шикарные автомобили,	One of them liked classy cars,
Его случайно в гараже придавило.	He was accidentally run over in the garage.
Второй сидел на LSD и героине,	The second was hooked on LSD and heroin,
Врачи поставили диагноз—передоз в теле.	The doctors' diagnosis: an overdose.
Третий впервые решил пригнуть с парашюта.	The third went skydiving for the first time.
Он не раскрылся как в злом анекдоте.	The chute didn't open, like in a bad joke.
Четвёртый понял, в чём дело, и удрал,	The fourth knew what was up, and took off,
Из города на долгие года, без вести пропал.	Left the city for years, and disappeared.[13]

Detsl's role as vampire slayer in "Blood, My Blood" is a phenomenon in the musical production of post-Soviet Russia. The reappearance of this venerable figure from the Russian and European past is not accidental. Like the rationalist slayers before him, Detsl's character wants to rid modern Russia of the trappings of folklore and fiction of the past so that it can move into a new progressive (European?) era. As Bruce McClelland contends in his study of the vampire slayer of the Age of Reason:

> [T]he rationalists' purpose was to completely destroy the imaginary and the folkloric and to replace them with the materialistic and scientific, partly as a reaction against the sort of violent, elaborate fantasies that had tormented the Inquisitors as much as their victim and led to cycles of extreme persecution and excessive punishment. Once science had explained away the vampire as unreal, it was no longer possible for this sort of folklore to have any autonomy among the folk—especially in those areas where the vampire was not native.[14]

With only slight revision, one can easily change McClelland's observation to read "Once modernity had explained away the 'vampire' (i.e., Soviet rule) as unreal, it was no longer possible for this sort of 'folklore' to have any autonomy among Russians." Indeed, Detsl's less-than-impressive rap skills are certainly overshadowed by the timely and direct message to the Russian youth to take charge of their destiny in New Russia.

The first years of the new millennium produced vampire-themed musical works of other genres in addition to rap. Like Nautilus Pompilius and others, the rock group Aria emerged on the musical scene during the halcyon days of Gorbachev's era of *glasnost'* and *perestroika*, when many of the constraints and restrictions on political voices, social commentaries, and cultural production were greatly relaxed. Prior to 1985, a band like Aria, with its heavy metal sound and even harder lyrics would have been relegated, at best, to the Soviet underground where it would have endured constant censorship and threat of arrest, not to mention a very small audience.

After enduring several changes of band members during the 1990s, the band reemerged in the new millennium with a decidedly more gothic sound on its 2001 album «Химера» [*Chimera*], which included a song titled simply «Вампир» ["The Vampire"]. Significantly, the title of the song names the creature overtly; other than that mention, however, the word *vampire* only occurs once more in the lyrics. That singular mention, still, is one more than appears in Detsl's composition, although the video for his song uses very overt images of vampires. Instead of naming the creature, both works rely more heavily on the listener's prior knowledge of the vampire myth to connect all of the lyrical dots, so to speak, and give vampiric meaning to the overall work. The Aria piece begins with an apocalyptic vision reminiscent of the collapse of the Soviet Union:

Рухнул мир, сгорел дотла,	The world's collapsed, burned to the ground,
Соблазны рвут тебя на части.	Temptations are tearing you to pieces.
Смертный страх и жажда зла	Deathly fear and a thirst for evil
Держат пари.	Are making a bet.

In a version of the vampire myth less optimistic than that of Detsl as vampire slayer, the Aria song invokes instead the inevitability of one's fate to become a vampire in this unhappy world:

Днём лихорадка—ночью пир.	Fever in the day, at night a feast,
Ты теперь демон, ты вампир.	You're a demon now, you're a vampire.
В поисках новой жертвы	In search of a new victim
В снег и зной,	in the snow and in the heat,
Вечной изгой.	An eternal hunt.
Но ты был одним из нас,	But you were one of us,
Жаль ангел тебя не спас.	A pity an angel didn't save you.[15]

From these most recent examples, it might seem that the contemporary Russian vampire—in popular music at least—is still often a product of Gorbachev-era "self-criticism" and, indeed, "self-othering," suggesting that the real monsters in modern Russia are the Russians themselves. However, such a view may be a bit too simplistic, given the additional data provided by examples of the Russian vampire in 21st-century film. Several of Russia's newest contributions to the vampire in film offer a modified portrait of the figure that is a far cry from the very tame and folkloric Soviet-era production of "Viy."

Vamps on Film: Russia's Newest Monsters

As the United States and the West indulged its fascination and appetite for vampire films with *30 Days of Night, Daybreakers, Fright Night,* and *Dark Shadows,* not to mention the ubiquitous contributions from the *Twilight* machine, plus television shows like HBO's *True Blood* and the CW's *Vampire Diaries,* among others, New Russia added its contributions to the "vampire mania" of the new millennium. Coinciding with the Western obsession with and prolific production of vampire-themed programs in the 2000s, Russia also embarked on the film production of the first two of Russian-Ukrainian-Tatar author Sergei Lukyanenko's multi-volume modern-day vampire saga, comprising *Night Watch, Day Watch, Twilight Watch, Last Watch,* and *New Watch.*

In 2004, all prior box office records in Russia were smashed with the release of Kazahkstan-born director Timur Bekmambetov's «Ночной дозор» [*Night Watch*], in many respects a classic tale of good and evil, in which vampires—both Light and Dark—own the Earth, and a young Chosen One must devote his own allegiance to one or the other side in order to determine the balance of power in the vampires' world. The vampires depicted in the film are real—as opposed to metaphorical, and the conflict in which they are engaged to gain complete power is to the death. The Night Watch, or the vampires of the Light, are tasked to protect Moscow and the rest of the world from dominance by the Day Watch, or the dark forces. In another historic battle between the imperialist and the subaltern, Russia's fate is once again in the balance.

In a scene central to understanding the portrayal of the vampires in *Night Watch*, a young boy, Yegor, whom the Night Watch has named the Chosen One, questions his two Night Watch protectors about the nature of "Otherness," the conflict between Light and Dark and Good and Evil, and his own identity:

Егор:	А как понять "иные"?
Yegor:	How do I understand "The Others?"
Она:	Иные? Ну, иные отличаются от обычных людей.
She:	The Others? Well, the Others are different from normal people.
	Иной обладает нечеловеческими способностями.
	The Other has inhuman abilities.
Егор:	Гм. Почему?
Yegor:	Hmm. Why?
Она:	Ну, потому что им пришлось в жизни пройти
She:	Well, Because they had to endure in life
	—нечеловеческие испытания. Понимаешь? И приложить
	—inhuman trials. Understand? And add
	к тому нечеловеческие усилия. Он становится иным.
	to this inhuman efforts. So he becomes an Other.
	И жизнь у них становится иная. И если в этот момент
	And their life becomes an Other as well. And then if there's
	рядом не будет того, кто смог бы обяснить ему что с
	no one close to him, who could explain to him what's
	ним происходит, и научит как жить среди людей с
	going on with him, and teach him how to live among people with
	такими способствиями. Тогда . . .
	such abilities. Then . . .
Егор:	А бы какие иные—тёмные, или светлые?
Boy:	So what Others are you—Dark or Light?
Она:	Мы? Мы светлые.
She:	Us? We're Light.
Егор:	А я?
Boy:	And me?
Он:	А это ты решишь сам.
He:	That you'll have to decide for yourself.
Она:	Понимаешь?
She:	Understand?
Егор:	А какая разница между тёмными и светлыми?

Boy:	So what's the difference between the Dark and the Light ones?
Она:	Все иные берут силу у людей. Тёные берут тёмную,
She:	All Others draw their power from people. Dark ones take what's dark,
	светлые светую. Ну, как пищу, как еду.
	the Light take what's light. Like what you eat, like food.

The not-so-subtle text of "light" and "dark" is certainly not lost on a Russian audience that has lived through nearly two decades of a very fraught war with the Chechens—a conflict that has often been racialized by Putin himself, earning him the moniker of "vampire" in the Western press, notably in the more conservative press, such as *The New American* and *The Telegraph*. *Night Watch*, like the earlier Slavic vampire tales of the 15th and 16th century, is a cautionary tale, a self-portrait intended to offer Russians a chance to learn from past mistakes and prepare for a better future.

The sequel to *Night Watch*, «Дневной дозор» *Day Watch*, was dubbed "The first film of 2006" and opened on New Year's Day, implying that it was, indeed, the first film of 2006 chronologically, and also the number 1 film in terms of box office draw for the year. Both assertions turned out to be true. The film continues the story begun by its predecessor and brings the conflict between the Light and Dark vampires to a filmic climax worthy of the film's grandiose epic premise. What is notable in this sequel is present in the original film as well: the portrait of present-day Russia as a cultural monolith hanging in the balance between to forces, represented metaphorically by the Light and Dark vampires. In reality, Russia is still that medieval nation-state geographically, philosophically, and emotionally caught between the East and the West, an Occidental victim of its own Orientalism, if you will.

This untenable dichotomy is brilliantly portrayed in the film's opening sequence, which depicts a reimagining of Tamberlane's 14th-century campaign in Samarkand and Central Asia. Sharing the same name as the film's director, Timur Bekmambetov, Tamberlane emerges as both an historic and a contemporary figure dangerously close to precipitating the end of the world as he pushes across the continent from East to West. Similarly, the vampires in the film represent both the historical and folkloric ties of Russia to the ancient and enduring mythology of the undead, as well as its current reluctant place in a globalized modern world, a world in which the vampires and other monsters sometimes turn out to be oneself.

As Russia moves forward in defining its ever-growing role in global affairs, economics, and culture, whether through its increasingly active role in the G-8 and beyond, or through its next literary, musical, and cinematic contributions to the arts, it will continue to use metaphor like the vampire to explore its own weaknesses and vulnerabilities. As Veronica Hollinger notes:

[The vampire] is the monster that used to be human; it is the undead that used to be alive; it is the monster that *looks like us*. . . . The figure of the vampire always has the potential to jeopardize conventional distinctions between human and monster, between life and death, between ourselves and the other. We look into the mirror it provides and we see a version of ourselves.[16]

In seeking to examine itself increasingly through a lens of self-criticism and objectivity, and placing itself in a position to see its own monsters more clearly, Russia will continue to be the progenitor and the perpetuator of the Western vampire myth.

Notes

1. Jan L. Perkowski, *Vampire Lore: From the Writings of Jan Louis Perkowski* (Bloomington: Slavica Publishers, 2006), 216.
2. Jan L. Perkowski, *The Darkling: A Treatise on Slavic Vampirism* (Columbus: Slavica Publishers, 1989), 54.
3. See Felix Oinas, "Heretics as Vampires and Demons in Russia," *Slavic and East European Journal*, 22 (1978): 433–441.
4. See Edward Saïd, *Orientalism* (New York: Vintage Books, 1978).
5. All translations included in this piece are the author's, and song lyrics appear in Thomas J. Garza, compiler and ed., *The Vampire in Slavic Culture*, revised ed. (San Diego: University Readers, 2010).
6. Garza, *The Vampire in Slavic Culture*, 539.
7. Garza, *The Vampire in Slavic Culture*, 545.
8. Garza, *The Vampire in Slavic Culture*, 563.
9. Garza, *The Vampire in Slavic Culture*, 541.
10. Garza, *The Vampire in Slavic Culture*, 541.
11. Garza, *The Vampire in Slavic Culture*, 567.
12. William F. Jasper, "Putin's Russia: The Return of the Iron Fist," *The New American* 23 (2007): 14.
13. Garza, *The Vampire in Slavic Culture*, 548.
14. Bruce McClelland, *Slayers and Their Vampires: A Cultural History of Killing the Dead* (Ann Arbor: University of Michigan Press, 2006), 128
15. Garza, *The Vampire in Slavic Culture*, 569.
16. Veronica Hollinger, "Fantasies of Absence: The Post-Modern Vampire," in *Blood Read: The Vampire as Metaphor in Contemporary Culture*, eds. Joan Gordon and Veronica Hollinger (Philadelphia: University of Pennsylvania Press, 1997), 201.

15

Dracula Comes to Mexico: Carlos Fuentes's *Vlad*, Echoes of Origins, and the Return of Colonialism

Adriana Gordillo

V AMPIRES, PARTICULARLY IN THE ANGLO-SAXON WORLD, have been a symbol that aids discussions related to race, gender, and capitalist production systems.[1] This symbol, suggests Howard L. Malchow (following Showalter), reflects a kind of panic about gender and racial anarchy, a fear that translates into that which is outside of the social norm, or that which is part of two different worlds exceeding modern categories, such as homosexuality, *mestizaje* (racial mixing), and the like.[2] In Hispanic America, this liminal space is part of a mestizo reality, a mixed and post-colonial reality that co-exists on a daily basis with that which *is* and at the same time *is not*. It is what Derrida in his readings of Heidegger's metaphysics of presence has called the *specter*, a notion that aims to question the hierarchical order articulated through pairs of opposites through the duality presence/absence (*to be* or *not to be*) that inevitably leads to the subordination of one of the parts within this order of beliefs.[3]

Both Derrida and Malchow's notions privilege a sense that coincides with a discussion that is at the core of Hispanic American identity, given the multiplicity of cultures that have co-existed, mixed, and survived after (and during) its conquest, colonial, and republican periods. Take for instance how, in Mexico in particular, as Octavio Paz says, "the opposition between life and death was not so absolute to the ancient Mexicans as it is to us. Life extended into death, and vice versa. Death was not the natural end of life but one face of an infinite cycle."[4] This pre-colonial imaginary, coupled with a strong baroque Spanish tradition—a ritualistic tradition where opposites do not exclude each other but co-exist—survives in the interstices of today's society through a number of cultural manifestations, the most popular of which is the *Day of the Dead*. The baroque aesthetic, one of unity and plurality at the same time, serves as an appropriate vehicle to express the Hispanic American complex reality, emphasizing either its conservative, guiding, and cohesive version[5] or its transgressive, revolutionary aspect. This latter trend, according to Mabel Moraña's study on colonial baroque,[6] is "the beginning of a process in which Latin America emerges into the world scenario with its own voice, although it is still articulated to the institutions and discourses of the empire."[7]

The baroque aesthetic has proliferated in Hispanic America as a symbol of excess, but also of what Cuban writer Lezama Lima has called "an aesthetic of 'curiosity,' of igneous, Luciferine, and Faustian knowledge, a daemonic *poiesis*."[8] In the Hispanic American literary scope, the baroque and neo-baroque traditions are a privileged mode that encompasses authors such as Jorge Luis Borges, Alejo Carpentier, Severo Sarduy, José Lezama Lima, Octavio Paz, and Carlos Fuentes, among others. The latter author, one of the most renowned Mexican writers of the 20th and 21st centuries, believes that the Hispanic American baroque mode is an adequate instrument to access an ambiguous world in which the pre-colonial world and various stages of modernity and post-modernity co-exist in the same space without annihilating each other, and where these stages are organized in a nonlinear progression. These stages are organized in a sort of spiral that allows a constant gaze toward the past, as well as a continuous wondering where one can recover the ruins of a past that is still alive, even though it sometimes appears to have just a spectral form. In his essays, Fuentes discusses the baroque mode directly. However, in his fictional works the baroque aesthetic comes alive in the craftsmanship of the texts: the importance of the reader, circular narrative, a burlesque tone, and a set of symbols, such as theater, mirrors, the idea of death, and vampire-like beings.[9]

The vampire is a symbol that points toward this ambiguous state associated with the baroque mode because it (the undead or the living-dead) refers to two contradictory states that co-exist in one being. Although the Hispanic American vampire does not have the prevalent place that it has in the European literary tradition, there are a good number of authors who have explored the symbol during the past couple of centuries, such as Rubén Darío, Delmira Agustini, Quiroga, Griselda Gambaro, Alejandra Pizarnik, Julio Cortázar, Luis Zapata, as well as more recent authors like Carmen Boullosa, Yolanda Pantin, Adriana Díaz-Enciso, Carlos Fuentes, and Carlos Franz. In this context, some questions come to mind when dealing with rewritings of this new-yet-old character: how is the vampire symbol reinvented and rearticulated in contemporary Hispanic American literature, in particular in Mexican literature? What elements does a text draw upon when picturing this figure and what categories can we attribute to it? Carlos Fuentes's work is an adequate referent for these questions because he often uses vampire-like references and attributes in many of his texts.[10] Through this symbol, Fuentes discusses notions of memory, the survival of *art* and *ideas* through their ruins (which become "living dead" after the death of their creator) and, following Schopenhauer's perspectives on nature, the constant struggle between humans and the environment, in which it is impossible to survive without feeding on another life.

Fuentes's "vampiric references" are brought to a concrete embodiment of the classic vampire story in his novella, *Vlad*.[11] This story is in direct dialogue with Bram Stoker's *Dracula*, as well as with Murnau's and Herzog's cinematic versions of the monster.[12] Fuentes's character can also be related to Béla Lugosi's[13] performance in the Broadway play (1927) and film version (1931), as well as to the horror satire portrayed by the same actor in Ed Wood's movies. In *Vlad*, the *lugosi* are part of a genealogy of monsters that oscillate between two worlds (the *moroni, nosferatu, lugosi, strigoli,* and *varcolaci*).[14] In this case, the two worlds juxtapose the animal and the human world, satiric and horror modes, as well as the written, oral, and visual traditions, creating a mixture of ideas that encompasses various levels of information and symbolism, as we will see.

Count Vlad Radu's story goes as follows: Yves Navarro, the narrator, was a Mexican lawyer who worked for a prestigious law firm whose head was Mr. Zurinaga, an old influential man who represents a generation of men enriched by the Mexican Revolution.[15] Yves's latest job at the firm entails helping his boss's friend, Count Radu from Transylvania, to find a house in Mexico City, a task that resembles Jonathan Harker's enterprise to Eastern Europe in Stoker's *Dracula*. Fortunately for Yves, his wife Asunción was a realtor who found the perfect location for the visitor. This house was on an isolated cliff, had all the windows sealed and was decorated with Fuseli's macabre and phantasmagoric paintings.[16] However, this house was also a "modern monastery . . . a house built for light, according to Scandinavian dictates."[17] To prolong the set of contradictions, the house was in the Colonia Roma neighborhood, a contradictory neighborhood known for its colonial environment, an aspect that emphasizes the notion of opposites, as well as what David Castillo understands as a "baroque condition": the exercise of "extreme," whether extreme overabundance or excessive simplicity, which refers both to fear and to the attraction that comes with absence or emptiness.[18]

Count Radu moved to Mexico, displaced by his country's last civil war, and came with his 10-year-old daughter, Minea, and his butler, Borgo. Asunción and Yves also had a 10-year-old daughter, Magdalena, who was the perfect role model of Mexican middle-class girls who followed French social trends, maintaining one of the most significant 19th-century Latin American cultural orientations. The couple also had a son who drowned in the ocean years ago, and whose death will be the driving force for Asunción's later actions. When Count Radu arrived at his new house, Yves noticed an uncanny resemblance between Minea and his own daughter, Magdalena. They looked like twins.

Later on, Yves finds out that his wife and daughter were kidnapped by Count Radu while he was at work, and when Yves tries to rescue them, Zurinaga, his boss, reveals the true story behind the Romanian visitor; Count Radu's story was basically Vlad Tepes's story, the historical character who possibly gave birth to Dracula's myth.

At this point, the text embarks in a spiral of stories behind stories, in a Chinese box structure or Matryoshka principle—common to Fuentes's texts—that invites the reader to question if there is another secret behind the latest secret revealed, and if it is at all possible, to know the original source of the monster's myth (or for that matter, any other myth).

Around 1448, said Zurinaga telling his version of the vampire's story, Vlad Tepes, from Wallachia, impaled thousands of people during his reign of terror. His atrocities were associated with both the Holy Roman Empire and the Ottoman Turks, each faction considering Vlad as its enemy's ally.[19] The myth around the bloody ruler grew in both Christian and Muslim imagery associated with the idea of the demon and the malignant enemy. Today, says Fuentes, accentuating the tenuous distinction between reality and fantasy, it seems "almost unrealistic that Ceausescu, the Romanian dictator, printed a stamp with the Impaler's image"; in that sense, Fuentes continues, "a monster paid tribute to another monster,"[20] validating and recontextualizing the myth's use.

When Yves's attempt to rescue his wife and daughter failed, he discovered the rest of Vlad's origins, which unexpectedly involved Minea. In this new layer of Fuentes's reinvention of the story, the Impaler was buried alive due to his crimes, which was the origin of his name, "the un-dead." When he was taken to his tomb, nobody looked at him except for a 10-year-old girl. In time, the place of the count's tomb was forgotten; however, local peasants felt the need to control the evil that lived in it and which seemed to be the cause of continuous malevolent episodes. There was an old tradition among the peasants that would help them find the monster's tomb: a naked girl should ride a horse and it would stop exactly at the location of the tomb. The same girl who looked at Vlad during his way to the tomb offered to perform the rite to find him. However, when the horse was about to stop, the girl sank the spurs in the animal so that nobody but her could find the tomb. At night, the girl went to the tomb and opened it, freeing Vlad from his prison. It was the girl who made him a vampire, depriving him of his sight so that his eyes "could not express more need than that of blood, and no sympathy than that of the night."[21] When Count Vlad told Yves his side of the story, he expected the Mexican to have sympathy for him since he, too, should have been subject to the devastating effects of time. However, it was the child who removed him from his path and took him to eternity.

In Fuentes's fiction it is common to find a discussion on the relationship between humans and nature, especially through the exploration of the fear sparked by our finite existence and our desire for transcendence. Our mortality comes with freedom, with the ability to grow, to change, and to create; whereas the notion of eternity is often associated with a state of immobility, a timeless and sterile existence. Fuentes believes that this difference is resolved through *writing* because the written text encompasses both concepts. Writing resembles the notion of immortality and is (in theory) permanent, timeless, and unchangeable once it becomes part of the printed world; and whether the text is visual, oral, or written (narrative, recordings, film, painting, photography, and so on), the medium that captures it also paralyzes it.[22] On the other hand, writing is also alive because it evolves in the hands of the reader who creates new meanings on every new reading. The vampire metaphor comes in handy to express the cohesion of these ideas. Similar to art and writing, the vampire is timeless; it transcends death (the death of the author) and, in doing so, its biological existence stops at the age in which the person was bitten by the monster. The vampire is frozen in time, paralyzed, just like a text both immobilizes its content and immortalizes it. The vampire reproduces through biting. It can procreate only through immortalizing another being. In this sense, we could argue that a text can only "procreate" when it "bites" the reader and promotes new meanings that will also, if in print, transcend death.

Moreover, this intersection between our mortality and our desire for survival comes with the need for a constant recreation of the idea of origin, a need for a beginning that explains our current mortality and explores the possibilities of transcendence. The notion of origin comes hand in hand with the act of naming as a vitalizing force, in a sort of Kabbalistic way, that promotes the creation of possible pasts and futures that come to life through the aesthetic experience. In this account of the story, Vlad is merely a creation of little Minea, not the "original" vampire as tradition tells us. The notion of origin is questioned to remind us that this "square one" exists because there is a tradition behind it, though such tradition is fluid and multiple, and there is always another secret to unveil (and to create).

In this story, Fuentes takes us back to a tradition associated with figures of evil that has gone from oral to written, from written to visual representations, and, from there, back to written. This process of appropriation and re-appropriation of a myth coincides with Fuentes's narrative program, which integrates the notion of *mestizaje*, not only in a racial sense but also in a literary sense: the vampire myth can be traced back to Indo-European, Slavic, Turkish-Iranian, and even Hispanic American oral traditions. However, it is in English, French, and German Romanticism that the myth becomes a recurrent literary topic. The modern idea of vampires is generally associated with Stoker's *Dracula*, an example of the opposition to modern values. The count is an aristocrat who lives in an isolated castle in the Carpathian Mountains at the margins of bourgeois capitalist society during the 19th century, at a time when the modern city was at center stage. Romania was then a region associated with superstition and religious conflicts between Christians and Muslims were common. This region, also known for its pagan mythology, was isolated from the capitalist circuits guided by Imperial Europe.[23] The colonial enterprise was behind the myth of the vampire. It became an allegory of progress and the division between civilization and barbarism that justified the appropriation of land, human beings, and the creation of policies that allowed the reproduction of one and only one version of reality.

In the case of Vlad, Minea, the eternal child—youth's utopia—is the reason behind the vampire's visit to the New World, as will be explained later. However, Vlad is not interested in visiting the United States, the American dream, or the New World that exemplifies progress and capitalism. Instead, the vampire decides to go to Mexico, the New World in which modernity is filled with pre-Columbian and colonial specters, and where multiple times and realities co-exist at the same time; that is to say, a place where his contradictory essence would not be noticed due to the fact that the place itself is a sort of palimpsest where multiple and diverse levels of realities coexist. Furthermore, Vlad comes to today's Mexico, where 20 million souls await his hunger. Fuentes's vampire appears here as a foreign, voracious, and uncontrolled force. It appears as the specter of an enterprise that was supposed to be eradicated, but that returns like a seasonal crop to take advantage of the impunity and poverty of a country such as Mexico. This topic connects also with Fuentes's *The Crystal Frontier*, where the author explores the incidence of U.S. neocolonial economic policies in Mexico. In this direction, Fuentes's vampire resembles the monster's 17th-century image, which is associated with the idea of a bourgeois exploiter who fed on poor people. In a time when social theories established an analogy between society and the human body, the bourgeoisie fed on people's "blood." Later on, in 19th-century England, the image of vampires was related to Irish immigrants, who were at the same time pictured as both victims and a menace to the economy.[24] Fuentes's retelling of the vampire myth feeds on this previous symbolism in this case to reflect on the new capitalist menace, the globalized neocolonial order, which comes like a monster to feed on his country. From this perspective, Fuentes's vampire examines a new type of exploiter that can be translated as big corporations and policies such as the North-American Free Trade Agreement (NAFTA) that have immigration as its major consequence.[25] If the 19th-century European vampire became the monster feared by the English due to his embodiment of that which was against the capitalist order, Fuentes's vampire becomes a mirror-like image that transforms the old fear into a new fear that situates the old victim as the new perpetrator, though covered by the old mythology.

Fuentes's vampire also emphasizes the questioning of a univocal point of view that comes alive through the re-appropriation and re-invention of a tradition that is not at center stage in Hispanic American literary studies, and which also corresponds to Malchow's gender and racial anarchy from various standpoints. On the one hand, despite Stoker's *Dracula* being the most common reference to the origin of the vampire, it is imperative to think about the female vampire when approaching Fuentes's text, for example Goethe's "The Bride of Corinth," Le Fanu's *Carmilla*, Coleridge's "Christabel," Keats's "Lamia," and countess Elizabeth Báthory's story. However, unlike these texts, *Vlad* does not demonize women who became more socially active, an attitude that inspired the fear of 19th-century European writers. Fuentes's story contests the notion of a masculine origin (Dracula), which represents the 19th-century idea of traditional forces that slow the advancement of modernity, but also the notion of a masculine origin that supports patriarchal society. Dracula is the image of death, and death, according to Fuentes in his readings of Bataille, is "origin in disguise."[26] In Fuentes's text, origin (origins in general) is expressed through myth, which pretends to reflect a perpetual present. The emphasis here should be in the "pretention" because myths are constantly traveling in a sort of "myth tourism" that results in its re-appropriation, transformation, and mixing, giving birth to amalgams of temporalities that co-exist despite their apparent dissonance and mutual exclusivity.[27]

Fuentes' rewriting of the feminine vampire refers to the ambiguous character of ancient Maya and Aztec feminine entities such as Ixchel, Tlazoltéotl, Tonantzin, Mictecacihuatl, or Toci, who are at the same time creators and destroyers, as well as other deities like Ninhursag and Inanna (Sumerian), Ishtar and Kubab (Babylonian), Astarte (Greek), and Artemisia (Phoenician).[28] This ambiguity reinforces Fuentes's notion of women as an enigma that men are incapable of understanding.[29] Fuentes uses women as a symbol of an enigma in order to refer to the idea of origin as an empty space, capable of re-inventing itself from within or from outside of literary tradition. Women become a symbol of constant flux, of what travels disguised with the clothing of the eternal, but which is constantly reinvented in its journey, like myth and literature. That is to say, Fuentes's feminine figures travel around all his literary work claiming, like the literary text, multiple meanings that oppose the univocal sense associated with the masculine origin that sprang from Judeo-Christian mythologies, which gave birth to capitalist modernity and its political, racial and religious totalitarian beliefs. The relationship between the women-enigma-origin-myth articulated in *Vlad* has a polyphonic, Bakhtinian sense that Fuentes considers part of his literary heritage where the novel becomes the "agora" in which infinite points of view coincide.[30]

The feminine origin of the vampire also evokes a number of symbols and references that recall Bataille's ideas of evil as that which is outside of the norm, as well as that which opposes categories of masculinity, such as reason, instrumental value, self-control, adulthood, technology, and so on. Minea, Vlad's maker and fake daughter in present times, seems like a 10-year-old girl. She is the "eternal girl of the night,"[31] an appearance that points toward Bataille's idea of the "recovered childhood," a state of ingenuity and innocence; but also a state of impulsiveness, immediacy, of irrationality and, therefore, a sense that points toward the world of the now and the freedom that opposes the world of adulthood. This adult world, in theory, is the world in which we control our instincts and are able to sacrifice desire in favor of a future benefit.[32] Vlad's comment to Yves comes to mind following this logic: "Kids are pure internal force, Mr. Navarro. A part of our vital strength is concentrated inside each child and we waste it, we want kids to stop being kids and become adults, workers, 'useful to society.'"[33] This comment takes us also toward discussions about desire and creation, which Fuentes mentions when he discusses vampire figures: "Dracula looks for blood, but he also looks for love, he wants to be recognized by the beings that he desires even though that recognition means the death of what he loves. Love is only a union if it first recognizes the original separation, of the fact that we love somebody else."[34] While Minea is a girl in her physical appearance, she was more than 300 years old when she gave life to Vlad in the 15th century. This inconsistency confronts the reader with the contradiction and impossibility of categorizing a being that gathers in itself two aspects that both terrify and seduce human beings: youth and immortality.

The concept of the "eternal child" refers as well to the classic mythic theme of Adonis, which corresponds to the Jungian "puer archetype." The eternal child has been read as a symbol of the agrarian world, in particular, to that of spices (barley, wheat, fennel, lettuce) that sprout early during the summer but have a very short cycle of life. Furthermore, this archetype has been linked to the development of ego, which—through institutions such as marriage and work—becomes the link to society and to the external world that takes place through politics, in opposition to the world of what in Jungian analysis corresponds to the "collective unconscious" symbolized by the archetype of the

Great Mother.[35] Adonis's death is a constant return to the womb—to earth in the vegetable symbolism—which, says Robert Segal, "is simply his permanent rather than temporary return to her,"[36] an act that in the end embodies "the negation of practices without which the polis cannot be conceived: exogamy and reproduction. The myth [Segal concludes] dramatizes the consequences of rejecting those practices: barrenness and death."[37] With this in mind, Minea, Fuentes's eternal child, can be read as a reiteration of the Great Mother archetype, as part of the collective unconsciousness from where ego will spring. Not in vain we learn that Minea is legion. She is part of a genealogy of monsters whose nature is associated with the veil of night and a state that is in constant flux between the animal and the human world; that is to say, a state that oscillates—in a symbolic way—between a childish, irresponsible, and selfish attitude (both within the self and toward the external world) and an adult who is capable of embracing the responsibilities and limitations of the biological, social, and political world.

Minea, like Adonis, is a "symbolic puer."[38] She will never grow up; however, unlike Adonis' infertile life, Minea can reproduce by creating more creatures like herself. Even though her reproduction is limited, she can spread her kind. Her childish, animalistic progeny keeps alive in the margins of society, contesting the notion of "barrenness and death" as the consequences of rejecting conventional practices of reproduction. In this sense, Minea is not only a metaphor for the collective unconsciousness but also a metaphor of the creative impulse that lies within that same collective unconscious, an impulse that, like art and literature, does not require notions of heteronormativity, adulthood, and binary categories in order to become alive.

At the end of the story, Asunción, Yves's wife, embodies a "historical puer" when she decides to become the vampire's lover while her daughter Magdalena grows up and marries the monster. In this case, we face the subversion of the life of a married woman who has a "normal" life. Asunción—surprisingly for Yves—has been in contact with Vlad for a while and she had an active part in her fake kidnapping. The woman follows the vampire in exchange for Magdalena's eternal life, which she considers a counterbalance of her son's early death. Asunción is also tired of her marriage's routine and of the sense of security that Yves provides her. She feels like a "prisoner of daily tedium" and repudiates her husband's "normality," throwing herself in the arms of a man who "can hurt her," who is "not good" like Yves whose fidelity seems to her like "a plague."[39] Asunción rebels against the institution of marriage, a union that in her case follows a pattern of respect and peaceful coexistence that she neglects in order to indulge her repressed instincts, which bring her closer to Bataille's recovered childhood and to the puer archetype.

Breaking Western society's rules will come only with new conditionings and new-yet-old traditions that keep Asunción in a marginal position subject to the vampire's will. Vlad wants the company of a woman who resembles his creator, Minea, but who, contrary to her, will not be limited to her childish state. The vampire wants a kind of woman who has not grown up yet, a woman who—despite her resemblance to the monster's maker and her symbolism—is also capable of growing, of transforming herself every day, at least until the day she becomes his wife leaving the effects of time. Vlad is not trying to revitalize an identical twin of his maker since this alternative implies the return to the collective unconsciousness and that is simply not possible if he wants to preserve his ego, which, in this case, coincides with a dominating, oppressive, and controlling force traduced as a neocolonial power.

Though Magdalena is Minea's mirror image, Fuentes's doubles are never identical; just like allegories, they always leave a little bit of room for a new interpretation since language is incapable of encompassing the totality of meanings. With this in mind, Magdalena and Minea's names invite the reader to post another set of symbols and relationships that differentiate the girls.[40] On the one hand, Minea's name reminds the reader of the young Cretan woman who—in Mika Waltari's *Sinuhe* (1945)—was sacrificed to continue the farce of a dead god and on the other her name resembles that of Mina Harker.[41] Mina, in Stoker's *Dracula*, is the person who types "the disparate material provided by many fictional participants" of the story.[42] Her narrative is "a copy of a copy," and therefore a story within a story, the same structure that Fuentes portrays in his own version of the vampire's tale.[43] In that sense, the feminine principle in both accounts of the vampire story (Stoker and Fuentes's) is that of a creative force that translates into a new, symbolically complex, and "mestiza" narrative; that is to say, into a "vampire-narrative." Mina's character has been read also as the "depiction of the New Woman" that terrified 19th-century authors who, like Stoker, had an "ambivalent response to assertive or independent women."[44] Despite Mina's skills—at the time seen as masculine-like skills (her organizational and written abilities, and her endurance to weather conditions)—she ends up surrendering to a male's protection.[45] Mina's character reverts to an infant state that resembles that of Minea's childish appearance. Minea's and Mina's resemblance—both linguistically and symbolically—ends up being a game of distorted mirrors that reflect one another, and, in doing so, allow us to recognize a set of characteristics (often associated with evil) that are constantly mixing and reproducing new, often twisted, versions of themselves.

Magdalena's name refers immediately to the biblical tradition. Magdalena is a prostitute redeemed thanks to her love for the Christ. Her transformation is that of a woman who commits the sin of altering the order of the nuclear family (again, gender anarchy). She trades her sexuality but is redeemed by following and venerating the word and the path of a man. In this sense, Fuentes's Magdalena will be a mirror image of Mary Magdalene since their paths seem similar yet rather opposite. Magdalena in *Vlad* is a child, a condition that faces the future in opposition to the past that Mary Magdalene rejects in favor of her Messiah. Magdalena, the girl, will also achieve eternal life, like Mary Magdalene, though in her case she will achieve this condition following the vampire, a symbol of evil, a vital (yet apparently dead) force connected to the collective unconsciousness and the creative impulse. However, is eternal life not a state similar to death? What is death but "eternal and immobile time . . . an instant without an end"?[46] Magdalena's eternal life will take place through her acceptance of her undead state, the eternity provided by the vampire. Magdalena's destiny as the vampire's future bride (as well as her mother's sexual attitude) connects her to Lucy Westenra's character in Stoker's *Dracula*. Lucy's character has been read as the consequences of an unleashed libido in Victorian times, revealing "the antithesis of decent womanhood: aggressive, demanding, powerful, and sexually uninhibited."[47] Moreover, according to William Hughes, Lucy is also a character that needs to be saved not only from her uncontrolled sexual instincts through "the corrective phallus of society," but also from a "predatory foreign invader."[48] Just like Lucy before she was transformed, Magdalena was a girl who followed the social norm, and whose destiny entails breaking her family's values when she embraces the vampire's world. Magdalena's social norm resembled that of 19th-century France, the colonial stepmother chosen by Hispanic American elites in their effort to distance themselves from Spain, the motherland and former imperial power. Magdalena, a Lucy-type character, is going to trade one colonial institution for a neocolonial one, which coincides with Mexico's cultural (and economic) dependency on France and more recently, on the United States, reconnecting the symbolism associated with the vampire to an imperialistic and oppressive force.[49]

Metaphors multiply in the text emphasizing its feminine and baroque aesthetics, which reflect on the text's ambiguity and fluidity. In this sense, the state of "undeadness" that we identify with vampires corresponds with Fuentes's notion of *ideas*, which, he believes, are never fully developed. For Fuentes,

> ideas come and go, sometimes retreating, hibernating like some beasts, waiting for the appropriate time to reappear. Thought does not die. It only measures its time. [It moves.] It duplicates and sometimes it even supplicates. When it disappears, we believe it is dead, however, with each word it resuscitates. . . . There is no word that is not filled with forgetfulness and memories, also tinged with

illusions and failures and yet, there is no word that does not overcome death because there is no word that does not come with an imminent renovation.[50]

Words, continues Fuentes,

> fight against death because they are also inseparable from death, since they announce it, steal it, or inherit it. There are no words that do not come with its imminent resurrection, since each and every word that we pronounce announces, simultaneously, another word that we do not know, because we forgot and because we desire it. This also happens with bodies and matter. All matter contains the aura of what it was before and after its existence, that is why we are the specters of our future.[51]

Vlad presents, then, the rewriting of myths of origin and their echoes in an inclusive way that contains its failures, its fears, and even history's shames. This contemporary retelling of the vampire legend is a glance at the past, the present and the future through multiple and constantly reinvented ideas of origins. These origins create a displaced spot that forces us to question the idea of a fixed, single origin in order to oppose it (or validate it). In creating possible and multiple origins that materialize through the metaphor of the vampire, Fuentes invites the reader to always look for a previous version of a certain reality and, in doing so, shake totalitarian beliefs that plead for a univocal and fixed idea of the world, whether in racial, gender, religious, or political ways. In Fuentes's own words: "A man installed in his origins also has been outside of them: he can interrogate them and, in doing so, invariably he will acquire an imagination of opposing and alternative realities that will conduct him, also, to a clandestine certainty, covered with myths, that there ever was an original unity, meaning, a history before separation."[52]

Notes

1. In *The History of Gothic Fiction*, Markman Ellis explores the *London Journal* discussions that started in 1730 and how they developed in the conception of the idea of vampires as a corrupt politician that bleeds the population. The economic transformations that made commercial ideology the dominant way of life came with the notion of money as "a kind of vitality that circulates in the economy like blood in the body" (Edinburgh: Edinburgh University Press, 2000), 167.

2. Howard L. Malchow, *Gothic Images of Race in Nineteenth-Century Britain* (Stanford, CA: Stanford University Press, 1996), 126.

3. All translations are by the author (A. G.).

4. Quoted in Barbara Brodman, *The Mexican Cult of Death in Myth and Literature* (Gainesville: University Presses of Florida 1976), xvi.

5. José Antonio Maravall, *La cultura del barroco: Análisis de una estructura histórica* (Barcelona: Editorial Ariel, 2007).

6. Mabel Moraña, *Relecturas del barroco de Indias* (Hanover, NH: Ediciones del Norte, 1994), i.

7. What these two trends of the baroque mode have in common is "an awareness that these phenomena must be understood within the larger frame of epistemic and/ or social crises," "Introduction: The Baroque and the Cultures of Crises," in *Hispanic Baroques. Reading Cultures in Context*, ed. Nicholas Spadaccini and Luis Martín-Estudillo (Nashville, TN: Vanderbilt University Press, 2005), ix–xxvi.

8. José Lezama Lima, *La expresión americana* (Santiago de Chile: Editorial Universitaria, 1969), 22.

9. Carlos Fuentes, *El espejo enterrado* (Madrid: Taurus, 1992), 281.

10. "Chac Mool," *Aura, Terra Nostra, Distant Relations*; "Constancia," among others.

11. Initially published as the last story of the collection *Inquieta compañía* (Disturbing Company) (México: Alfaguara, 2004) and later republished as a stand-alone novella in 2010.

12. Mauricio Molina, "Escrito con sangre de ángeles, fantasmas y vampiros: Notas sobre *Inquieta compañía* de Carlos Fuentes," *Revista de la Universidad de México* 3 (2004): 30–36.

13. The actor took his name from his hometown *Lugos* in present-day western Romania. On the other hand, "Bela Lugosi's Dead" (1979), a song by the British gothic band *Bauhaus* revitalized the actor's name, making another pop culture referent out of it.

14. For further information on Fuentes's interest in film, particularly in German Expressionism, see Fernando Salcedo, "Técnicas derivadas del cine en la obra de Carlos Fuentes," *Cuadernos Americanos* 3 (1975): 175–196.

15. This character echoes another of Fuentes's stories, "El prisionero de Las Lomas," in which Sarmiento, also a lawyer, obtains his money after the social reorganization of the country that came with the Revolution, along with the displacements from rural areas to urban centers: published in *Constancia y otras novelas para vírgenes* (México: Alfaguara, 2001).

16. Fuentes, *Inquieta compañía*, 215.

17. Fuentes, *Inquieta compañía*, 230.

18. David Castillo, "Horror (Vacui): The Baroque Condition," in *Hispanic Baroques: Reading Cultures in Context*, 87.

19. The historical Vlad Tepes was a prince, not a count like in Fuentes's recreation of the story.

20. Fuentes's comment questions the role of a heroic figure since Vlad is viewed as a hero in Romania; see Hugo Beccacece, "Carlos Fuentes: Entre el terror y la belleza," *La Nación,* May 9, 2010, http://www.lanacion.com.ar/599325-carlos-fuentes-entre-el-terror-y-la-belleza, accessed September 2, 2012,.

21. Fuentes, *Inquieta compañía*, 277.

22. This concept may be challenged by today's electronic world in which working boards such as wikis allow multiple authors and changes within one document.

23. Katri Lethinen, "Twentieth-Century Vampire Literature: Intimations of Evil and Power," in *This Thing of Darkness: Perspectives on Evil and Human Wickedness*, ed. Richard Paul Hamilton and Margaret Sönser Breen (Amsterdam-New York: Editions Rodopi, 2004), 1–19.

24. See Ellis, *The History of Gothic Fiction*, and Malchow, *Gothic Images*.

25. In this same direction of economic and social policies reflected as vampires, the image of G. W. Bush with fangs and sucking the blood of the Statue of Liberty comes to mind, an image created by artist and illustrator Alex Ross to accompany Rick Perlstein's article in *The Village Voice*. Matt Haber "2004 *Village Voice* Cover Makes Cameo on HBO Vampire Series," September 30, 2008, accessed April 8, 2012, http://www.observer.com/2008/media/2004-village-voice-cover-makes-cameo-hbo-vampire-series.

26. Carlos Fuentes, *En esto creo* (México: Seix Barral, 2002), 167.

27. Marcelo Coddou, "*Terra Nostra* o la crítica de los cielos: Entrevista a Carlos Fuentes," *The American Hispanist* 3 (1978): 8–10.

28. Lucía Guerra, *La mujer fragmentada: Historias de un signo* (Colombia: Colcultura-Ediciones Casa de las Américas, 1994), 35. See also James E. Doan's essay in Part Three of this collection.

29. Hugo Beccacece, "Carlos Fuentes: Entre el terror y la belleza," *La Nación*, May 9, 2004, http://www.lanacion.com.ar/599325-carlos-fuentes-entre-el-terror-y-la-belleza, accessed April 8, 2012.

30. Michael Wutz, "The Reality of the Imagination: A Conversation with Carlos Fuentes at 70," *Weber: The Contemporary West* 17 (Winter 2000), http://weberstudies.weber.edu/archive/archive%20c%20vol.%2016.2-8.1/vol.%2017.2/wutz.htm, accessed April 12, 2012.

31. Fuentes, *Inquieta compañía*, 277.

32. Georges Bataille, *La literatura y el mal*, Ediciones elaleph.com: 2000, www.elaleph.com/libro/La-Literatura-y-el-Mal-de-Georges-Bataille/691710/, 23–24.

33. Fuentes, *Inquieta compañía*, 277.

34. Beccacece, "Entre el terror."

35. Robert Segal, "Adonis: A Greek Eternal Child," in *Myth and the Polis*, ed. Dora C. Pozzi and John M. Wickersham (New York: Cornell University Press, 1991), 64–85.

36. Segal, "Adonis," 80.

37. Segal, "Adonis," 80, 85.

38. According to Segal, "A puer can thus be either an actual person or a symbol. Indeed, some famous historical pueri eventually become symbols themselves. While a historical puer is biologically an adult, a symbolic one may never grow up. These symbolic pueri exemplify exactly the eternally young life that actual puer personalities strive to emulate. Other symbolic pueri are Peter Pan, Little Prince, and of course Adonis," Segal, "Adonis," 77.

39. Fuentes, *Inquieta compañía*, 280–281.

40. Fuentes, following Socrates, asks about the importance of naming: "Why do we give names? Does a name have an intrinsic meaning or just the formal value that we attribute to it or . . . is it what allows the relationship among things? Without

names we would not know how to relate things," Luisa Valenzuela, "La transparencia en la opacidad," *La Nación*, April 5, 2008, http://www.lanacion.com.ar/1000479-la-transparencia-en-la-opacidad, accessed April 12, 2011.

41. Many thanks to James E. Doan for his comments on this subject.

42. William Hughes, *Reader's Guides: Bram Stoker's Dracula* (London, GBR: Continuum International Publishing, 2009), 14.

43. Hughes, *Reader's Guides*, 14.

44. Hughes, *Reader's Guides*, 100.

45. Hughes, *Reader's Guides*, 6, 101.

46. Fuentes, *En esto creo*, 167.

47. Lethinen, "Twentieth-Century Vampire Literature," 2.

48. Lethinen, "Twentieth-Century Vampire Literature," 4, 17.

49. This topic of colonial-neocolonial cultural and economic dependency in Mexico is at the core of many of the stories in *Inquieta compañía*, the volume that includes *Vlad*.

50. Fuentes, *Inquieta compañía*, 168.

51. Fuentes, *Inquieta compañía*, 168.

52. Carlos Fuentes, *Los reinos originarios (teatro hispano-americano)* (Barcelona: Barral Editores, 1971), 13.

16

Sublime Horror: Transparency, Melodrama, and the *Mise-en-Scène* of Two Mexican Vampire Films

Raúl Rodríguez-Hernández and Claudia Schaefer

MOVING PICTURES WERE ESTABLISHED IN MEXICO in the 1890s, fostered by the Lumière cinematograph, a device that captured and documented the nation's transition into modernity and gave spectators an insight into revolutionary changes in their society as well as a window on the strange world outside. Imported from that cradle of the modern, France, the *cinematógrafo* arrived in time to accompany and echo the revolutionary social changes occurring over the first half of the 20th century.

The 1940s Golden Age of cinema that followed the Revolution of 1910 added to the primarily historical genre, the *mise-en-scène* of melodrama that would become one of the foundations of 20th-century Mexican cinema. Following the Golden Age, Mexican popular cinema has continued to develop around the mass audience staples of melodrama and the *cine de espantos* [horror or scary movies], opening a window on the estranged and unfamiliar but now within Mexican culture itself. While the purveyors of earlier cinema fare profited from bringing the music, dance, clothing styles, and daily life of exotic places into Mexican theaters, mid-century entrepreneurs combined low-budget productions with star vehicles to inject "an array of vampires, Aztec mummies, mad scientists, ape-men, and various other macabre menaces[1] into an evolving consumer society that still contained strong vestiges of nationalism promoted by the state. That varied mix of cinematic codes would create fertile grounds for the introduction of the myth of an unbroken heritage—the Aztec mummy appearing alongside contemporary wrestling heroes, for example—that struggled to maintain its coherent vision of modernity as the next step in the development of the Mexican nation as it sought to reach the masses who flocked to theaters. Popular culture icons such as *El Santo* were joined by Fernando Méndez's 1957 *El vampiro* (a character played with elegance and grace by Spanish immigrant Germán Robles) as part of a series of hybrid artifacts that were successful vehicles of commercial entertainment as well as ideological messages of the need for unity when faced with menacing danger. Its "melodramatics"[2] influenced the Hammer dynasty of horror films as well as Christopher Lee's own take on the character. *El vampiro* is also filled with light-hearted characters (Enrique), dramatic irony (the audience "sees" so much more than the characters do), humor (especially linguistic), and no small amount of kitsch, especially in the low-budget technology of the *mise-en-scène*. Encounters between insiders and outsiders—the foreign menace of the vampire from Bakonia appears to infiltrate the social space of *El Santo* and a whole entourage of home-grown heroes—constantly negotiating between sets of generic codes and giving rise to a series of films with mass appeal that include variations on horror, melodrama, but not the American staple of space invaders popular at the time. The jeopardy to the nation does not come from other worlds but from this one: the United States and Europe. From *El vampiro* to Guillermo del Toro's 1993 *La invención de Cronos*, images that juxtapose the "look" of the modern with the shadowy vestiges of disappearing tradition fill vampire, wrestling (*lucha libre*), and melodrama or a combination of all three. Settings—haciendas, catacombs, outdated laboratories, the countryside, a city made unfamiliar, antiquarian shops—combine with objects that do not belong in those spaces to produce a combination of familiarity and estrangement.

Incorporating and recycling those images that produce heightened feelings of fear and distress, those which Sigmund Freud saw as belonging to "that class of the frightening which leads back to what is known of old and long familiar"[3]; the conventions of melodrama in particular allow for the addition of the traces, phantoms, and the limited knowledge of a state of "intellectual uncertainty"[4] Freud found necessary to produce the unfamiliar and the dreadful from the recognizable and homely. The "something" that Freud proposed needed to be added to the novel to produce the uncanny is, in Mexican films, the vampire. With the vampire as an integral aspect of the *mise-en-scène*, directors could create the look of a *locus suspectus* or questionable space that gives origin to fears within the comfortable physical environs of home (nation). This is accomplished through the deploying of set design, stage lighting, and character movement as well as by means of *mise-en-shot* scale (how images are edited into moving pictures by camera position, movement, pacing, depth of focus), editing, pace, and close up focus. The vampire was just made for melodrama, as evidenced in films ranging from *El vampiro* [The Vampire] (1957), *El ataúd del vampiro* [The Vampire's Coffin] (1958),

El Santo en el tesoro de Drácula [El Santo in Dracula's Treasure] (1968) to *La invención de Cronos* [The Cronos Device] (1993). The contradictions of modernity play out in these films on the human body made "helpless"[5] in the face of ambiguity and mystery.

As Freud concludes, not about *mise-en-scène* directly but in terms that recall those very acts of staging and duration, of "the surplus of objects and interior décor"[6] associated with the genre, the uncanny "is like a buried spring or dried-up pond. One cannot walk over it without always having the feeling that water might come up there again."[7] Persons and things unseen but perhaps there and hidden, sinister in their belonging to the place but not always a visible part of it, create doubt and unease. The excitation of the senses by the animation of the apparently lifeless—dolls, mannequins, human bodies—throws standard conclusions into disarray and notions of temporality into chaos. With the problematic—some might even say monstrous—advent of modernization as a purportedly collective, if elusive, goal, melodrama and its attendant domestic figures such as the vampire still "attempt to make sense of modernism and of the family."[8] Traditional values that are under threat by changes that accompany capitalist development are addressed in melodramatic films of the 1950s in the metonymic space of the home into which all sorts of invaders and "phantoms of horror"[9] penetrate. The films are so successful that by the turn of the 21st century, the vampire—or vampire capitalism—is a familiar member of the family. He (or she) may not be the favorite relative, but the terrors of the unfamiliar have finally become, by the time Guillermo del Toro takes them up with some evident black humor in 1993, the uncanny figure that audiences have become used to. So, we propose that modernity and the vampire unite in Mexican cinema as flip sides of the same cinematic coin: the dead brought to life and the reanimation of what appeared to be dead issues.

The components of the formal framing of shots through the *mise-en-scène*—domestic ruins or the jumble of ruined objects in an antique shop; scarce, low-key, or stark lighting; the abandoned architecture of old mansions, streets, and dank rooms; generic rather than period costumes that disorient the spectator into not recognizing what should be familiar; seemingly anachronistic props amid contemporary technologies; the vehicles of technological innovation (a passenger train, a stagecoach, automobiles), and the use of sounds (rushing wind) and silence to manipulate and distort our everyday experience of reality—establish fascinating interiors and shadowy exterior shots as spaces of the sublime.

In Edmund Burke's division between beauty and the sublime, beauty is composed of those qualities of things that relax the viewer, including picturesque elements pleasing to the eye. Audiences used to the sweeping panoramic shots of cinematographer Gabriel Figueroa would come to expect no less than the joining of the two ideal states of the beautiful and the sublime evidenced in the stately actress María Félix displayed in close up against a vast and dramatic, even terrible, panorama of desert cactus, a figure of dark and mysterious beauty amid the stark natural backdrop. Mexican Golden Age cinema naturalized the spectacle of a national authenticity tied to the land, a look that continued into the 1950s despite the government's agenda of modernization that brought Hollywood productions and television into the economy. Zuzana M. Pick calls the survival and reincorporation of the spectacle of such cinematic conventions the state's branding of them as "fetish objects of Mexico's cinematic patrimony."[10] The settings, whether urban or rural, are familiar even as the story twists in uncanny ways.

In director Fernando Méndez's *El vampiro* (1957), Burke's notion of beauty appears in the emblematic opening shots as "coercive, irresistible, a species of seduction."[11] The submission of the spectator to the seduction of Marta González (Ariadna Welter), a young blonde woman alighting from a Mexican National Railroad car at the beginning of what will subsequently become her encounter with the sublime, accords well with Burke's erotic meanderings through the image of a woman's body. He writes: "it is like a deceitful maze, through which the unsteady eye glides giddily, without knowing where to fix, or whither it is carried."[12] She is an innocent young thing, attractive in appearance, soft of voice, about to enter the shadowy woods beyond the train station as a prime *locus suspectus* in search of her aunt who has been taken ill. Faced with a landslide that has kept her ride away, Marta, Enrique (another stranded traveler), and a large box of soil arrived from Hungary all get stranded at the Sierra Negra station. The agreeable relaxation that lulls an audience into the narrative is both produced by the tight focus on the faces of the characters (and box of earth) and emphasized by the lack of expected establishing panoramic shots.

At the other end of the chronological spectrum is *La invención de Cronos*, the 1993 directorial debut of Guillermo del Toro. There is a prologue with a voiceover by the director that frames the opening sequence, launching the contemporary story into the terrain of myth and mystery. Instead of creating more certainty and an atmosphere of seduction by the beautiful "smoothness"[13] of images, bells toll, a ghostly figure is pursued by forces of repression, human bodies are dehumanized, and death rather than life fills the screen. The following narrative opens in a modern global city—the street signs are in Arabic letters but the storefronts, taxicabs, and houses can be easily matched to the *Centro Historico* [historic downtown of Mexico City]—but the building interiors soon become the focus of the melodrama. That is the last panoramic shot until near the end of the film when a night view of the twinkling lights of the metropolis appear as backdrop for a violent encounter between the living and the dead. The visible signs of loss—of a homeland, a sense of alienation from one's turf, and the invasion of outsiders—quickly disappear as the comfortable interior of an apartment comes into focus: a man, a woman, and a child are eating breakfast. The relaxation of vision begins with the usual trials of making a recalcitrant little girl eat her food, a wife admonish her husband he will be late, and the gray-haired grandfather taking the girl by the hand to uncover their car and head off to work. Perhaps the nuclear family is a bit skewed as it skips a generation—there are no parents—but the rest has the look of routine. Burke reminds us that curiosity, the "pleasure we take in novelty,"[14] is not foreign even if superficial in its affection and is required to keep the mind challenged. So, spectators may fix their gaze upon the strident city inhabited by gentle families and wonder what might connect the first sequence with the rest. If "Beauty is a lure, the Sublime is a rape,"[15] how do they co-exist?

In contrast to beauty, Burke writes, sublimity is made up of "fierce and terrible qualities, elements that excite wonder, astonishment, and even horror."[16] Pleasure may be the closer object of focus, but pain or terror may accompany it if appearing to be at a distance. In *El Vampiro*, Marta's fellow traveler Enrique is the humorous bridge between the outside (known, recognizable, distant, and only suggested) world and the gloomy, timeless, lugubrious space of the woods on whose edge her relatives' house is embedded. The leafless trees, like the lifeless town, are shadowy, uninviting, and astonishing in density and in number. The birds'-eye view of the camera turns them into a maze that the hapless travelers, bonding harmlessly over their shared predicament, must traverse.

In order to reach the realm of the sublime, Marta must cross the transitional space of a wood filled with fog, strange sounds, and the imminent fall of darkness. Obscurity of vision is accompanied by "a feeling of helplessness and uncanniness . . . as when caught in a mist, . . . [or] lost one's way in a mountain forest [with] every attempt to find the marker or familiar path [lost]."[17] Los Sicomoros [The Sycamores] as a familiar landmark seems more and more remote; Enrique keeps asking how much farther they have to walk. Each scene appears enclosed by either natural or architectural arches so that a sense of foreboding in the story is echoed in the limited vision as if we were all inhabitants of a tomb. Her modern vehicle—even in 1957 Mexico this is an uncanny one—is a stagecoach whose driver has been bribed by a fellow traveler on the railroad to take them to the family hacienda, Los Sicomoros. Marta and Enrique exchange light banter as they make their way to the ruins of the family home, unaware that Aunt Eloísa, an ageless figure in black, follows them on the path or that her other aunt has already died.

Eloísa is accompanied onscreen by ominous violin screeches, sudden gusts of wind, and great quantities of smoke. The rumors of Marta's aunt, María Teresa's insanity do not rest easily on the family, for she desperately (and rightly) feared a vampire out for her blood. It is revealed to the audience that Enrique is actually a doctor hired by the family to sort out the mental state of the ill woman; it is a fact that Marta does not know. Science is proposed as intervening where logic and reason have been useless weapons against the foreign neighbor whose presence has caused the flight of everyone else for miles around. In point of fact, the ghost town could be the result of a migration of *campesinos* to the growing capital city, but in the film the cause is the mysterious outsiders. Enrique's investigative talents will include recourse to an old leather-bound book that accidentally falls off a library shelf at his feet. The hidden story of the land and its hacienda will open up the history of the families and their neighbors the Duvals, the addressees on the box of soil sent from Hungary that was delivered to the station. That night's reading matter reveals secrets, as do the screams from Marta's room as the first bat enters through her open balcony, winging its way clumsily on visible wires to claim her as the next victim. Clearly, the process of "translating [an audience] into a state of feeling"[18] has begun.

Wonder, astonishment, and, yes, even horror, coincide in two-staged spaces. First, the seemingly abandoned, deteriorated family home is filled with a new dread: the possible sale of the property to an outsider, neighbor, and rumored vampire Señor Duval (Germán Robles), ending the familiarity of a family space and definitely creating the horror of the foreign and strange within one's own walls. Marta is cast in the role of the tiebreaker as her two other relatives cannot decide whether to sell.

Second, there is already a breach in the walls of the homely as Aunt Eloísa, the black figure shadowing their walk, is also a vampire and she stalks the property along with Duval. They just need to turn Marta into one of them and the vote will be unanimous; the two Duval brothers (the second is in the box of dirt from the original family plot) thinly disguised as the Lavuds (Duval spelled in reverse) will then rise again and inhabit the Mexican hacienda where "normal" life had gone on for so long. Secret passages behind a bookcase, a stone staircase down to a maze of tunnels, and the appearance of Duval's crypt within the space linked to the family home all unite to produce an estrangement from the setting filled with fierce and terrible qualities that alternate in their effect on the audience. What Hayward calls the "paranoid" aspect of melodrama[19] or the polarization of values from within and without, assails the eye of the spectator who is left indecisive and anxious. An open balcony door, the entry of bats on visible wires jerking into the sacrosanct space of Marta's bedroom, and the uncanny apparition of both Eloísa the vampire and María Teresa who is neither dead nor a vampire reinforce the terrible nature of the beautiful as it co-exists with the sublime. The cleansing of that domestic space, what was previously a nurturing place for Marta when she was growing up, has become that uncanny dried up spring or pond under whose surface troubled waters—the whole Duval/Lavud story—might bubble at any time can only be accomplished through ritual fire. That is the destiny of the ruined family home and those buried in the mausoleum.

Thirty-six years later, the setting could not be more urban but the tale is remarkably similar. In the opening scenes of *Cronos*, evidence of the implementation of the North American Free Trade Agreement (NAFTA) is everywhere in commercial advertisements on walls, the diversity of automobiles, trilingual street signs, and the congested business district of a megalopolis. Yet, amid the clutter and chaos of what is no longer really foreign but frighteningly domestic, walking hand in hand, antique dealer Jesús Gris (Federico Luppi) and his granddaughter Aurora (Tamara Shanath) traverse the equally knotty labyrinth of the global city to arrive at a destination where familiar objects quickly become uncanny vestiges of the dream of eternal life and even painful reminders of what life might be like if it were eternal. The cultural economy has filled Mexico's streets with goods—that overinvestment with "things" that melodrama thrives on—but old myths and fears survive intact under the surface. In Latin America, circular historical nightmares and unresolved social issues form a questionable backdrop for the promises of the cronos device, a gleaming gold-hued artifact hidden away by Spanish alchemist Huberto Fulcanelli on the run from the tortures of the Inquisition as a heretic. A 16th-century wooden statue of an archangel—the ultimate confluence of aesthetics and theology—is like the ground that hides the uncanny spring when it turns up among the items for sale in Gris's store of ruins. Wrapped in brown paper, hidden from the naked eye, the statue sits on a counter amid a collection of ticking clocks of varied quality and provenance. The sound of time passing is appropriate to accompany the device that, according to myth, promises to extend the life of its possessor indefinitely. If it were successful, the cronos device would abolish the need for scientific measurement such as the hours and minutes steadily marked by the clocks.

The jewel-incrusted, scarab-like device that launches sharp claws at intervals and holds in its center a strange and uncanny animated creature, harkens back to colonial Mexico and the era of the Baroque. It combines the metallic surface of a modern machine and the invisible enigma of faith in a mysterious force, the epitome of a confluence of the beautiful and the sublime for it lures us in only to invade the body. The Baroque mode, whether referring to "an episode in the history of art, or of religion, or of absolutist politics, or of consciousness,"[20] placed great value on "aiming to stir the spectator's emotions actively."[21] It could therefore lure the eye with beauty as it prepared to take its victim (as in Burke's sublime). Housing both beauty and the sublime in one small and fascinating apparatus, Gris cannot take his eyes off it and, later, becomes addicted to its workings. But there is more to the story of the seduction; the cronos device is also the holy grail of modern industrialist Dieter de la Guardia (Claudio Brook) whose fatal disease has sent him on a quest for time and back into the past for remedies no longer available in modern times. The "disruptive impulses"[22] of the Baroque aesthetic that wished to break free from classical restraints find an echo in the contemporary entrepreneur's search for a source of energy and life that might cancel his terminal diagnosis in favor of continuation, transformation, and "the impossible."[23] Burke's conclusion that, in addition to the direct threat of danger in things sublime, there is another effect transmitted by our encounter with terror suggests this "impossibility." He concludes: "I know of nothing sublime which is not some modification of power,"[24] with eternal life a clear example of the power of the impossible over the imagination.

Once again, the wisdom contained in the pages of a long-lost document, like the pages of the yellowed volume that falls at the feet of Enrique, unfolds unexpected processes and exuberant promises. The true story of the alchemist's device that was anathema to the Inquisition informs the film's narrative of a modern choice between life and eternal life. On the rooftop of the de la Guardia factory, an anachronistic architectural structure that we are asked to believe is part of the landscape of 1993, turns into the ultimate encounter between angels and demons. De la Guardia sends his bodyguard Angel (Ron Perlman) to steal the device from Gris, and the ensuing bloodbath is reminiscent of the archangels' punishing the fallen angel (the devil) by casting him out of heaven. Yet, the winner of this encounter is Gris since he cannot be killed as the effects of the cronos device continue. When the context of cut-throat capitalism is considered, one must ponder just what a businessman is capable of in order to keep his factory running. Uncanny, clumsy technologies inhabit de la Guardia's canny universe; his factory looks like a transnational corporation whose production line manufactures medieval objects, a link between the (lost) time of understanding (the era of the alchemical) and the supposed modern, rational comprehension of the universe.

Yet, the real horror of the narrative is that, for all the excruciating scenes of Gris's experimentation and the humor of the mortuary scene with Gris leaving the premises as a vampire unable to be buried, the device is proved to work, making Gris cursed with eternal life. At the breakfast table with his wife and granddaughter, walking the dark streets of the city at night, death never comes to relieve him of the burden of modern life until the very last scene. Like the 17th century itself, cronos "has a Janus-like aspect: an age of extraordinary advances in philosophy and science, and of sweeping changes in the economic sphere, and in the development of the modern state but an age characterized also by continuing . . . controversy."[25] As such, the 20th century gives the Baroque a second round of life as it too looks to past and future in a difficult and unstable point of equilibrium.

Beauty is to be found in the care with which the old man clasps the hand of his young granddaughter in the opening sequence, in the soft tones of Gris's voice, in the genuine enthrallment with the mysterious device, in his deathbed scene that comes as a liberation from the suffering of eternal life. The interiors of home, office, social club, public restroom, and even de la Guardia's factory retain the notion of closed spaced and protected life until the invasion of the outside through the cronos device. Like those invisible barriers of the nation, the walls of familiarity are breached by outside invaders who might bring tempting and dangerous objects and ideas into the *mise-en-scène*. Cronos, the primordial Titan god of time and of the ages, devouring and destructive, ruled the cosmos in the golden age according to the Greeks. Fearful of being overthrown by his own children, he devoured each as he was born, with only Zeus hidden away and protected from such a fate. In the end, Cronos is freed by Zeus and sent to rule the Elysian Islands as the land of the blessed dead. Only in del Toro's version, the beauty of the Elysian fields is the ruinous lure of the modern industrial city, and death is not Elysian but sublime—fearful and horror-filled not in its natural presence but in its uncanny absence.

The tight cinematic focus of the opening scenes in both films places the spectator alongside the characters, with shot–counter-shot techniques establishing the paranoia of dealing with the uncanny. We share with Marta, Enrique, Jesús, and Aurora the experience of the intrusion of the familiar—fog, ethereal old women in black, cockroaches in rotted wood, a traumatized and mute child in a happy setting, the lure of life everlasting in difficult economic times—into new spaces, allowing for what Burke calls a vicarious sense of sublime excitation, trepidation, and delight. The philosopher addresses this: "The passions which belong to self-preservation, turn on pain and danger; they are simply painful when their causes immediately affect us; they are delightful when we have an idea of pain and danger, without actually being in such circumstances."[26] The images of Jesús Gris fighting Angel on a rooftop filled with industrial debris and flickering neon lights, or Marta fleeing the hostile intent of Duval, are scenes of self-preservation, but a continuity of life premised on natural cycles and not on alchemical or scientific falsehoods.

Cinematic techniques that produce physiological effects on the viewer—such as the rhythmically slow rising of the vampire from the coffin at the start of three separate scenes, a visible vestige of the return of the repressed and repetition compulsion that hypnotizes as much as it repels sight; extreme close-ups of the vampire's eyes as a stand-in perhaps for the eye of the cinema and not just the hypnotic power of the vampire; or the visual sequence involved in the deploying of the cronos device as it is placed on Gris's unearthly white skin, extends its claws, and whirs into life as it pierces flesh and injects something mysterious—reiterate a commingling of recognition and estrangement, of the natural and the unnatural. This vestigial figure of the frightening, repressed into an anxiety, is made visible in the cinematic structure as "an element that recurs."[27] Burke asserts that "the sublime experience is one of domination,"[28] therefore uniting Gris whose closed eyes seem to be imagining the future rather than the present with the spectator in the immediacy and subjugation of the device over the will of the body. Burke's association of the fear of death, dismemberment, terror, and darkness (here, literally a "howling wilderness") with feelings of the sublime makes it impossible to ascertain one's safety in the space of the disjunction between what the mind expects and what actually occurs on screen. The *mise-en-scéne* that actually proposes to overcome the fear of death by associating it instead with the enthrallment of the unknown and the horrifyingly sublime always includes domesticity: the kitchen, a stairway, a refrigerator, a bathroom sink. Gris's enticement to use the device a second time, for instance, creates that disjunction in the spectator between the recognized act of what happened before with all of its concomitant pain and winced expression, and that hope and fear of eternal life that come with this. Burke's theory of the beautiful concludes with its positive evocation of the passions, something visible on the face of Gris as he gives himself over to the device. Yet the parallel "pain, admiration and disorientation"[29] associated with the sublime combine into a moment when "agreeable relaxation" of the beautiful carries us into a scenario of loss and uncertainty.

Marta's companion Enrique, perhaps a predictable love interest in the melodramatic narrative that accompanies the enigmas of Los Sicomoros, is actually an incognito physician invited to make sense of the aunt's illness and perhaps come to her rescue from the dark forces of the vampire. Enrique embodies reason, empiricism, and scientific thinking, all of those qualities that modernity is associated with as a rupture from the superstition of the past. However, he is confronted with sights and sounds that evoke and confirm those superstitions, and make such methods and measurements unfeasible. Mere observation does not reveal the truth about their circumscribed world; the family is not suffering economically although their domestic space exhibits symptoms of decadence, decay, and death. There is no order to the piles of furniture, cobwebs in corners, or locked rooms that preserve a lost space of (Marta's) childhood, or the anachronistic look of the interior spaces. There is sheer accumulation that looks impenetrable to the eye and to the mind, much like the in-between spaces of E. T. A. Hoffmann's Sandman narrative that Møller finds outside the realm of Freud's analysis, "aspects for which his archaeological reconstruction cannot account."[30] Like a fairy tale brought home, it takes a narrative of antiquity (the leather-bound volume in the family library) to unravel the story, not the enlightenment of modern times.

Although the crypt of the Duval family contains the layers of their history embodied in the niches filled by successive generations, the home is not equally stratified and chronological. Piles of "things" have replaced history, and the metonymical relationship between production and reproduction that Hayward emphasizes in melodrama has come to a screeching halt. Los Sicomoros is not the site of any production but only of the reproduction of the sublime myth associated with the Duvals. Ghostly apparitions, the undead (Marta's aunt, Duval, the "moonlight and marble" paleness of Gris), and the visible ravages of time and history on material artifacts occupy the screen simultaneously with modern modes of transportation and, in the case of *Cronos*, the effects of globalization. With almost 40 years between them, both films rob scientific reason of its power and make spectators aliens in their own land. Outside the chronology of history, the viewer, like the vampire, is cast into the limbo of a social eternity, disconnected from the real, much as modern politics is not so much transparent as opaque, dark, and dangerously familiar. They also devour their own in order to survive. The figure of the vampire has made a transition from the countryside to the city, joining the throngs of migrating workers and the young in a venue that offers more opportunities for blood. As Joan Gordon and Veronica Hollinger suggest regarding more modern vampire stories, "perhaps death has become more terrible, now that it can strike when we are among strangers, now that it is no longer hedged about with ritual and poetry."[31] When the world was less inhabited, each geographic portion smaller and more remote, the vampire and the ceremonial fire co-existed; today, the vampire is a timeless myth with a timeless character whose remoteness seems both familiar and uncanny as it is resurrected in modern capital cities.

Ambiguous by nature, as luring and anxiety-producing as Burke found in images and objects not smooth and relaxing to the eye but instead complicated and textured, the vampire functions as a metonymy for modernity as the home was metonymy for the state. Duval and Gris are not repulsive figures but carefully groomed as uncannily domestic and familiar ones that do not lose their appeal across time or generations (much as the vampire is an equal-opportunity feaster on the blood of all without consideration of gender, ethnicity, or social class). In a de-mythified modern society based on capital, whether in 1957 or 1993, a sophisticated, well-dressed, soft-spoken, enticingly suave seducer of women young and old is merely a neighbor or relative. Gris is just another member of the Mexican family. Duval's nocturnal habits, telepathic communication, and uncanny ability to sniff out new blood when Marta arrives, are all acceptable quirks. As Burke writes, "the effect produced on the view"[32] of the body deemed beautiful, be it in its parts or the whole, include the attraction of the glance to linger. If the ultimate result of that beauty and grace is submission, disorientation, and the "rape"[33] of vision, then the "buried spring or dried-up pond" that Freud warns of in the experience of the uncanny is revealed just underneath the surface. That the vampire, the mummy, or the werewolf "commands our interest despite our modern rationality"[34] contributes to talking about, if not entirely understanding, our fascination with cultural survivals. Walter Benjamin's angel of history inhabits the mound of rubble produced by modernity's progress, but the vampire of history does not try to make sense of that past. Instead, his presence evokes the past's uncanny permanence regardless of modernity's persistent narrative of "transience" and progress.[35]

Freud's insistent categorizing of the uncanny within aesthetics leads us to take up the sublime as what exists beyond empirical human experience, concealed (or disguised) from the eyes of ordinary, mundane human beings but brought into the frame of sight and cast over our eyes as if possessed by spirits not our own. Exerting rapidly alternating attraction and repulsion over the spectator, the sublime cloaks objects in obscurity and darkness, it evokes solitude inhabited by mystery, and it reveals the incompetence of human speech by resorting to silence. In *El vampiro*, Marta traverses silent forests only to arrive at a silent mansion; the camera lingers on closed-mouth faces whose eyes do all the talking. Duval and María Teresa, his latest recruit, gaze into the night as we hear voiceovers of their words to one another. In *Cronos*, Aurora only utters one word in the whole film: *abuelo* (grandpa). Although her grandparents try to evoke speech, she has been traumatized into silence. Yet that family tie breaks down with the loss of time and generations; something irreplaceable has been lost in the years sacrificed to the Dirty Wars in Argentina (Luppi's accent is unmistakable). Those who have disappeared are not vampires but the truly dead. Jesús's son has been disappeared in the Dirty War; his granddaughter represents the dawn of something new, something that could be endangered by the temptations of the Cronos device. Gris remains in limbo, neither fully dead nor alive, for most of the film. As the decibels of the voices in modern Mexican politics rose to heightened levels during the post-revolutionary "miracle decades" between the 1950s and the 1990s, and exhortations of transparency filled the airwaves and the media, the omnipresent image of the vampire is simultaneously overwhelming and hauntingly attractive.

Whether set in a crumbling hacienda; a mansion, crypt, apartment, or an industrial complex; a railroad station; the confines of an antiquarian shop, a funeral home, an attic; with a "new" family made up of a niece and her dead and living relatives; or the grandparents and grandchild left orphaned by the Dirty Wars of the 1970s, these films move from a more positive reading of the conquest of time with the idea that living forever is good or affirmational, to a setting that uses the intervention of an outsider (Enrique) to solve a mystery or a set of mysterious technologies to bring an old man back to care for his granddaughter eternally without a resolution of the crisis that brought about the death of his son that triggered it all. In addition to the home and the nation, the cinema itself has become a *locus suspectus* filled with images of the frightening that do not cease to challenge the audience's "intellectual certainty" that Freud posited as the basis of the uncanny.

Notes

1. Doyle Greene, *Mexploitation Cinema: A Critical History of Mexican Vampire, Wrestler, Ape-Man and Similar Films, 1957–1977* (Jefferson, NC: McFarland, 2005), 1.

2. Greene, *Mexploitation*, 8.

3. Neil Hertz, foreword to Sigmund Freud, "The Uncanny," in *Writings on Art and Literature: Sigmund Freud* (Stanford, CA: Stanford University Press, 1997), 195.

4. Freud, "The Uncanny," 195.

5. Freud, "The Uncanny," 213.

6. Susan Hayward, *Cinema Studies: The Key Concepts*, 2nd ed. (London: Routledge, 2000), 215.

7. Freud, "The Uncanny," 198.

8. Hayward, *Cinema Studies*, 215.

9. Freud, "The Uncanny," 204.

10. Zuzana M. Pick, *Constructing the Image of the Mexican Revolution: Cinema and the Archive* (Austin: University of Texas Press, 2010), 145.

11. Adam Phillips, introduction to Edmund Burke, *A Philosophical Inquiry into the Origin of our Ideas of the Sublime and Beautiful*. Oxford World's Classics (Oxford: Oxford University Press, 2008), xxiii.

12. Phillips, introduction, xxiii.

13. Phillips, introduction, xvi.

14. Burke, *A Philosophical Inquiry*, 29.

15. Phillips, xxiii.

16. Philip Prodger, *Darwin's Camera: Art and Photography in the Theory of Evolution.* (Oxford: Oxford University Press, 2009), 11.

17. Freud, "The Uncanny," 213.

18. Freud, "The Uncanny," 194.

19. Hayward, *Cinema Studies*, 215.

20. Robert Harbison, *Reflections on Baroque* (Chicago: University of Chicago Press, 2000), vii.

21. Harbison, *Reflections*, viii.
22. Harbison, *Reflections*, 1.
23. Harbison, *Reflections*, 1.
24. Burke, *A Philosophical Enquiry*, 59.
25. John Rupert Martin, *Baroque* (Boulder, CO: Westview Press, 1977), 12.
26. Burke, *A Philosophical Enquiry*, 84–85.
27. Freud, "The Uncanny," 217.
28. Phillips, introduction, xxii.
29. Phillips, introduction, xxiii.
30. Freud, "The Uncanny," 112.
31. Joan Gordon and Veronica Hollinger, "Introduction: The Shape of Vampires," in *Blood Read: The Vampire as Metaphor in Contemporary Culture*, ed. Joan Gordon and Veronica Hollinger (Philadelphia, University of Pennsylavnia Press, 1997), ix.
32. Burke, *A Philosophical Enquiry*, 88.
33. Phillips, introduction, xxiii.
34. Peter Hutchings, *The Horror Film* (New York and London: Longman, 2004), 70.
35. Beatrice Hanssen, *Walter Benjamin's Other History: Of Stones, Animals, Human Beings, and Angels* (Berkeley: University of California Press, 1998), 66.

Selected Bibliography

Auerbach, Nina. *Our Vampires, Ourselves*. Chicago and London: University of Chicago Press, 1995.

Barber, Paul. *Vampires, Burial and Death. Folklore and Reality*. New York: Yale University Press, 2010.

Bell, Michael. *Food for the Dead: On the Trail of New England's Vampires*. New York: Carroll & Graf Publishers, 2002.

Beresford, Matthew. *From Demons to Dracula. The Creation of the Modern Vampire Myth*. London: Reaktion Books, 2008.

Bunson, Matthew. *The Vampire Encyclopedia*. London: Thames & Hudson, 1993.

Burns, Stu. "And With All That, Who Believes in Vampires? Undead Legends and Enlightenment Culture," in *European Studies Conference Selected Proceedings*. Omaha: University of Nebraska, 2007.

Butler, Erik. *Metamorphosis of the Vampire in Literature and Film: Cultural Transformations in Europe, 1732–1933*. Rochester: Camden House, 2010.

Byron, Glennis, ed. *Dracula*. Basingstoke: Macmillan Press Ltd., 1999.

Calmet, Dom Augustine. *Treatise on Vampires and Revenants: The Phantom World*, trans. Henry Christmas. Brighton: Desert Island Books, 1993.

Day, Peter, ed. *Vampires: Myths and Metaphors of Enduring Evil*, Amsterdam: Rodopi, 2006.

Dundes, Alan, ed. *The Vampire: A Casebook*. Madison: University of Wisconsin Press, 1998.

Frost, Brian. *The Monster with a Thousand Faces. Guises of the Vampire in Myth and Literature*. Bowling Green: Bowling Green State University Popular Press, 1989.

Glover, David. *Vampires, Mummies and Liberals*. London: Duke University Press, 1996.

Gordon, Joan and Veronica Hollinger, eds. *Blood Read: The Vampire as Metaphor in Contemporary Culture*. Philadelphia: University of Pennsylvania Press, 1997.

Greene, Doyle. *Mexploitation Cinema: A Critical History of Mexican Vampire, Wrestler, Ape-Man and Similar Films, 1957–1977.* Jefferson, NC: McFarland, 2005.

Heick, Alex. "Prince Dracula, Rabies and the Vampire Legend," *Annals of Internal Medicine* 117 (1992): 172.

Jakobsson, Ármann. "The Fearless Vampire Killers: A Note about the Icelandic Draugr and Demonic Contamination in Grettis Saga." *Folklore* 120 (2009): 307–316.

Jenkins, Mark Collins. *Vampire Forensics.* Washington, D.C.: National Geographic Society, 2011.

Kimberly, Steven. "A Psychological Analysis of the Vampire Myth," *Estro: Essex Student Research Online* 1 (2010): 38.

Le Fanu, Joseph Sheridan. *Carmilla*, ed. Jamieson Ridenhour. Kansas City: Valancourt, 2009.

McClelland, Bruce. *Slayers and Their Vampires: A Cultural History of Killing the Dead.* Ann Arbor: University of Michigan Press, 2006.

Meyer, Stephenie. *Twilight.* Oxford: Oxford University Press, 2005.

Murray, Paul. *From The Shadow of Dracula: A Life of Bram Stoker.* London: Jonathan Cape, 2004.

Oinas, Felix. "Heretics as Vampires and Demons in Russia," *Slavic and East European Journal*, 22 (1978): 433–441.

Perkowski, Jan L. *Vampire Lore: From the Writings of Jan Louis Perkowski.* Bloomington: Slavica Publishers, 2006.

Perkowski, Jan L. *The Darkling: A Treatise on Slavic Vampirism.* Columbus: Slavica Publishers, 1989.

Radford, Benjamin. *Tracking the Chupacabra: The Vampire Beast in Fact, Fiction, and Folklore.* Albuquerque: University of New Mexico Press, 2011.

Rodrigues de la Sierra, L. "Origin of the Myth of Vampirism," *Journal of the Royal Society of Medicine* 91 (1998): 290.

Rudkin, David. *Vampyr.* London: British Film Institute, 2005.

Skal, David J. *Hollywood Gothic: The Tangled Web of Dracula from Novel to Stage to Screen.* New York: Norton, 1990.

Stoker, Bram. *Dracula.* Peterborough, Ontario: Broadview, 2000.

Stoker, Bram. *Dracula: A Case Study in Contemporary Criticism*, ed. John Paul Riquelme. New York: Bedford/St. Martin's, 2002.

Stoker, Bram. *The New Annotated Dracula*, ed. Leslie S. Klinger. New York: W. W. Norton, 2008.

Summers, Montague. *The Vampire in Europe.* London: Kegan Paul, 1929.

Summers, Montague. *The Vampire, His Kith and Kin: The History of Vampirism.* Scotts Valley, IAP: 2009.

Theodorides, J. "Origin of the Myth of Vampirism," *Journal of the Royal Society of Medicine* 91 (1998):114.

Tiziani, Moreno. "Vampires and vampirism: pathological roots of a myth," *Antrocom* 5 (2009): 133.

Trow, M. J. *Vlad The Impaler: In Search Of The Real Dracula.* Stroud: Sutton Publishing, 2003.

Twitchell, James. *The Living Dead: A Study of the Vampire in Romantic Literature.* Durham, NC: Duke University Press, 1997.

Wright, Dudley. *Vampires and Vampirism: Legends from Around the World.* Maple Shade, NJ: Lethe Press, 2001.

Index

About the Editors

Photo Credit: Bob Eighmie

James E. Doan is professor of Humanities at Nova Southeastern University (NSU), where he teaches courses in literature, the arts, folklore, and mythology, including a course on the vampire, which he has taught for twenty years. He has published widely in the fields of folklore and Celtic studies and has recently written a play, *The Irish Dracula: A Melodrama in Five Acts*. He and Brodman are also planning to host an Irish studies conference on Ireland and the Supernatural in Ft. Lauderdale, Florida, in February 2014.

Barbara Brodman is professor of Humanities at Nova Southeastern University in Fort Lauderdale, Florida. She holds master and doctoral degrees in Hispanic languages and literature, Latin American Studies, and International Business and has published a variety of scholarly works that deal with international arts and affairs. Her 1997 journey through South America, retracing Che Guevara's 1952 motorcycle journey, was widely covered by the media, while thousands followed her adventures online or read her book about the adventure. In her present endeavors as co-editor with James Doan of the Universal Vampire series and as co-coordinator with Doan of a 2014 international conference on the Supernatural in Fort Lauderdale, Florida, Brodman pursues the theme of the Other as revolutionary, focusing on the Don Juan and vampire legends.

About the Contributors

Katherine Allocco is Associate Professor of History and Chair of the Women's Studies program at Western Connecticut State University. She specializes in medieval Europe, especially gender and politics in 14th-century England and France. She has presented several papers about medieval women in comics with a particular focus on female villains, sex, and power.

Cristina Artenie is a Ph.D. candidate at Laval University, Canada. She was born and raised in Transylvania and speaks the three main languages of the province: Romanian, Hungarian, and German. Before moving to Canada, she worked as a foreign affairs journalist, in which capacity she traveled and wrote extensively about East-Central Europe. Her interests range from post-colonialism to feminism, discourse analysis to scholarship on the novel *Dracula*.

Paul E. H. Davis is a Research Fellow at the University of Buckingham, England. He is currently working on the "Dickens Journals Online" project, based at the university. He has been researching 19th-century Anglo-Irish literature for nearly two decades, beginning with Joseph Sheridan Le Fanu, the acclaimed writer of ghost stories (including tales of vampires), and is the author of *From Castle Rackrent to Castle Dracula: Anglo-Irish Agrarian Fiction from the 19th Century* (2011).

Thomas Jesús Garza is University Distinguished Teaching Associate Professor of Slavic and Eurasian Studies at the University of Texas at Austin. He teaches courses on Russian language and literature, and contemporary Russian culture. His course, "The Vampire in Slavic Cultures," has been taught since 1997 and attracts more than 150 students each year. The reader for that course, *The Vampire in Slavic Cultures*, was published in 2010.

Adriana Gordillo is Assistant Professor of Spanish at University of Minnesota, Mankato. She has published articles that explore figures such as vampires, angels, ghosts, and contemporary reinventions of fairy tales, all from a Latin-American standpoint. She is currently finishing a book on the phantasmagoric work of Carlos Fuentes and how it anchors his literary and cultural criticism. She is also editing a volume that explores monsters and monstrosities in Hispanic literatures and cultures.

Edward O. Keith worked at Nova Southeastern University (NSU) from October 1986 until his untimely death in September 2012. He conducted research on marine mammals and the biochemical aspects of tear protein adhesion to contact lenses. He taught biochemistry, clinical chemistry, general biology, human nutrition, marine mammalogy, and other courses at NSU, in the Farquhar Colleges of Arts and Sciences and in the Oceanographic Center.

Alexis M. Milmine specializes in 19th-century British literature with an emphasis on Gothic literature. Her ongoing research includes the topic of Bram Stoker's *Dracula* and folklore, an historical analysis of Dracula, research on Thomas Hardy's use of tragedy in his novels, various research projects concerning Edgar Allan Poe's use of the revenant, and William Shakespeare's use of the supernatural.

Jamieson Ridenhour is a scholar of Victorian Gothic literature at the University of Mary in Bismarck, North Dakota, where he serves as Chair of Language and Literature. He is the editor of the Valancourt edition of *Carmilla*, as well as a novelist and filmmaker. Ridenhour's published academic essays include work on Charles Dickens, Iris Murdoch, and Joseph Sheridan Le Fanu.

Raúl Rodríguez-Hernández is Associate Professor of Spanish and Comparative Literature, and of Film and Media Studies at the University of Rochester.

He has published several dozen articles on Mexican film, popular cultural artifacts, Latin American literature and philosophy, the artist as monster, and on modernism and postmodernism. With co-author Claudia Schaefer he published "Cronos and the Man of Science" on Guillermo del Toro's vampire film in *Revista de Estudios Hispánicos*.

Leo Ruickbie has been investigating and sometimes experiencing the darker side of life—from Black Masses to haunted houses—for most of his career. He is the author of *Witchcraft Out of the Shadows, Faustus: The Life and Times of a Renaissance Magician*, and *A Brief Guide to the Supernatural*. He is a member of Societas Magica, the European Society for the Study of Western Esotericism, the Society for Psychical Research, and the Ghost Club.

Clemens Ruthner is currently Assistant Professor of German & European Studies and Director of Research of the School of Languages, Literatures and Cultural Studies (SLLCS) at Trinity College, Dublin. He is presently writing a literary history of vampirism in the German-speaking world from the 18th century to the present. In April 2012 he organized the conference "Vampire (&) Science" for the centenary of Bram Stoker's death at Trinity College; the proceedings will be published in 2013.

Claudia Schaefer is Rush Rhees Chair, Professor of Spanish and Comparative Literature, and of Film and Media Studies at the University of Rochester. She is the author of 5 books and more than 75 articles dealing with Mexican art, cultural identity, literature, and the horror film genre. She is co-author with Raúl Rodríguez-Hernández of "Cronos and the Man of Science," published in *Revista de Estudios Hispánicos*.

Nancy Schumann has been researching, reading, and writing vampires for several years. She has an M.A. in English Literature and her thesis dealt with the female vampire and its representations in Anglo-American literature. The thesis was expanded into *Take A Bite*, published in 2011 and is currently in the process of being translated into German for publication.

Masaya Shimokusu is Professor in English at Doshisha University, Kyoto, Japan. He was the former secretary of the Japan branch of the International Association for the Study of Irish Literatures. His main research interests are James Joyce and Bram Stoker, and he has published books and articles on those subjects. He also has translated both literary and critical works including Bob Curran's Irish vampire stories, *Bloody Irish*. His translation of Ian Mac-Donald's "The Djinn's Wife" received the 2007 S-F Magazine Readers' Award.

Matthias Teichert, an Assistant Professor in Old Norse Philology, Literature, and Culture at Goettingen University, Germany. His publications include studies on the heroic sagas (*Heldensage*), the Icelandic *Edda*, the werewolf episode in chapter 8 of *Völsunga saga*, game-boards and gaming pieces in Old Norse fiction, and the Norse undead in their Germanic-European context.

Angela Tumini is an Associate Professor of Italian Studies at Chapman University in California. She is the author of *Il Mito nell'Anima*, a book that discusses the influence of myth and folklore on Gabriele D'Annunzio's works; *An Unintentional Liaison: Lars von Trier and Italian Cinema and Culture*, a book that assesses the analogies between Italian Cinema and of Lars von Trier's works. Her current research focuses on the representation of the feminine in Scandinavian and Italian cinema.